WORKING CAPITAL MANAGEMENT

— A CONCEPTUAL APPROACH

DHIRAJ SHARMA
Sr. Lecturer, Regional Institute of Management & Technology,
Mandi Gobindgarh (Punjab.)

Himalaya Publishing House
ISO 9001 : 2015 CERTIFIED

First Edition : 2023
Edition : 2008
Edition : 2009
Edition : 2010
Edition : 2014
Edition : 2023

Published by : Mrs. Meena Pandey
for **HIMALAYA PUBLISHING HOUSE PVT. LTD.,**
"Ramdoot", Dr. Bhalerao Marg, Girgaon, Mumbai - 400 004.
Phone: 022-23860170, 23863863; **Fax:** 022-23877178
E-mail: himpub@bharatmail.co.in; **Website:** www.himpub.com

Branch Offices :

New Delhi : "Pooja Apartments", 4-B, Murari Lal Street, Ansari Road, Darya Ganj, New Delhi - 110 002. Phone: 011-23270392, 23278631; Fax: 011-23256286

Nagpur : Kundanlal Chandak Industrial Estate, Ghat Road, Nagpur - 440 018. Phone: 0712-2721215, 2721216

Bengaluru : Plot No. 91-33, 2nd Main Road, Seshadripuram, Behind Nataraja Theatre, Bengaluru - 560 020. Phone: 080-41138821; Mobile: 09379847017, 09379847005

Hyderabad : No. 3-4-184, Lingampally, Besides Raghavendra Swamy Matham, Kachiguda, Hyderabad - 500 027. Phone: 040-27560041, 27550139

Chennai : No. 34/44, Motilal Street, T. Nagar, Chennai - 600 017. Mobile: 09380460419

Pune : "Laksha" Apartment, First Floor, No. 527, Mehunpura, Shaniwarpeth (Near Prabhat Theatre), Pune - 411 030. Phone: 020-24496323, 24496333; Mobile: 09370579333

Cuttack : Plot No 5F-755/4, Sector-9, CDA Market Nagar, Cuttack - 753 014, Odisha. Mobile: 09338746007

Kolkata : 3, S.M. Bose Road, Near Gate No. 5, Agarpara Railway Station, North 24 Parganas, West Bengal - 700109. Mobile: 09674536325

Printed at : Trinity Academy, Mumbai. On behalf of HPH.

DEDICATED

to my mother,
Smt. Dev Ichhya Sharma,
with love, affection and respect.

FOREWORD

The volume in hand: Working Capital Management — A Conceptual Approach written by Dhiraj Sharma is one of the first books I have seen on this subject. My experience has been that generally the books available on Working Capital Management refer only to the management of accounts, cleaning of account — books and accounting technicalities. But in this book Dhiraj Sharma has given the concepts governing the subject of Working Capital and the theory of management techniques that can be effectively employed to ensure proper financial management.

In fact, the inadequacy of Working Capital Management or WCM is one major factor, which has led to an economy wide massive upsurge in the NPAs. In the Government sector also, the revenue budget is nothing but working capital management. The Government also has done no better in this field than the erring private sector that is why zero- based budgeting and many other techniques have been invented and employed; their success has yet to be seen. From my experience as a Financial Advisor in Central Ministries, I can safety say that much has to be learnt for the management of Revenue budget which is working — capital management of the Government. Revenue — deficits of the Central and State Government and NPAs of the Banking sector and Financial Institutions are primarily due to mismanagement and mishandling of Working Capital.

I have no hesitation in saying that this book fills up the gap in the availability of literature providing conceptual insights into issues related to WCM. The chapterisation in the book has also been done in a very intelligent manner as are the subjects discussed in each chapter. Dhiraj Sharma, himself a young professional in the field deserves all the congratulations for this path-breaking effort. Student and Professional community shall have all the reasons to be grateful to him for this.

This book would make an interesting and important reading for the young men and women aspiring to become professionals; young professionals and event middle level managers. This book can also be used by senior management professionals for handy referencing needs. Sure enough this would be an essential volume for all the libraries — personal and institutional — of the accounting professionals, in public as well as private sector. My congratulations to Dhiraj Sharma for this book and best wishes for bringing out many more such useful volumes.

DR. JIVTESH SINGH MAINI

I.A.S.

PREFACE

There are financial implications in virtually all organisational decisions, whether the organisation is a business firm, a non-profit organisation, or a government enterprise. Thus, financial executives are of central importance to overall planning and control, and non-financial executives must know enough finance fundamentals to work the financial implications into their areas of expertise. The increasing importance of finance for any organisation has accompanied the evolution of the field of finance itself. Finance has evolved since the early 1900s from a descriptive to an analytical discipline recognized as a genuine science. Finance builds on economic theory to focus on both sides of the organisation's balance sheet, asset analysis and the optimal mix of liabilities and equity, including the implications of working capital for the firm.

Working Capital Management is the management for the short-term finances. Managers spend about 70% of their working time on short-term financial decisions. Every day companies receive and manage cash, make payments, balance cheque-books, grant credit, record receivables, manage inventory and so on. Maintaining adequate working capital is not just important in the short-term. Sufficient liquidity must be maintained in order to ensure the survival of the business in the long-term as well.

The purpose of *Working Capital Management — A Conceptual Approach* is to enable the reader to understand short-term financial decision-making process and to interpret the impact of these decisions on a firm's performance. The book, therefore, deals with the major areas in Working Capital Management: Cash Management, Receivable Management, Inventory Management, Banking and Financing aspect. The utmost care has been taken in exploring the area of Working Capital, in easy to understand and user-friendly manner. Although the book is designed for specialized courses in finance, it can be used by all those professionals and students who are directly/indirectly gaining from financial principles. There is a mistaken belief that the understanding of Working Capital Management concepts requires the knowledge of high-level mathematics. Also, some students mistakenly believe that Working Capital Management is an area in which they do not need competency. In spite of this every finance specialization in a college of business, and many majors in other finance courses, require the knowledge of short-term financial management fundamentals. The purpose of this book is to enable the reader to understand the short-term financial decision-making and to interpret the impact of these decisions on firm's performance.

The combined resources making up current assets are the working capital of the company. So, it is appropriate to look at the overall size of this working capital in order to verify that sufficient resources have been devoted for that purpose. In other words, working capital is the money and assets (excluding fixed assets i.e. buildings, machinery etc.) that a business uses to finance the day-to-day operations that produce the goods or services supplied to customers. Working capital is also the difference between current assets and current liabilities and is known as 'net working capital'. There are two types of capital needs for a business firm: 'fixed capital' to invest in things such as buildings, plant and equipment; and 'working capital' principally to pay for stock and to cover the amount of credit extended to customers. Fixed capital, as the name implies, do not vary in the short term but varies as the major investment decisions are made or assets are sold. Working capital, on the other hand, is much more fluid and fluctuates with the level of business. The management of working capital is, therefore, important to the financial health of businesses of all sizes. It is a critical factor in the sustainability and viability of any business. The funds invested in working capital are often high in proportion to the total assets employed, so it is vital that these funds are used in an efficient and effective way, but most companies concentrate their managerial efforts on controlling profits only. They try to increase sales revenue, reduce their production cost and control their overheads. Operational budgets are drawn up, standard costs are set and considerable efforts are made on identifying and rectifying variances of actual results against these budgets and standards. However, a few companies worry about managing another, equally important, part of their business — the area of working capital management. Many profitable companies fail each year because their management teams fail to manage working capital effectively. These companies may be profitable, but they are not able to pay their current obligations. Therefore, when businesses make investment decisions they must not only consider the financial outlay involved with acquiring the new machine or building, etc, but must also take account of the additional current assets that are usually involved with any expansion of activity. Increased production engenders a need to hold additional stocks of raw materials and work-in-progress. Increased sales usually mean that the level of debtors will increase. A general increase in the firm's scale of operations tends to imply a need for greater levels of cash. Therefore, managing the working capital can make the difference between business survival and business failure. Further, financing working capital can be very costly, so the proper management of working capital is of vital importance.

Thus, the area of working capital management is concerned with the management of all aspects of both current assets and current liabilities, so as to minimise the risk of insolvency while maximising return on assets. This way, working capital management influences both a firm's risks and its expected returns. As such, it is an important determinant of a firm's market value. A firm's investment and financing decisions are interconnected, thus they cannot be made independently. Financial planning and management of current assets makes a manager think systematically about the relationships among firm's goals for growth, investment, and financing. The manager judges the risk-return tradeoffs that are implied in financial forecasting, the process of financial planning, the importance of managing cash inflows and outflows, and evaluates how to finance short-term assets, and make the right decisions on financing and investment for the firm.

In nutshell, the importance of having working capital can be best understood as costs incurred before payment received for goods or services provided to the customer. Therefore, no capital means no production and therefore, no customers, which means no capital. Working Capital Management is concerned with making sure we have exactly the right amount of funds and lines of credit available to the business at all times. Smart companies know that Working Capital Management is a strategic tool that can fund research and development, acquisitions, share buybacks, and higher dividends. This text defines what is meant by working capital, examines the issues involved, and outlines a number of different ways in which the components of working capital can be managed. The primary objective of this book is to develop a broad understanding of the short-term financial activities and decisions to provide thorough understanding in the fundamental tools of working capital analysis. In order to make the book more accessible to non-finance readers the book extracts most of the technical terms from various chapters and places it in the last chapter 'Glossary of Financial Terms'.

ACKNOWLEDGEMENTS

In preparation of the present text, I have received encouragement and support from various quarters acknowledged here. First of all, I express my indebtedness to the thinkers and authors, too numerous to acknowledge here individually, who have enriched knowledge area of working capital on which I have heavily drawn.

My father as well as my mother has provided me, once again, with continual support and encouragement during the writing of book. To *Neeraj*, whose unfailing guidance and encouragement never wavered, I owe all the things that can be owed to an extra-ordinarily gifted brother. I have benefited from helpful comments by *Ms. Poonam*, an authority on accounting and finance. The cheerfulness of *Shubhi* and *Mourya*, my nephew and niece, kept me active and smiling all the time.

Many thanks are due to Dr. Jivtesh Singh Maini, IAS (Former Financial Adviser to the Govt. of India, Presently Principal Resident Commissioner) for his encouragement and expert comments on the book.

I am profoundly thankful to *Shri Dharminder Pal* and *Smt. Janak Bala* for their consistent care and support.

My wife, *Chetna* deserves special appreciation for her support during the time I spent in developing the present text.

For their dedication and skill, I owe special thanks to the able staff at Himalaya Publishing House, especially to *Late Shri. D.P. Pandey* and *Shri. K.N. Pandey* for their timely efforts and assistance.

Readers' valuable suggestions and recommendations are always welcome. I hope that the readers will share my enthusiasm for this vast knowledge area of working capital by providing me their honest feedback.

DHIRAJ SHARMA

dhiraj2001@indiatimes.com

CONTENTS

Chapter 1

INTRODUCTION TO FINANCIAL MANAGEMENT

(**Contents:** Goal of Financial Management, Profit Maximisation, Wealth Maximisation, The Agency Problem, Corporate Governance, Functions of a Finance Manager, Traditional Approach, Modern Approach, Indian Financial Scenario, Indian Financial System, Financial Reforms, Financial Management In Public Sector, Corruption and Malpractices, Integrated Financial Management System (IFMS), Components of an IFMS, Financial Management in a Small Firm.)

"You have to learn to treat people as a resource...you have to ask not what do they cost, but what is the yield, what can they produce?"

— Peter F. Drucker

Finance is the study of money management, the acquiring of funds (cash) and the directing of these funds to meet particular objectives. Good financial management helps businesses to maximize returns while simultaneously minimizing risks. It is essential to define the objectives and functions of financial management before identifying its major element – Short-term financial management or Working capital management. This section discusses some of the fundamental facets of financial management.

Financial management is concerned with the maintenance and creation of economic value or wealth. Value creation occurs when we maximize the share price for equity shareholders. Financial Management is concerned with the activities involving planning and control by which an organisation administers financial resources in order to maintain its market share, increase its profitability, and to maximize the organisation's rate of return on equity. Financial management deals with financial decisions such as when to introduce a new product, when to invest in new assets, when to replace existing assets, when to borrow from banks, when to issue stocks or bonds, when to extend credit to a customer, and how much cash to maintain.

GOAL OF FINANCIAL MANAGEMENT

The management of a company strives to achieve a number of objectives, some of which conflict with each other. Such conflicts arise because the firm has a number of constituents, such as stockholders, employees, customers, creditors, suppliers, and the local community, whose desires do not necessarily coincide. It is management's responsibility to satisfy such differing desires. Hence, the conflicting objectives confronting management raise the problem of setting priorities. In addition, it is essential for management to set priorities for the most efficient use of a company's scarce resources. Setting priorities in an organisation is particularly important and difficult because it has highly diversified groups of individuals and firms.

There is a difference of opinion amongst economists and financial managers as to what should be the main objective of financial management in a firm. The economists feel that wealth maximisation should be the main objective while financial managers in general opine that profit maximisation should be the objective. For a better understanding of the goals, let us discuss each goal in detail.

PROFIT MAXIMISATION

In Economics, profit maximisation means maximizing total revenue. In Finance, it is a little different. It is the maximisation of the firm's net income i.e. Revenue minus Expenses. Business enterprise aims at earning profit and hence it may be argued that profit maximisation is the directing goal of the enterprise, which in turn is the responsibility of financial management. The finance manager makes available need-based funds at a competitive cost, and oversees its effective deployment. The commercial firm is thereby enabled a smooth and unhindered operations yielding optimum business results. Profit earning is the purpose of the business. Earning profit sustains its continued existence. The destination of financial management centers therefore towards the goal of earning profit or earning maximum profit.

In this objective, the firm takes steps to ensure that the company makes maximum amount of profits at the end of the year. Profit is the difference between the sales price and the costs. So profit maximisation can be done by getting the maximum sales price and by spending the least amount of money. The sales price is determined by the demand and supply forces of the market, so a firm does not have any control over it. The business firm can only control the costs which mainly comprise of two elements — cost of goods sold and the efficiency of operation. Again the purchase price being determined by the market forces, the firm cannot control it. In that case the profit maximisation can be achieved only by working at the maximum operational efficiency.

Profit maximisation assumes perfect competition in the market place, which for all practical purposes does not exist. Profit maximisation objective ignores many real-world complexities that financial managers must address in their decisions. Business managers must deal every day with two major factors not considered by the goal of profit maximisation: uncertainty and timing. Profit maximisation does not reflect — the timing of profits and the riskiness of different operating plans. However, both of these factors are reflected in stock price maximisation. Thus, profit maximisation would not necessarily lead to stock price maximisation. Projects and investment alternatives are compared by examining their expected values or weighted average profits. In considering investment opportunities available for funds in hand, we are not indifferent to the timing of the returns. A firm always likes to have profits in the current year instead of receiving them on a distant future date. Business involves risk factor, and highly speculative decisions may in the initial stages return very attractive profits. Whether one project is riskier than another does not enter into these calculations. Projects differ a great deal with respect to risk characteristics, and to ignore these differences can result in incorrect and fatal decisions. Thus the real-world factors of uncertainty and timing force us to look beyond a simple goal of profit maximisation as a decision criterion.

The term Profit itself is somewhat vague and ambiguous. Is it short-term profit or long-term profit? Short-term profits may endanger the long-term survival. Is it before tax profit or after tax profit? In this case it is profit after tax, the profit can be enhance by tax manipulation rather than better performance. Is it total operating profit or the percentage profit per share? The profit maximisation does not consider the time value of money. The profit made today and the profit made after one year is treated to be the same. In an inflationary economy, a rupee today is much more valuable than one rupee one year after. Do we maximize profits over the current year, or do we maximize profits over some longer period? A financial manager could easily increase current profits by eliminating research and development expenditures and cutting down on routine maintenance. In the short run, this might result in increased profits, but this clearly is not in the best long-run interests of the firm. If we are to base financial decisions on a goal, that goal must be precise, not allow for misinterpretation, and deal with all the complexities of the real world.

Profit maximisation may benefit the shareholders, but the business thrives successfully only when different stakeholders (Stakeholders include creditors, employees, and customers) are made happy with its policies and functions. They are the employees, the customers, and the credit institutions. Others to be taken care of are rating agencies, the stock exchanges, the Government etc. The business enterprise has also specific social obligations to the society at large. Profit maximisation at the cost of social and ethical standards is a shortsighted policy. The objective of profit maximisation cannot be achieved if any one of the other stakeholders withdraws or even reduces the level of support. Similarly certain steps like periodical shutdown of the plant for maintenance are required in the interest of their better upkeep. A firm, in order to maximize its profits, should not minimise expenditure on such items like advertisement and publicity; vendor development; after sale service, employee training and development. Good public relations with influential stakeholders like bankers, suppliers, government officials; etc. are equally important to promote the all round progress of the firm. In case of a small firm where the owner is single, the sole aim remains enhancing his individual wealth and personal power which is satisfied by the goal of profit maximisation. But in case of a limited company, the single owner is replaced by professional managers who are salaried employees, and equity shareholders. The business firm also has to deal with other interested parties which are the government, customers, employees and the society. Therefore, profit maximisation is not the final objective of corporate.

WEALTH MAXIMISATION

It is believed that the primary goal of financial management is the maximisation of shareholder's wealth. Not only will this goal be in the best interest of the shareholders, but it will also provide the most benefits to society. This will come about as scarce resources are directed to their most productive use by business competing to create wealth. A business firm should also attach importance for its social responsibilities, business ethics etc. which is totally ignored in the profit maximisation goal of the firm. Social responsibility is the concept that businesses should be partly responsible for the welfare of society at large. Wealth maximisation does not preclude the firm from being socially responsible. Business ethics can be thought of as a company's attitude and conduct toward its employees, customers, community, and stockholders. A firm's commitment to business ethics can be measured by the tendency of the firm and its employees to adhere to laws and regulations relating to such factors as product safety and quality, fair employment practices, and the like. The wealth maximisation objective is consistent with maximizing the owners' economic welfare. As for the shareholders the wealth created by the firm reflects in the market value of the share. Thus the fundamental objective of the financial manager is to maximize the market value of the shares of the company.

Wealth maximisation means maximizing the net present value of a course of action.

Net present value = Net present value of cash inflows — Net present value of costs

The financial action which generates positive net present value adds to the wealth of the firm and thus is desirable. If there are a number of mutually exclusive projects, then the project that gives the maximum net present value should be chosen.

The goal of profit maximisation merely maximises the net income (earnings) of the firm. Because of factors such as risk, timing of earnings, number of shares outstanding, and so on, profit maximisation does not necessarily lead to shareholder wealth maximisation. A better approach is to accept wealth maximisation as the primary objective of the business firm. The risk and timing associated with expected earnings per share and cash flows are considered in order to maximize the price of the firm's common stock. Thus the objective of wealth maximisation solves the two problems faced in profit maximisation. It considers the time value of money and secondly it considers the risks involved in going for the various alternatives. Wealth maximisation is reflected in the earnings per share of the firm and the market price of its shares. If the shares of the firm are traded in stock exchange, a good performance of the firm results in the price at which the shares are traded. When the firms shares attracts a good price, the owners or shareholders are better off, because the market value of their investment appreciates. The market price of a stock represents the judgement of all market participants, as to what the value of the particular firm is. The market price serves as a performance index of the firm's progress. It indicates how well management is doing on behalf of the stakeholders. The modern thinking on management goes further and considers wealth as consisting not only physical or tangible assets, but also intangible assets, like human capital, knowledge capital and relations capital.

The goal of maximisation of shareholder wealth is nothing more than modified goal of profit maximisation which is required to deal with the complexities of the complicated business environment. The goal of wealth maximisation means maximisation of shareholders' wealth which means the maximisation of the market value of the shareholders' stock. Investors react to poor investment or dividend decisions by causing the total value of the firm's stock to fall, and they react to good decisions by pushing up the price of the stock. In effect, under this goal, good decisions are those that create wealth for the shareholder. Unlike profit maximisation, stockholder wealth maximisation is a long-term goal. Companies, and consequently the stockholders, prosper by management making decisions which will produce long-term increases in earnings. But there are many practical problems in following this goal and in using changes in the company's market share price to evaluate financial decisions. The price of a firm's stock fluctuates often for no apparent reason. However, in the long run, the value of the firm is reflected through its stock price. Although, wealth maximisation is generally accepted as the primary goal of a company, in some places, however, the goal of a company is to maximize corporate wealth. Corporate wealth includes not only the company's stockholder wealth but also its marketing, technical, and human resources. In this approach, a company should treat shareholders at par with other corporate constituents. In other words, management strives to increase the corporate wealth for the benefit of all constituents.

There are a number of reasons for management to focus on stockholder wealth maximisation. Managers are also concerned with their salaries and perks. Usually, these are tied to improved return on investments (ROI), return on equity (ROE), return on assets (ROA), or return on net assets (RONA). Since the shareholders are the owners of the company, management has a fiduciary obligation to act in their best interests. Moreover, the owners or shareholders provide the risk capital that protects the welfare of other constituents. The wealth maximisation approach provides the protection from a hostile takeover or a forced corporate restructuring. The another reason in favour of this goal is that, if a company enhances shareholder value, it is easier for the company to attract additional equity capital. The share price reflects the market's evaluation of the firm's prospective earnings stream over time, the riskiness of this stream, the dividend policy, and quality aspects of the firm's future activities. Quality aspects of future activities include stability, diversification, and growth of sales. Therefore, shareholders' wealth maximisation can be accepted as the primary objective of financial management.

THE AGENCY PROBLEM

Agency problem deals with the conflict of interest between managers and shareholders. There exists a relationship between shareholders and managers that is known as the Agency Relationship. This occurs when one party (principal) hires another (agent) to act on their behalf. So, the possibility of conflicts of interest between the parties is termed as the agency problem. Shareholders (principals) and management team (agents) work under a contract— Contract that the management team will run the firm for the shareholders under the direction of the Board of Directors. Board of Directors (agents) act on behalf of the shareholders (principal). Shareholders delegate decision-making authority to managers on the condition that the agents will act in the stockholders' best interest. Problems can arise when directors or managers do not act in the best interests of their shareholders, choosing instead to satisfy their own personal goals. Because the stockholders of most companies today are well diversified, the control of these companies is separated from ownership. This situation allows managers to act in their own best interest rather than in the best interest of the stockholders. Thus, some managers may be concerned with their own welfare, such as their own gain, position, power, and prestige. Therefore, the management decisions may be concerned with the welfare of managers only, ultimately resulting in lower stockholder wealth.

On the other hand, management may be keen on developing the company through its qualified managers while shareholders are interested in their returns only. So, there exist problems of differential of interests where investment, cash flows, financial management and reporting are concerned. These mechanisms are considered to be the lifeblood of an organisation yet they have often been subjected to agency issues. What are the basic reasons behind it? Why managers' interest diverge from shareholders? Following are some of the major reasons for agency problem:

- Management's perks and salaries may not be linked to performance.
- Executives may be very highly paid.
- Management may be concerned with another stakeholders.
- The Board of Directors may not be able to exercise proper control.
- No one, among owners, has an incentive to oversee managers.
- Excess expenditure on items of perks which do not increase the value of the company's stock and benefit others.

It is the existence of asymmetry of information, which makes it difficult for shareholders to monitor managerial decisions, and gives the opportunity for managers to follow their own welfare maximising decisions. The term information asymmetry is used when Management knows more about the company than outsiders including shareholders, debt holders, creditors, customers and employees. Each firm has a different level of information asymmetry and a different cost of lower information asymmetry depending upon many things including corporate policy, competitive pressures and level of business complexity. This problem applies to all the contracts of a firm, not just the contract between principals and agents.

Agency costs are the incentives and monitoring costs incurred by the principal and losses due to the divergence of the agent's decisions relative to the principal. There are two types of agency costs: direct and indirect. Direct costs come about in compensation and perquisites for management. Indirect costs are the result of monitoring managers and of poor decisions by management. Factors, such as a compensation system that is based on management performance (bonuses tied to profits, stock option plans) as well as the possibility of being removed from office (voted out of office, an unfriendly tender offer by another firm) serve to keep management's focus on stockholders' interests. Moreover, in the long run, management's own growth, including survival, will largely depend on the value of the firm.

The agency problem can be overcome by voting mechanisms and managerial incentives. Through voting shareholders can change and appoint the board of directors. Thus, shareholders control Board of Directors, who in turn selects the management team. The performance of managers can be monitored by reviewing management perquisites, auditing financial statements, and limiting management decisions. Incentives can also be used to motivate the managers to work efficiently. Managerial incentives include the performance plans linked to accounting income or equity participation in the shape of executive stock options and performance shares. Performance shares are shares of the firm's stock given to executives on the basis of performance as measured by earnings per share, return on assets, return on equity, and so on. Executive stock options are performance-based incentive plans which allow managers to purchase stock at some time in the future at a given price.

From an agency perspective ownership acts as an incentive to make value creating decisions rather than maximising personal benefits. Collective ownership may be an incentive for managers to become wholly committed, and devote more effort and time to profitable and innovative projects. This way another solution to this problem can be Management Buyout. The reuniting of ownership and control via a Management Buyout may result in a lowering of agency costs. The equity incentive can in many cases be a key motivator for the management team to make a success of the new venture and ultimately control their own future. Many Management Buyouts are heavily leveraged and the existence of this debt can in many cases put an onus on managers to achieve targets in order to service this debt. Additionally many third party institutions such as venture capitalists hold substantial amounts of debt and equity in the new company and thus retain a strong desire to monitor its performance.

CORPORATE GOVERNANCE[1]

Based on the theory of agency is the concept of Corporate Governance. Corporate Governance is concerned with the methods and styles in which the suppliers of capital

1 "Worldwide corporate debacles in recent times have amply demonstrated that undue emphasis on profits and market expansion at the cost of good governance is disastrous. Many corporate erroneously feel that profits and ethical corporate management practices are incompatible. For them wealth making can only be promoted through unethical practices. Corporate often ignore the interest of the public on whose money they have built their industrial empire. Small investors are often at the receiving end of corporate manipulation and mismanagement. The investing public becoming steadily more vigilant and investors both institutional and overseas mindful of governance benchmarks in place, corporate governance is used to evaluate a company's competitiveness, to attract investment and its overall potential world. Excellence in performance of the corporate sector can be achieved only through accountability, transparency, quality of information and by fulfilling their obligations towards society". The Vice President, Bhairon Singh Shekhawat, in his speech at 'Corporate Excellence Awards 2002' instituted by the Institute of Company Secretaries of India (ICSI), New Delhi, Dec. 31st 2002.

to business firm assure a return on their investments. In other words, corporate governance is an Agency perspective sometimes referred to as separation of ownership and management.

Corporate governance has a direct impact on the efficiency of a business firm, thus it also influences the effectiveness of a country's corporate governance system which in turn shapes economic performance at a country level. If managers are getting sound incentives, they will be more likely to use and allocate firm's resources and capital efficiently. If managers, however, have enormous discretion to act in their own interests rather than the interests of the firm's equity and debt holders, then this will adversely affect corporate governance. In particular, managers will allocate capital less efficiently and may behave in ways that favour their personal interests but damage overall firm's growth. Thus, the corporate governance is crucial for shaping capital allocation at the firm level and at the country level.

Most of the successful companies are treating shareholder value maximization as their primary goal. It is through effective corporate governance only that today many companies are doing something that was not the rule of thumb in their respective industries. They are restructuring their business operations to enhance shareholder wealth. For example, multinationals like IBM, Unilever etc. are laying off thousands of workers, closing offices, and quitting non-core businesses to maximize their investors' wealth. To maximize shareholder value, companies are avoiding over investments, increasing dividend rates, utilizing assets, increasing mergers and acquisitions. These days most of the large business firms are linking a significant portion of executives' pay to the company's market stock price performance. So when shareholders earn more profits, management also gets richer.

Agency theory, as discussed earlier, defines the corporate governance problem in terms how equity and debt holders influence managers to act in the best interests of the owners. To the extent that shareholders and creditors induce managers to maximize firm value, this will improve the efficiency with which firms allocate resources. These mechanisms, however, do not work well throughout the world. Small investors face problems exercising corporate governance because of informational asymmetries and poor legal, and regulatory systems. Corporate governance mechanisms are economic and legal mechanisms that can be altered through the political process only. Moreover, ensuring that capital allocation and lending practices are adequate is not simple in practice. The ability of authorities to influence managers is enhanced if regulators can impose penalties when there is evidence of fraud or of improper conduct. Similarly, the incentives of managers will clearly be enhanced if small shareholders can use an efficient court system that supports their rights.

In March 2003, a committee was formed by SEBI to discuss the scope of Corporate Governance in India which is headed by Mr. Narayana Murthy, the CEO of Infosys. The committee suggested that a company is a congregation of various stakeholders, namely, customers, employees, investors, vendor partners, government and society. A company should be fair and transparent to its stakeholders in all its transactions. This has become imperative in today's globalized business world where corporations need to access global pools of capital, need to attract and retain the best human capital from various parts of the world, need to partner with vendors on mega collaborations and need to live in harmony with the community. Unless a company embraces and demonstrates ethical conduct, it will not be able to succeed. Corporate governance is about ethical conduct in business. It stems from the culture and mindset of management, and cannot be regulated by legislation alone. Therefore, corporate governance is beyond the realm of law. Corporate governance deals with conducting the affairs of a company such that there is fairness to all stakeholders and that its actions benefit the greatest number of stakeholders.

Companies need to recognize that their growth requires the cooperation of all the stakeholders; and such cooperation is enhanced by the corporation adhering to the best corporate governance practices. In this regard, the management needs to act as trustees of the shareholders at large and prevent asymmetry of benefits between various sections of shareholders, especially between the managers and the shareholders. Therefore, corporate governance is a key element in improving the economic efficiency of a firm. Good corporate governance also helps ensure that companies take into account the interests of a wide range of communities within which they operate. Further, it ensures that their BOD is accountable to the shareholders. This helps assure that companies operate for the benefit of society as a whole. While large profits can be made taking advantage of the asymmetry between stakeholders in the short run, balancing the interests of all stakeholders alone will ensure survival and growth in the long run.

FUNCTIONS OF A FINANCE MANAGER

The main job of financial manager is to procure money for the firm at the cheapest rates, and utilize it to the best possible use, and to keep proper records of the money transactions. The functions of a finance manager, in a business organisation, are oriented towards realisation of the firm's overall objectives. These can be summarised as under:

- Mobilization of required funds
- Deployment of the funds into various profitable projects and activities
- Long-term and short-term investment decisions
- Plowing back of profits and dividend policy decision
- Deciding Risk-return criteria for the firm
- Getting market information
- Co-ordinating with other departments.

Mobilisation of funds requires the accurate estimation of the cost of the project or investment undertaken. This also involves finding the cost-effective means of finance. The finance mix is then planned for lowest cost of capital by choosing among the different mix of equity, debentures, Bank credit, Term Loans etc. Working capital needs are also assessed thoroughly. This is termed as capital structure decision. After mobilizing the funds, the finance manager is responsible for its proper allocation and use. In a manufacturing organisation the two major functions of the organisation are Production and Sales. The Finance manager supports the manufacturing by making money available for purchase of raw material, purchase of machinery and payments for personnel employed while it supports the sales by making money available for advertising campaigns, marketing infrastructure and sales and service functions.

However, the above discussed functions are very traditional. Let us now discuss the recent developments with reference to the functions of the finance manager. The Finance Manager, in addition to the above mentioned operations, takes care of treasury operations i.e. short-term productive investment of surplus funds in the money market; tax-planning; maintenance of the market price of share; fighting against hostile take-over etc. The finance manager's role has changed a lot in recent years. Now the finance manager in a business organisation is assuming the role of a strategic planner. In the past, the finance manager had to be an accounting man. Now the conceptual and managerial skills have become more important. The role of accounting and bookkeeping has become smaller and smaller within the organisation while the role of finance has increased. The role of accounting and bookkeeping has reduced largely due to the technological innovations, computers and so on. The role of accounting, book keeping totalling and tallying is relegated to variety of machines. The job skills required by the finance manager have changed considerably. Instead of merely mobilizing and deploying funds among various projects, finance manager is now directly concerned with corporate strategy and business policy decisions. With the globalization of markets and the world financial markets becoming one, the financial management is passing through the fundamental changes. The subject is becoming more vast and complicated.

Now the finance function is no more merely a support function. It has percolated into all aspects of corporate management and a business is made or lost through the finances.

Managerial approach to finance evolved with the recognition of Corporate Finance as a distinct field of study at the turn of the 20th century. Its evolution may be divided into two broad phases, i.e. traditional phase and modern phase. A transitional phase in between the two is also sometimes recognised.

TRADITIONAL APPROACH

In the start of 20th century, the corporate finance was based on certain episodic events in the life cycle of the firm-formation, issuance of capital, major expansion, merger, reorganisation, and liquidation. The approach, known as the Traditional Approach, was not analytical but descriptive and institutional in nature. The sources of finance, the mechanism and institutions in the capital markets, and legal framework of financial activities formed the basis of corporate finance. This approach followed the outsider's point of view i.e. corporate finance was viewed mainly from the perspective of the investment bankers, lenders, and other outside parties. The brief Transitional Period which started during the 1940s, and continued through the early 1950s, the basic approach was emphasis on the day-to-day problems faced by financial managers in the area of funds analysis, planning and control. A limited analytical framework characterised this period.

MODERN APPROACH

In the middle of 1950s, the modern approach came into being. This approach led to an accelerated pace of development with the infusion of ideas from economic theory and application of quantitative techniques. This approach views the discipline if finance in a broad sense and provides a conceptual and analytical framework for financial decision-making. The theme of financial management is considered to be a rational matching of funds to their uses in the light of appropriate decision criteria. The finance function covers both acquisition of funds as well as the efficient and wise allocation of funds to various uses. The approach of financial management has become more analytical and quantitative. Unlike traditional approach, this approach is dominated by insider's viewpoint i.e. the perspective of managerial decision-maker. The scope of the financial management has broadened and it is treated as an integral part of general management.

Since the beginning of the modern phase many significant and seminal developments have occurred in the fields of capital budgeting, capital structure theory, efficient market theory, option pricing theory, agency theory, arbitrage pricing theory, valuation models, dividend policy, working capital management and financial modelling. As the Managerial approach to Finance has turned into a subject of growing complexity, many more exciting developments are making finance a fascinating and challenging field.

INDIAN FINANCIAL SCENARIO

With the starting of Liberalization Era from 90s and the onset of Economic Reforms have changed the finance scenario in India. The emergence of financial services sector and SEBI as a watchdog for investor protection and regulating body of capital market is contributing towards the prominence of finance manager's job. The innovative tools of fund raising like zero coupon bonds, flexible bonds are some of the examples of developments during the recent years having a direct impact on the corporate financial policies.

In earlier years financial managers used to function in an environment, where sellers' market prevailed. Nearly monopoly was the state of Indian business. Finance was coming from traditional sources, i.e. Banks and Financial Institutions. The satisfaction of shareholders' was not the concern of the promoters, since most companies were closely held. But the situation is totally changed today. Because of opening of the economy and dismantling of tariff walls, the competition is getting intense. Markets are becoming buyers' market at a rapid rate. The development of Internet in the field of Information Technology has brought new challenges before Indian managers. Now the Indian concerns have not only to compete domestically, but also internationally.

As the finance manager has now global reach through computers, the finance function has become even more important. Also on the other hand as the repetitive work is delegated to lower levels — due to computers — the level of each employee in the company is improving. As each employee goes up the rung of organisation, it becomes imperative that he understand the financial consequences of his actions and thus today everyone in the organisation has to have a basic understanding of finance to enable them to make a positive contribution to the bottomline.

FINANCIAL MANAGEMENT IN INDIAN PUBLIC SECTOR

The objective of financial management is to provide information on which decision-makers can base wise and prudent judgements. In the Indian public sector organisations, however, financial management has been more concerned with compliance with legal requirements than it has been with providing inputs into decision-making. As a consequence, many key financial management decisions in the public sector tend to be based upon present political realities, rather than on a careful analysis of future outcomes. It is this mixture of politics, law and public scrutiny that makes governmental financial management so much more difficult and complex than financial management in the business world. As a result, governmental financial management can be much more challenging than it is in the private sector. However, it is very important that the objectives for public sector financial management be reformulated along the lines of private sector dynamics.

The scope of financial management in government or business includes funding, custodial, analytical and reporting functions, among other elements. The following tasks characterise financial management in both sectors:

- Analysing and assessing the financial impact of management decisions
- Ensuring the necessary cash flow to finance planned activities and operations
- Safeguarding resources through appropriate financial controls
- Providing a financial framework for planning future activities and operations
- Managing all types of information systems which controls the planned activities and operations
- Ensuring legality and regularity in the use of public funds
- Paying attention to concepts of efficiency and effectiveness and
- Reporting and interpreting the results of activities and operations measured in financial terms and thereafter audit and evaluation.

As the demands on government have increased, and as new revenue sources have been exhausted, there has been a shift in emphasis among the financial management functions.

India is a cash-poor country in relation to the accepted demand made on its government. Hence, the spotlight of financial management should be on getting and managing liquidity (cash) – for without cash, budgets have no relevance. The existence of uncontrollable external economic influences, the questionable reliability of traditional revenue sources, and the high demand for more and more public services, have all acted to bring working capital management (especially cash and debt management) to the forefront of public sector interest. The fragmentation of the central financial management functions is another characteristic peculiar to the public sector. Although businesses commonly designate qualified individuals as Chief Financial Officers etc, but, is it possible in the case of India and can the government identify its own key financial executives? The basic financial management functions are often divided among agencies which compete for influence, instead of collaborating for the common goal. Usually, the financial information is not available or is not timely or is not reliable and sometimes, is not used in making the key decisions of government. A sense of financial management consciousness is direly needed in the Indian public sector. Government needs an appropriate financial management philosophy, and a clear definition of the scope of the financial management function. Then, it must assure competent professional financial management leadership for that function and provide adequate staffing and support.

As the country develops, the need for coordinated professional financial management increases. Thus, there arises the need to integrate basic financial management functions and responsibilities into a coordinated single system under competent professional leadership. This can be done even without the extensive use of sophisticated computerised systems. However, increasingly new microcomputer technology and decreasing costs are bringing integrated financial management systems within the reach of our country.

INDIAN FINANCIAL SYSTEM

The financial system of a country consists of specialized and non-specialized financial institutions, of organized and unorganized financial markets, of financial instruments and services, which facilitate transfer of funds. Procedures and practices adopted in the markets, and financial inter-relationships are also parts of this system.

The Indian financial system can be broadly classified into two sectors: Organized Sector and Unorganized Sector. The organized financial system is made up of a vast network of banks, other financial and investment institutions and a range of financial instruments, which together function in fairly developed capital and money markets. The commercial and cooperative banking structures mainly provide short-term funds. About 90% of such banking business is managed by 28 leading banks, which are in the public sector. In addition to commercial banks there is the network of cooperative banks and land development banks at State, district and block levels. There is an increasing trend of private banks and with nearly 65% of the total assets of the financial system held by banks, they play an important role in the Indian Financial Industry. There is a growing trend among Development Financial Institutions changing their traditional roles of providers of long-term finance to 'Universal Banking' institutions.

The unorganised financial system comprises of moneylenders, indigenous bankers, lending brokers, landlords, traders, etc. There are also a host of financial companies, investment companies, chit funds, etc. in the unorganised sector. These are not regulated by the Central Bank or the government in a systematic manner.

In product or other service markets, purchasers part with their money in exchange for something in the present. In finance, money in the present is exchanged for a promise to pay in the future. However, in product or service markets, if the product sold is defective, the buyers often find out relatively soon. On the other hand, loan quality is not readily observable for quite some time and can be hidden for extensive periods. Moreover, banks and non-bank financial intermediaries can also alter the risk composition of their assets more quickly than most non-financial industries, and banks can readily hide problems by extending loans to clients that cannot service previous debt obligations.

Theoretically, the financial market facilitates allocation of resources efficiently, which involves quick dissemination of information and reaction to it. The financial markets are susceptible to manipulation as some participants have information that others do not have and this is known as information asymmetry. To overcome this problem corporate governance is required to ensure that suppliers of finance to companies are assured that they get their return on their investment. Despite the existence of institutional and legal framework numerous financial scams continue to be reported both in developed and developing countries.

Financial Liberalization is a phenomenon that is almost pervasive in all over the world today. While liberalization has led to substantial benefits in terms of increased transparency, it has also given birth to the chances of corporate mis-governance. This implies that the mechanism by which legal institutions ensure that suppliers of funds receive the return on investment is not appropriate. Recent trends after the 1990s in India reveal how corporate governance has not been effective permitting unscrupulous and opportunistic individuals to manipulate the market in their favour, the case of Harshad Mehta scam is an appropriate example in this regard. The process of financial market regulation ensures that important guidelines are issued regarding how primary dealers (brokers) should operate with regards to mode of operation, conduct, litigation, amount of business to be handled, management of risk, internal control etc.

The financial scandals and scams, occurring every day in India, involve the manipulation of huge amounts of money. The occurrence of such scams and scandals can be attributed to a failure of corporate governance in finance, despite the existence of a functioning regulatory authority empowered with the legal sanctions.

Though, the Indian financial system is broad-based, yet it is inadequate and inefficient. The establishment of efficient financial systems will help India to grow, partly by mobilizing additional financial resources and partly by allocating those resources to best uses. In the future, we can hope that the Indian financial system will grow in size and complexity, different segments of the market will become closely linked and inter-dependent. Influencing only one market segment without affecting others will become increasingly difficult.

As is the case in many industrially advanced countries these days, the major link connecting the various segments is the interest rate. In order to influence the entire system, the monetary authorities will have to act on interest rates. There will be increasing specialization and there can emerge financial system dealing in different financial products and services. The existence of healthy and sound financial institutions should be able to exercise control over investors and other borrowers to use resources in an efficient and productive manner in order to repay existing obligations and to raise new finances. Banks will begin to function increasingly under cooperative pressures. These pressures may work from within the banking system, as well as from non-banking financial institutions. With the increasing participation of private shareholders even in public sector banks, there will be greater accountability to shareholders, including the Government.

FINANCIAL REFORMS[2]

India has entered into 21st millennium and has largely completed the first phase of financial sector reforms and is in process of the second phase to meet new challenges. The first phase — liberalization of interest rate and directed credit — began in the early 1990s, jointly with real sector deregulation. With prices in the real economy reflecting economic costs and with greater reliance on the private sector, it naturally became important to move from a financial system that was traditionally a system of centralized

2. Data used in this section is taken from various RBI and other banking bulletins, annual reports of banks and internet uploads.

public finance, directed credit allocations to a system where financial institutions play a greater role in allocating resources based on their evaluation of risk and return.

Giving financial sector institutions a greater role in credit allocations brings many changes — not just freeing interest rates and credit allocations but giving more attention to legal, regulatory and supervisory issues and incentives. The changes involve not only individual institutions and sectors of the financial system, but also inter-sectoral issues, such as the roles of banks, development banks and the capital market. If these changes occur, India will reap the benefits of a financial system appropriate to its development and to the changes that are taking place globally.

The Indian financial system is still dominated by the public sector. Lack of appropriate incentives in public sector financial firms add to the above mentioned problems. Public sector banks have 80% of commercial bank assets and are heavily involved in other financial institutions; development banks, among the largest institutions, are either government-owned or have much of their equity owned by public sector banks; the publicly owned Unit Trust of India (UTI) and the public banks' mutual funds are the largest players in the stock market; insurance was a government monopoly until recently. It is generally understood that in the case of public sector institutions where the owner is the Government itself, it typically lacks both the incentive and the means to ensure an adequate return on its investment. Political decisions, as opposed to the ROI criteria, are often important in determining resource allocation. Debt collection service may be low, relative to private financial firms. Political pressure and interference generates decisions that lead to economic instability. Managers and staff in public firms have little incentive to gather and use information to make investment decisions that maximize the risk adjusted rate of return.

A public sector firm's competition to improve services and cut costs is very limited. Lenders, investors and depositors in public banks and mutual funds do not worry much about the use of their funds because there is a public guarantee that taxpayer will make good the promised returns.

All these problems suggest that resolving these issues are critical to the success of India's financial reforms. Improvements in the legal, regulatory and supervisory framework are a key to financial reforms. The legal and judicial system, the regulations and the supervision of the regulations are a major factor in the effectiveness of a financial system. For example, the quality of the legal and judicial framework affects the incentives to service debt promptly. The rules on minimum capital, risk weighting, exposure, lender of last resort and deposit insurance affect the size and nature of transactions in the system.

Good quality supervision ensures the rules are followed and that weak institutions are either made strong promptly or are sold-off. The role of regulation and supervision is to include the reduction of market risk and economic instability. A sound legal framework for collateral and loan recovery is also very important.

The pre-reform era from the mid 60s to the early 90s, India's Governments treated the financial system as an instrument of public finance. A complex web of regulations fixed the details of deposit and lending rates and loan amounts, channelling credit to the government and priority sectors at below-market rates. Public institutions dominated the financial system; competition was limited — between banks and between the banking sector, the capital market and international financial markets. When problems and irregularities occurred, regulations were changed to prevent the same in future, without much attention to their impact on the financial system as a whole. Despite the restrictions on deposit rates, India had a relatively strong financial system for a low-income country. The stock market was also large in terms of number of listings and market capitalization.

On the lending side, financial repression was greater than on the deposit side. Substantial and increasing volumes of credit were channelled to the government at below-market rates through high and increasing cash reserve requirements (CRR) and statutory liquidity requirements (SLR), in order to fund a large and increasing government deficit at relatively low cost. In addition, 40% of advances were to offer to priority sectors, mainly agriculture and small-scale industry. An additional 10% went to export credit. And credit to fund food procurement was about 10% of advances during the 1980s. Thus, over 80% of portfolio allocations were fixed by sector. Moreover, interest rates and credit volumes on individual loans were regulated in minute detail. The public sector, through the CRR and the statutory liquidity requirement, and agriculture received the largest average cross subsidies.

India's reforms of the early 1990s began in response to the balance of payments crisis of 1991-92; it also included a stabilization programme. The reforms specifically included financial reform. The financial reforms sought to improve resource mobilization and allocate credit to its most efficient uses. The first Narasimham Committee Report (1991) provided a blueprint, particularly in the banking sector. The recommendations of this committee were largely carried out. From 1992 onwards, India gradually liberalized interest rates (except savings deposit rates). Deposit rates were liberalized by first setting an overall ceiling for term deposit rates. Trading of stocks and bonds was, however, relatively low. Also, the size of the debt market was difficult to measure. Although large volumes of government debt were bought, the buyers were largely the banks, which bought debt and held it to maturity to satisfy the statutory liquidity requirement, which at one point was 38.5% of deposits. Regulations kept the interest rates low on public sector debt. After 1992, rates on priority lending were also gradually allowed to be set more freely, and the number of categories was reduced sharply. Finally, interest rates on Government debt were increasingly determined in auctions. However, the rules of the auction effectively allowed RBI to set the rate.

Additional measures liberalized credit allocation, improved regulation and supervision, liberalized the capital account, and introduced more competition over the post-1992 period. These additional measures included: Reduced Cash Reserve and Statutory Liquidity Requirements, tightening of prudential norms and improvement of banking supervision. Recognition of non-performing assets gradually tightened, so that by March 1995 most loans with past due interest of more than two quarters were considered non-performing.

Non-bank financial corporations were allowed to grow under a regime of less directed credit requirements (lower cash reserve and statutory liquidity requirements, no priority lending requirement) and limited regulation and supervision. After reform, the growth of bank deposits, relative to GDP, resumed, though somewhat more slowly than in the 1980s. Deposits in non-bank financial companies (NBFCs), grew rapidly, by over 40% p.a.

between 1992 and 1997. However, a crisis[3] in one of the NBFCs in 1997 led to runs against many of them. The Government appropriately refused to extend deposit insurance to them. The weakest NBFCs were wound up and the remaining institutions are being more tightly regulated.

The reforms strengthened banking regulation and supervision, as mentioned above. Regarding non-performing assets, the tighter regulations led to recognition of the large volume of existing non-performing assets (NPAs). However, by 1998-99 the ratio of banks' NPAs to Total Assets had fallen to about 6%. Regarding the capital market, larger firms raised most of their funding through the capital market or private placements. Banks still provide much of these funds, but under competitive conditions that have depressed margins. The increased competition has been a major factor in the decline in banks' interest rate spreads and profit rates over the last few years.

Financial Sector Reforms were initiated as part of the overall structural reforms aimed at improving the productivity and efficiency of the economy. The Financial Sector Reforms recognise the fact that the Indian Banking System had over the years grown and that the geographical and functional coverage of the banking system have been truly impressive. However, questions have been raised from time to time on the viability of the banking institutions. Concerns have also been expressed about the deterioration in the quality of services provided by banks. It was with a view to these problems that Financial Sector reforms were initiated. The major merit of these reforms has been the cautious sequencing of reforms and the consistent reinforcing nature of the various measures taken. Even as the new prudential norms are being introduced, the capital base of the banks has been strengthened and organisational improvements are being made consistently. Through FDI and Portfolio investments, the Foreign Exchange Reserve of India has steadily increased to reach a level of US$ 34.87 billion as of January 2000. The reforms have generated encouraging results, however, there is a great deal of economic development required before India is competitive in all aspects on an international level.

CORRUPTION AND MALPRACTICES

We all know that corruption itself has become a part of our system, day by day it is eating up our reserves and values. One of the most powerful anti-corruption devices is the establishment of sound financial management practices, with timely and efficient accounting systems combined with professional reviews by internal and independent auditors. To achieve this involvement of top-level management and political commitment is inevitable. Such a commitment is a missing element in our country today, and that too, in both the public and the private sector.

One of the major objectives of a sound financial management system in business is to check and disclose internal flaws and crimes. Annual audit is one of the most common solutions prescribed for this. However, auditors' hands are tied where inadequate accounting practices hinders the audit trails which should permit auditors to find irregularities and determine who is responsible for them. Poor, disconnected and untimely accounting systems and disintegrated approaches to financial management provide opportunities for fraud. Auditors also serve to cover up the frauds, and, if fraud is

3. C.R. Bhansali, the promoter of a NBFC ran away with Rs. 1000 crore collected as fixed deposits from public.

discovered, they make it impossible to identify and punish those responsible. On the other hand, clear and transparent audit trails not only serve to find the guilty but they also provide a powerful prevention.

A sound system of financial management and accounting discloses and helps to identify corrupt practices and corrupt people in the following ways:

- It provides sound information for the various anti-corruption agencies and watchdogs
- It forces a disciplined on-time approach to public activity and financial reporting.
- Sound financial management includes requirements that all transactions adhere to the same rules, eliminating the loopholes and alternative mechanisms which foster and cover up corrupt activities;
- It promotes the development of strong internal managerial controls. These include appropriate audit trails (requisites of sound financial management), which strengthen the probability that corrupt practices are discovered and identified as such, so permitting more prompt investigation;
- Managerial control is further strengthened with regards to oversight of discretionary power over resources and expenditures which are subject to a high degree of vulnerability.
- It facilitates audit. Professional and timely internal and independent audit which focuses on highest risk areas is made possible where financial management, especially accounting systems are adequate; and
- It provides psychological control. The knowledge that internal managerial controls are in place, constantly being emphasised and improved, and subject to selective audit review, is a powerful danger to the potentially corrupt.

So, the responsibility of a government is not limited to ensure the proper financial management of funds in accordance with standards and procedures. It extends over the whole of the government sector, including regions, districts and municipalities, as well as government institutions. This task can be extremely difficult where there is a large degree of decentralisation accompanied by shortages in management and audits, or where ineffective democracy and subsidiary are a part of political culture.

The government should also ensure that strong financial management systems are introduced into public corporations that are subject to government regulation and agencies that are interfacing the public and private sectors. With fraud and corruption, legal and disciplinary measures are directly attached, and there is a lot to do to improve our legal system.

INTEGRATED FINANCIAL MANAGEMENT SYSTEM (IFMS)

An Integrated Financial management System (IFMS) is a very important tool of financial management. An IFMS consists of an inter-related set of sub-systems which plan, process, report resources, and quantify them in financial terms. The basic sub-systems normally are accounting, budgeting, cash management, receivable management, and their related internal controls. Other sub-systems, sometimes, included are collection and receivable management, acquisitions and supply management, information management, tax and customs administration, retirement or social security system administration, etc. One of the most important elements of modern internal control in any organisation consists of an independent and professional internal audit function, which constitutes, an integral part of an IFMS.

The principal factor, which integrates the system, is a common, single, reliable database or several interconnected databases in which all data is expressed in financial terms. All of the sub-systems, and all users of financial data, are required to participate in common data sharing. The validation, classification and recording of data is a function of the accounting sub-system which produces timely reports of classified data for use by all systems, and others who use financial information.

An IFMS can be developed regardless of a specific organisational structure, but it is likely to function better where the four basic sub-systems — accounting, budgeting, cash management, and receivable management — are closely related within the organisational structure, under a common, professionally qualified financial management executive.

The failure to integrate financial management information results in:

- Fragmented and unreliable data;
- Duplications of data and difficult to reconcile;
- Failure to utilise actual results in the planning and budgeting processes;
- Failure to fully/publicly report results of operations and financial conditions;
- Hidden transactions;
- Undue emphasis on one of the component sub-systems (usually budgeting) which tends to dominate, duplicate and fades out the others.

COMPONENTS OF AN IFMS

The principal four components of an IFMS are accounting, budgeting, cash management and credit management. These component sub-systems of the IFMS must be permeated by sound internal managerial controls. Each of them must be supported by an environment of ethics and integrity, which must stem from the top levels of management.

ACCOUNTING

An accounting system is the collection of methods and records established to identify, assemble, analyze, classify, record, and reports a firm's transactions. The system is created to safeguard and maintain accountability for the entity's assets and liabilities. The accounting sub-system is at the heart of the IFMS, because the other sub-systems depend on it for useful, timely and reliable data. If the accounting sub-system fails to produce timely data, the remaining sub-systems cannot function properly. In this case, substitute data is often sought, new ad hoc records are set up to produce indispensable data, and management decisions are made without the information necessary to apply good judgement. Thus, sound development and maintenance of the accounting sub-system is absolutely necessary to the success of the IFMS, and constitutes a very important factor in its integration.

Among other things, the accounting system allows for:

- Providing information to programme managers for use in making informed decisions;
- The independence of financial transactions based upon duly organised supporting documentation;
- Making it possible to report results in financial terms, and where performance data is maintained, to report costs;
- Control over current year's disbursements and preparing future budgets based upon actual expenditures made; and,
- Providing periodic financial reporting and auditing.

It is very important that all accounting and budgeting classification or coding schemes be fully integrated into a single common classification which remains constant over a period of years. Changes in classifications from year to year impair the ability to compare data and to analyse trends.

The accounting system should maintain general ledger controls over all valuable resources which are independent of operations. Typical and repetitive transactions should be pre-coded according to type and amount entered, and therefore appropriate accounting entries should be made automatically, reducing the need for accounting expertise while at the same time reducing the possibility that transaction data can be manipulated. Timely entry of transaction data at the point of origin permits internal auditors to pay immediate attention to areas and activities identified as being vulnerable to corrupt practices.

BUDGETING

Budgeting is the process of stating in quantitative terms the planned activities of the organisation for given period of time. Budgets, the quantitative statements prepared with the help of accounting data, include such figures as projected income and expenditure. Budget execution data must be derived from the accounting system, and not separately recorded and processed. It is extremely important to highlight the fact that budgeting must be integrated with the other financial management areas.

Budgeting sub-system supports decision making by providing all the units and departments with regular reports, and other information that help them to-

(a) control their area of responsibility and

(b) allocate their resources to pursue the organisation's goals. Managers of subunits also may use budgets to help track progress of their own units.

Budgetary principles require that all forecast revenues and expenditures of all types should be accounted for within the budget. This means that any use of special revenues from the general pool of revenues, should be minimised.

The budgetary sub-system should be designed in such a simple and practical manner as to facilitate smooth operation in co-ordination with the other IFMS sub-systems. It is essential to ensure that the budget made for a year does not over-run by a substantial margin the figures set in the budget itself.

A budgeting system often is closely related to the general ledger system. The computerized general ledger system should permit budget amounts be entered by account number. Actual amounts spend or received are registered by means of the general ledger system or by means of subsystems for account payable.

Periodically (weekly, monthly, annually) or on ad hoc basis budgeted amounts and the actual expenditures should be compared and reported. Examples of budget reports are: current budget allocations compared with year-to-date income and expenditures; budget variances or differences between projected amounts and actual costs; current budget allocations compared to the previous year's allocations.

CASH MANAGEMENT

The objective of cash management is to collect, maintain, and disburse funds in a way that minimizes the risk of misuse, maximizes profitable cash flow, and supports the organisation's operations and mission. Cash is both a fundamental resource and the means by which the firm acquires other resources. To manage cash is to manage the firm's ability to purchase assets, service debt, pay employees, and control operations. Thus, effective cash management directly correlates with the firm's ability to realize its mission, goals, and objectives.

The cash management process combines:

- Cash management tools, such as cash budgets and cash forecasting, for controlling cash availability and maximizing the investment of idle funds
- Procedures for collecting, disbursing, and investing cash
- Internal controls for safeguarding, recording, and reporting cash

The cash management process has three major subsystems:

- Collection
- Disbursement
- Investment

These subsystems have very different control objectives. For example, the collection subsystem should reduce the time between point of collection and actual deposit. It is concerned with identifying the methods and procedures to be used to collect receipts and minimise collection delays.

The disbursement subsystem, on the other hand, should increase the time from point of disbursement to actual reduction of cash balances. In other words, this sub-system establishes payment dates and payment methods to maximise disbursement float (delay).

Investment subsystem identifies types and amounts of investments allowed, setting standards for dealers or brokers for investments. Therefore, compatibility and co-ordination between all the subsystems is necessary for overall cash management objectives to meet. Specific cash management policies should be developed for these subsystems.

Cash management seeks to ensure that the achievement of budgeted goals and objectives are not hindered by a lack of cash liquidity. Meeting cash management objectives requires forecasting the combined flow of funds, and planning to meet financing needs, including short-term borrowing, as budgeted. The scarcity of financial resources has increased the problems posed by traditional practices of maintaining multiple idle accounts, with various banks, and for multi-purposes. All the accounts having some minimum idle cash balance. Thus, in the modern and efficient financial management system it is obligatory to unite all cash flows in the 'single bank account'. Every financial inflow from any source should be deposited directly into the single cash depository account. In the same way, all disbursements should be drawn against the same account. The management should carefully plan and forecast their cash flows to avoid idle cash maintained in accounts, and to ensure that liabilities are met when they fall due.

RECEIVABLE MANAGEMENT

Receivable or debtors reflect money, goods, or services which have been earned but not received. They are shown as assets on the balance sheet, allowing the asset to be recognized during the period in which the revenue is earned. It is important not to lose sight of the fact that receivable management cannot be isolated from the rest of the financial management system. Planning credit is just as essential as planning cash flow, and these two sub-systems should be considered as one due to their close relationship. The basic phases of a receivables process are:

- Establish policies and procedures to control the granting of credit.
- Ensure that the system properly records, reports, and safeguards receivables.
- Ensure the process provides for the analysis and aging of receivables.
- Collect due and past-due accounts.
- Monitor and reevaluate the system.

The firm should ensure that reported receivables accurately reflect all receivables and provide the data necessary to forecast cash availability and analyse efficiency of the collection process while safeguarding assets. The cash management system relies upon the control system of the receivables process as surety that receivables are recorded and reported accurately. The data provided by the accurate recording of receivables is used to make aging schedule and analyze receivables to determine efficient and effective collection. Accounts receivable aging analysis is a review of amounts and percentage of outstanding accounts receivable falling into each of several defined billing periods. This analysis should be done at regular intervals.

Accounts receivable turnover analysis is used to measure the effectiveness of the management of accounts receivable. The commonly used turnover formulas used are turnover ratio and days sales outstanding ratio (DSO). Regardless of the method used, budgeted target turnover to compare to actual is helpful in planning and goal setting.

INTERNAL CONTROL

Internal controls are comprised of the plan of organisation and all methods and measures adopted within a firm to safeguard its assets, check the accuracy and reliability of its accounting data, promote operational efficiency, and encourage adherence to prescribed managerial policies[4]. Internal control, which is a type of managerial control, is of great importance within each of the IFMS sub-systems. Appropriate internal control measures should be integrated within each sub-system in such a manner that their application becomes an integral part of the normal processing of transactions. Internal control comprises all the coordinated measures and methods adopted within an entity to:

- Safeguard its resources;
- Promote the reliability and accuracy of financial and operational information;
- Promote efficiency in operations;
- Stimulate adherence to legal provisions, policies and standards; and to
- Achieve programmed goals and objectives.

Internal control measures and procedures should be installed and integrated within its operating procedures. Internal audit is a part of the internal control structure dedicated to measuring and evaluating the other internal controls. Thus, internal auditors must be professionally independent and should not participate in administrative functions or financial transactions of the transactions. Exception reports can be designed to provide prompt feedback to managers in areas where weaknesses are becoming a trend.

FINANCIAL MANAGEMENT IN A SMALL FIRM

Financial management in the small firm is characterized by a different set of problems and opportunities than those confronted by a large industrial house. One obvious difference is that a majority of small firms do not normally have the opportunity to publicly sell issues of stocks or bonds in order to raise funds. The owner/manager of a small firm rely primarily on trade credit, bank financing, lease financing, and personal equity to finance the business. Therefore, a small business firm faces limited financing alternatives than those faced by the financial manager of a large company. On the other hand, many financial problems facing the small firm are very similar to those of larger companies. For example, the analysis required for a long-term investment decision such as the purchase of plant and machinery or the evaluation of lease-buy alternatives, is essentially the same regardless of the size of the firm. Once the decision is made, the financing alternatives available to the firm may be radically different, but the decision process will be generally similar.

One major area of particular concern for the smaller business firms lies in the effective management of working capital. Working capital is the deployment of current assets in the business and net working capital is defined as the difference between current assets and current liabilities and is often termed as 'circulating capital' of the business. Lack of control in this crucial area is a primary cause of business failure in both small and large firms. The finance manager must continually be alert to changes in working capital accounts, the cause of these changes and the implications of these changes for the financial health of the company. One convenient and effective method to highlight the key managerial requirements in this area is to view working capital in terms of its major components such as Cash, Inventory and Receivables. All these components are dealt with thoroughly in the subsequent chapters.

4. Defliese, Philip L. Montgomery's Auditing, New York: John Wiley & Sons, 1975.

Chapter 2

AN OVERVIEW OF WORKING CAPITAL

(**Contents**: Introduction, Working Capital Defined, Dangers of Too Much Working Capital, Dangers of Too Little Working Capital, Defining Working Capital, Characteristics, Operating Cycle, Cash Conversion Cycle, Components of Working Capital Management, Assessment of Working Capital Requirement (WCR), Modern Mantra — Zero Working Capital, Factors Influencing Working Capital Requirements, Profitability Vs. Liquidity, Risk-Return Trade-Off, Working Capital Policy, Investment in Current Assets, Working Capital Financing Policy, Working Capital Management in Multinational Environment.)

"If things do not turn out as we wish, we should wish for them as they turn out".

— Aristotle

INTRODUCTION

Working capital is one of the most fundamental measures of a company's financial strength. If a company possesses a significant value of liquid assets, it can easily fund its day-to-day business obligations. If, however, a company is under cash crunch, whether by way of a lack of cash, trouble in collecting its accounts receivable, or a dearth of inventory, it may face difficulties keeping up with demand for its products/services. This directly affects a company's revenues, as it foregoes sales that it could have otherwise made to its customers. Working capital, therefore, also provides insight on how efficiently a company's management is able to oversee the company's operations. The speed at which the company is able to manage its short-term assets and short-term liabilities is also crucial to its business success. If a company uses a certain sum to purchase raw materials, it is important that the company processes those raw materials into finished products as soon as possible. Once the finished products are supplied to its customers, it is then critical to collect payment from the customers (collection of accounts receivable) within a reasonable period of time. This way, stock eventually becomes cash, but in the meantime represents working capital tied up in the business. Keeping working capital level to the minimum required for efficient operations keeps costs down. This means controlling buying, handling, storing, and managing stock properly. It is critical, therefore, that the company reduces its inventories, both of raw materials and finished products. Similarly, it is imperative that the company is able to collect on its receivables as quickly as possible. As the excessive working capital leads to over-capitalisation, resulting into waste through under-utilisation of resources and hence, leads to poor returns to stockholders. This also causes overtrading for the company which means extending liberal credit terms, therefore, more sales which brings more debtors and higher working capital requirements i.e. trying to maintain a level of sales which is higher than adequate level of working capital can sustain.

WORKING CAPITAL DEFINED

In simple terms, Working capital refers to the cash a company requires in order to finance its day-to-day business operations or in other words, working capital refers to the amount of capital which is readily available to an organisation.

The term Working capital (WC) is more an accounting term than a management concept. There are two concepts of Working capital for the purpose of definition – Gross Concept and Net Concept. As per Gross concept of working capital, it refers to the firm's current assets. The firm's total current assets are termed as gross working capital.

From the perspective of financing working capital needs, Gross concept of working capital is—the investment in circulating assets, or in inventory and accounts receivable comprising the operating cycle of a manufacturing firm. Investment in assets comprising the gross operating cycle is termed as Current Assets (CA). Current Assets are resources which are in cash or will soon be converted into cash in the ordinary course of business or in other words, current assets are defined as assets which in normal course of operations are meant to be converted into cash within a period not exceeding one year. Correspondingly, Current Liabilities (CL) are commitments which, within a short period of time usually within a year, require cash settlement in the ordinary course of business.

Net concept or Net working capital refers to current assets less current liabilities. That means, working capital is the difference between resources in cash or readily convertible into cash (Current Assets) and organisational commitments for which cash will soon be required (Current Liabilities). It is defined as the difference between the current assets and the current liabilities. Thus:

Working Capital = Current Assets – Current Liabilities

This definition leads to the principle that the entire amount of current assets should not be financed out of current liabilities (short-term debt) or the current ratio (ratio between the current assets and the current liabilities) should always be greater than one. The excess of current assets over current liabilities or the net working capital represents the liquidity or the margin of safety available to the lenders of the firm. To a large extent, liquidity strength determines the reputation of the firm in the market. The other conclusion from this concept leads to the notion that the major part of investment in working capital assets should be financed with long-term sources of finance.

So, there is no universal definition of working capital that is accepted by everyone. Some have made it quite simple stating it is the difference between current assets and current liabilities. Others consider it as being equal to the total of current assets. Whatever is the concept or definition we choose; the prime goal of every business remains 'increasing profits'. Whether or not this is accomplished depends to a great extent on the management of working capital. The research on the management of working capital covers such areas as Cash Management, Accounts Receivable, Inventory and other concerned areas. Thus, working capital is of paramount importance to a company's smooth functioning and is one of the major measures of evaluation of a firm's financial performance. The management of working capital is important for several reasons:

- Current asset management involves the largest portion of financial manager's time.
- Working Capital is continually required for a going concern so it is practically impossible to avoid an investment in current assets.
- There is a close relationship between sales growth and the level of current assets and current liabilities. Changes in the level of current assets and current liabilities are to be matched to the variations in the sales level. Therefore, the quantum of working capital fluctuates depending on the level of activity.

Working capital management is concerned with the activities such as arranging short-term sources of finance, deciding favourable credit terms and policies, managing cash inflows and outflows, controlling accounts receivables and their collection, and administrating the investment in various types of inventory. Moreover, the management of working capital requires to maintain a balance between too much investment in current assets and having a too little level of current assets. Following are the implications of both the extremes.

DANGERS OF TOO MUCH WORKING CAPITAL

(1) High investment in working capital denotes idling of funds which earns no returns on its investment.

(2) High level of inventory and receivable demands more supervision and good amount of control which has its cost too.

(3) Chances of wastages in inventory and bad debt losses are more when the level of working capital is very high.

(4) Idling and accumulation of funds may bring inefficiencies in the system.

(5) High liquidity in the business result into low profitability which can shake the confidence of shareholders and the market price of share may fall.

DANGERS OF TOO LITTLE WORKING CAPITAL

(1) Illiquidity is the biggest danger of inadequate working capital. A firm, which is not able to meet its short-term obligations, endangers its goodwill and long-term survival.

(2) Inadequacy of working capital leads to frequent and regular stoppages in the production.

(3) A firm short of liquidity cannot incash short-term environmental opportunities due to lack of funds.

(4) Advantages of bulk purchases are forgone.

(5) In case of emergency, the firm has to resort to external borrowing which has a very high cost.

Therefore, Working capital management or short-term financial management is a significant facet of financial management. Despite the importance of working capital management, concern for this management area is neglected for a variety of reasons. First, decisions on working capital are routine and frequent. Second, these routine decisions are easily reversible. Third, working capital management requires cash flow projections; however, cash flows cannot be forecasted by the finance manager alone. In addition to this, the difference between profit and present value is insignificant because of short-term period horizon. Let us discuss the major characteristics in detail.

CHARACTERISTICS OF WORKING CAPITAL

Following are the major characteristics of working capital:

(i) *Short Life Span:* Current assets like cash, bank balance, marketable securities, accounts receivable and inventories etc all are short lived. Usually their life span (or the conversion into some other form of CA) does not go beyond one year. Cash balances are usually held only for a week or so; accounts receivables are held for a duration of one month to three months and inventories are held not more than six months. Short life span of current assets depends upon the length of operating cycle of the firm. Time taken by various activities such as procurement of raw material, production process, sales and collection of bills; all these activities and their time duration decides the life span of current assets. Greater the time duration of operating cycle greater will be the life of current assets and vice-versa.

(ii) *Swift Transformation:* Swift transformation of current asset into other form of current asset is another major feature of working capital. The cash is utilized to procure raw material. Raw material is transformed into work in progress and then finished product which is usually sold or credit and creates accounts receivable which after collection are converted back into cash. Operating cycle

is nothing but a transformation cycle of various current assets into other forms of current assets, sequence of transformation of one asset into other from of asset.

(iii) *Short-term Focus:* The other significant feature of working capital is its attention on the short-term financial position. The entire focus is on the procurement & management of assets in the short sum i.e usually one year or in other words present value of money is not significant for the purpose of analysing financial condition here.

(iv) *Repetitive and Frequent:* Working capital management involves repetitive and frequent activities as explained in detail under the heading of operating cycle. Also, these activities are unsynchronized and non-instantaneous concerning production, sales and collection of accounts receivable. Had these activities been perfectly synchronized and instantaneous there would not have any need for the study of working capital management.

(v) *Liquidity:* The essence of working capital management is in providing liquidity all the time in business in such a way that neither the risk is very high nor the return on investment should fall. This is a difficult task for finance manager for the reason investment in CA keeps in changing and so does the financing required.

(vi) *Inter-Relation among Assets:* Just as the current assets are swiftly transformed into other form of assets so they are also inter-related to each other. That is, are current assets cannot be viewed in isolation because the decision related to this asset will also affect other current assets, for example the decision for investment in inventory cannot be taken without analyzing the expected level of sales and accounts receivable non-synchronization of production and sales give birth to inventory. Similarly, if there were cash sales only there would not have been any accounts receivable.

OPERATING CYCLE

Working capital has become one of the most difficult financial areas to understand. As mentioned earlier, the term working capital means different things to different people. By definition, working capital is the excess of current assets over current liabilities. However, with the help of this calculation we cannot judge what are the working capital needs and how to meet them. A useful tool in this regard is the operating cycle. The operating cycle analyzes the accounts receivable, inventory and accounts payable cycles in terms of days. In other words, accounts receivable are analyzed by the average number of days it takes to collect an account. Inventory is analyzed by the average number of days it takes to turn over the sale of a product (from the point it is procured to the point it is converted to cash or an account receivable). Accounts payable are analyzed by the average number of days it takes to pay a supplier invoice. The entire gamut of operations in a company can be summarised as follows:

Capital (cash) is put into the business –

- To purchase raw materials
- To pay salaries and wages
- To deliver goods/services

To allow a credit period to a customer

To raise an invoice

To collect dues

To pay suppliers/short-term loans

To purchase raw materials again

The operating cycle is the average time between purchasing or acquiring inventory and receiving cash proceeds from the sale of finished products. In other words, it is the time period, which elapses between the point at which cash is spent on the production of a product, and the collection of cash from the customer. The operating cycle for a company begins with the purchase of raw materials, but the payment is not done immediately. This leads to the creation of accounts payables. The raw material is then converted by the production process into finished goods and then sold. The time lag between the purchase of raw materials and the sale of finished goods is known as the inventory period. Upon sale of finished goods on credit terms, there exists a time lag between the sale of finished goods and the collection of cash on sale. This period is known as the accounts receivables period. Therefore, companies use some of their funds to finance inventory, through the manufacturing process, from raw materials to finished goods, and also the time lag between delivery of the finished goods/services and the payments by the customers, the accounts receivable. Business firms cannot finance the operating cycle (Accounts Receivable days + Inventory days) with Accounts Payable financing alone. Consequently, financing for working capital is needed. This shortfall is covered by the net profits generated internally or by externally borrowed funds or by a combination of both. Business firms also need short-term working capital at seasonal peak times. Even a business that is not seasonal, occasionally experiences peak months when sales are unusually high. This creates a need for extra working capital to fund the resulting high level of inventory and accounts receivable.

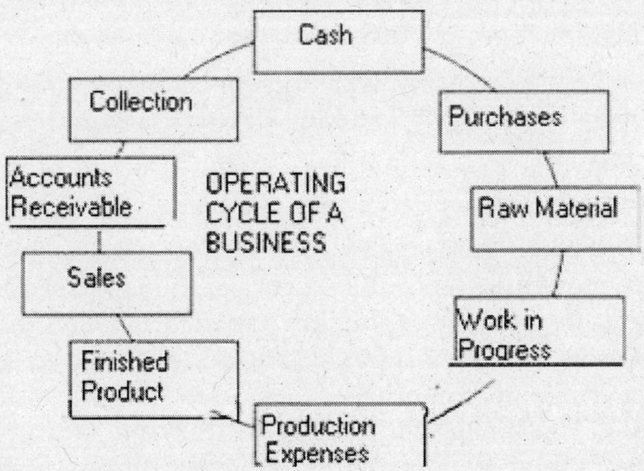

Fig. 2.1

As the above figure explains, the operating cycle or cash-to-cash cycle is the process of using cash to purchase current assets that are to be sold at a profit and collected as cash. Therefore, in nutshell, the operating cycle of a manufacturing company shows how the funds are used to purchase raw material inventory which is processed into finished goods inventory, sold at a profit to create receivables and collected as cash once again. The cash is then used to pay the suppliers (maturity of accounts payable) or short-term loans, with the profits left in the business. Sound working capital management involves matching the sources and uses of cash so that obligations come due as assets mature into cash.

COMPONENTS OF WORKING CAPITAL MANAGEMENT

A business firm must have sufficient cash balance to meet its immediate needs while ensuring that idle cash is invested to the organisation's best possible advantage. It is of paramount importance to have clear and accurate reports on each of the components of working capital and an awareness of the potential impact of external influences. Therefore, managing working capital is a matter of balance. The objective of working capital management is to maintain the optimum balance of each of the working capital components. This includes making sure that funds are held as cash/bank deposits for as long as and in the largest amounts possible, thereby maximising the interest earned. However, such cash may be invested in other assets or in paying other liabilities. Money invested in one area may cost opportunities for investment in other areas. If a firm is operating with more working capital than is necessary, this over-investment represents an unnecessary cost to the organisation and implies operating inefficiencies.

Working capital management involves the relationship between a firm's short-term assets and its short-term liabilities. The goal of working capital management is to ensure that a firm is able to continue its operations and that it has sufficient ability to satisfy both maturing short-term debt and upcoming operational expenses. The management of working capital involves managing inventories, accounts receivable and payable, and cash.

Working Capital Management takes place on two levels:

- The individual components of working capital (Cash, Receivable and Inventory) can be effectively managed by using various techniques and strategies.
- Financial tools like Ratio analysis can be used to monitor overall trends in working capital and to identify areas requiring closer management (see Chapter Financial Analysis).

Thus, principal current assets for a typical business are its inventories, its receivables, and its cash on hand. The key applications of working capital include maintaining the necessary stocks of the raw materials needed to create the products and funding the manufacturing and labour costs needed to transform those raw materials into finished goods for sale. Another important use of working capital in many businesses is providing the short-term financing for their customers' purchases by deferring collections for some period of time without interest charges.

When considering the techniques and strategies for working capital, we need to recognise that each company has a unique mix of working capital components. The emphasis that needs to be placed on each component varies according to the needs of the company. For example, some companies have significant inventory levels; others have little, if any, inventory. Moreover, working capital management is not an end in itself. It is an integral part of the company's overall management. The needs of efficient working capital management must be considered in relation to other aspects of the company's financial and non-financial performance.

A good practice in the management of working capital is to set benchmarks for every activity and determine how the actual figures are different from competitor firms. The benchmarks may include the rates of turnover in raw materials and finished-goods inventory, the average age of each receivable due from debtors, and the average length of time it takes to actually pay each bill to the trade creditors. But it should be kept in mind that no single level of any benchmark is right for every business.

The major components of working capital have been dealt with comprehensively in the subsequent chapters. Here, they are explained in brief.

1. Cash

Cash is the most liquid form of current assets. After this, in order of liquidity, come cash equivalents i.e. marketable securities or short-term investments. Cash and cash equivalents requires constant supervision. A well planned and maintained cash budgeting system is essential to answer key questions such as: Is the cash level adequate to meet current expenses as they come due? What is the time lag between cash inflows and outflows? When is the peak season which requires high volume of cash? What will be the magnitude of bank borrowing required to meet any cash shortfalls? When will this borrowing be necessary and when may repayment be expected? Following are the key strategies for efficient cash management.

- Inventory should be turned over as quickly as possible, while avoiding stockouts that may result in excessive lost sales.
- Accounts receivable should be collected as quickly as possible without losing future sales because of high pressure collection techniques, using cash discounts whenever economically justifiable.
- Accounts payable should be paid as late as possible without damaging the firm's credit rating, considering any cash discounts offered.

Good cash management requires regular cash forecasts. To maintain control over cash flow it is crucial that a cash flow plan or statement is prepared on a month-by-month or week-by-week basis, and which is continually reviewed and revised in the light of actual performance. Forecasts must be based on information provided by those managers responsible for the amounts and timing of expenditure. Capital expenditure and operating expenditure must be taken into account. It is also necessary to collect information about impending cash transactions from other financial systems, such as creditors and payroll.

Cash shortage is a common reason for business failure. However, businesses that are cash rich may also fail to take full advantage of opportunities to maximise the return on capital employed in the business. All investments should as a matter of company policy be appraised using one of the recognised discounted cash flow techniques such as NPV

(Net Present Value), IRR (Internal Rate of Return) or PI (Profitability Index). A company should determine whether each project is likely to pay back an acceptable return.

The finance manager must make decisions about how much cash should be available all the times in the firm's bank account and how much should be on term deposit at the various terms available. Cash receipts should be processed and banked as quickly as possible because they cannot earn interest or reduce overdraft until they are banked. Information about the existence and amounts of cash receipts is usually not available until they are processed. Good relationships with the bank should be maintained at all times with frequent interactions and meetings.

In nutshell, cash is a central component of working capital, so more efficient payment and collection practices can enhance any business's level of working capital. For example, business firms that receive frequent cheque payments from geographically dispersed locations can use lockboxes to collect remittances. In the lockbox arrangement, cheques can be processed more quickly than cheques mailed to a single location for batch processing. However, this facility has a cost. In addition to more efficient payment and collection systems, firms can enhance working capital by investing idle cash. Short-term investments can produce some additional income. A business's ability to invest idle cash effectively depends on its ability to forecast cash needs accurately. If the operating cash is tied up excessively, the costs of a missed opportunity or a late payment may exceed the additional income.

2. Inventory

Inventory often makes up more than forty per cent of a firm's current assets and therefore, requires close scrutiny. Inventory is kept in many forms— raw materials, work in progress and finished goods. The questions that must be answered in inventory management are: what is the reasonable level of inventory in relation to sales? What is the inventory turn over rate in relation to similar firms in the same industry? Is there any slow moving inventory? Is the firm loosing sales due to inadequate inventory levels? What action should be taken to increase or decrease inventory?

The total balance of inventory is the sum of the value of each individual stock line. Stock records are needed to provide an account of activity within each stock line and as evidence to support the balances used in financial reports. A company also needs a system of internal controls to efficiently manage stocks and to ensure that stock records provide reliable information.

Financial reports show only the total inventory balance. Analysts from outside the firm can examine this balance by using ratio analysis or other techniques. However, this gives only a limited assessment of inventory management and is not adequate for internal management. Good financial management necessitates the careful analysis of individual inventory lines. Inventory management is an important aspect of working capital management because inventories themselves do not earn any revenue. Holding either too little or too much inventory incurs costs. There is a trade-off to be made between carrying costs, ordering costs, and stockout costs.

Costs of carrying too much inventory are: Opportunity cost of capital, Storage costs, Theft, damage and pilferage costs, Obsolescence Risk, Insurance costs.

Costs of carrying too little inventory are stock out costs: Lost sales due to non-availability of material, Delayed delivery to customers, Loss of goodwill.

Ordering costs are: Freight and wages, Order documentation and administration cost, Loss of discounts.

Carrying costs can be minimised by making frequent small orders but this increases ordering costs and the risk of stock-outs. Risk of stock-outs can be reduced by carrying safety stocks (at a cost) and re-ordering ahead of time. The best ordering strategy requires balancing the various cost factors to ensure the firm incurs minimum inventory costs. The optimum inventory position is known as the Economic Order Quantity (EOQ).

In a manufacturing concern, main areas of waste, that relate mainly to inventory in terms of their handling and storage are overproduction, waiting, inappropriate processing, unnecessary inventory, unnecessary movement, product defects etc. These areas of waste emphasise the importance for companies to identify and take the appropriate action for improvements in this aspect of the management of working capital. Stock levels should be optimised so that neither too little is held to meet orders or too much held so that waste occurs.

Analytical review of inventories can help to identify areas where inventory management can be improved. Slow moving items, continual stockouts, obsolescence, stock reconciliation problems and excess spoilage are signals that stock lines need closer analysis and control.

However, it is important to keep an overall perspective. It is not cost-effective to closely manage a large number of low value inventory lines, nor is it necessary. A usual feature of inventories is that a small number of high value lines account for a large proportion of inventory value. The total value of inventory is represented by only 20% of the number of inventory items. Those high value lines need reasonably close management. The remaining 80% of inventory lines can be managed in routine without giving much stress.

Inventory management is part of the overall management strategy. The overall management philosophy of an organisation can affect the way in which inventory is managed. For example, Just In Time system organises production so that finished goods are not produced until the customer needs them (minimising finished goods carrying costs), and raw materials are not accepted from suppliers until they are needed. Thus, JIT inventory system reduces bottlenecks and stock holding costs.

3. Accounts Receivable

Accounts Receivable are the debtors/customers who have not yet made payment for the goods or services which the firm has provided. Almost all businesses are required to extend credit to their customers. The credit policies for customers offer an opportunity to manage the investment in working capital. The objective of receivable management is to minimise the time-gap between completion of sales and receipt of payments. Shortening this time interval can speed up the collections.

Effective management and control of debtors requires the establishment of appropriate policies covering the choice of customers, the way in which sales are made, trading terms, the sales invoicing system, the means of settlement, and the implementation of a credit management and overdue accounts collection system. The major questions that a business firm must answer, in order to have effective debt management, are: what is the amount of accounts receivable in relation to sales? How rapidly are accounts receivable converted into cash? Who are the doubtful customers? What action should be taken to speed up collections?

There should be a proper system established to see when the invoices become overdue. Accurate and up-to-date debtor information should be available, including all the invoices that have been issued and for all the payments that have been received, before calling a customer to follow payment.

Business firms also offer discounts for early payments, or add some charges for late payments. Some business firms follow aggressive collection activities such as frequent reminders and visits. Some firms experience that speeding up demands for payment put them at a competitive disadvantage. Therefore, the working capital calculations can suggest areas for potential efficiency, but they can be effectively implemented only after consideration of broader customer relationship management issues.

4. Accounts Payable

Trade creditors provide the company with an additional source of short-term finance. Accounts Payable are the suppliers of goods/services whose invoices have not yet been paid. Accounts or bills payable to creditors or banks are a second major source of financing for the business. Important questions in this class include: What is the amount of bank borrowing employed? Is this debt amount reasonable in relation to the equity financing of the firm? When will principal and interest payments fall due? Will funds be available to meet these payments on time? All these questions are very important for this aspect of working capital management.

Organisations often regard the amount owing to creditors as a free source of credit. However, creditor administration systems are expensive and time-consuming to run. The key concern in this area should be to minimise costs with simple procedures. While it is not advisable to pay accounts before they fall due, it is also not worthwhile to delay payments and forego discounts. Effective management and control of creditors requires the establishment of appropriate policies covering the choice of suppliers, the way in which purchases are made, trading terms, the purchase invoicing system, and the means of settlement.

The finance manager must maintain the level of payables and cash outflows in line with company policy, and at the same time ensuring no interruption to any manufacturing processes or the operations of the business. The manager must have accurate accounts payable information that is up-to-date in terms of all invoices received, invoices awaited and payments made.

5. Accrued Expenses

Accrued expenses are those current liabilities which are accrued but not yet paid for. Accrued expenses includes salaries payable, interest payable on bank borrowings, insurance premiums payable etc. Taxes and dividends, if any, should also be given due consideration. The key concern in this area, with regard to taxes and dividends payable is the magnitude, timing, and availability of funds for payment. Timely planning is required to ensure that these liabilities are paid on time.

It is important to remember here that although the working capital components mentioned above are listed separately but they must also be viewed in total and their inter-relatedness must be considered. Effective management of inventory, cash, receivables, and liabilities — the components of working capital — all have a powerful influence on the ultimate success or failure of the business.

ASSESSMENT OF WORKING CAPITAL REQUIREMENT

The investment in the operating cycle is called the working capital requirement. The working capital requirement (WCR) is normally financed by short-term bank loan because of its flexibility in accommodating the fluctuating nature of net current assets, and the lower cost of financing. Mathematically, we can calculate working capital with the help of following formula:

WCR = Inventory + Accounts Receivable – Accounts Payable – Pre-paid Expenses

We know that WC (Working capital) = CA (Current Assets) – CL (Current Liabilities)

or WC = Inventory + Debtors + Cash – Creditors – Pre-paid Expenses – Short-term Loans

Therefore, WC = WCR + Cash – Short-term Loans

Or in other words, the difference between working capital (WC) and working capital requirement (WCR) is Cash less Short-term Loans.

Since, Fixed Assets + Inventory + Debtors – Creditors – Pre-paid Expenses

= Equity + Financial Debt (Loans) – Cash

We know that financial debt comprises of long-term loans and short-term loans. So, an alternative equation for working capital is:

WC = Equity + Long-term Debt – Fixed Assets

In most manufacturing concerns, the working capital requirement remains positive. The smaller the WCR, the smaller is the total financing requirement, and the stronger is the financial base of the company. Some business firms may have limited inventory and zero accounts receivable, but high accounts payable. In such cases, WCR may be negative and these companies are effectively able to finance acquisition of fixed assets with funds payable to their suppliers. As a general rule, normally working capital (CA–CL) should always be positive in the long run because if it were negative then the company would be financing its fixed assets with current liabilities (short-term debt). The fundamental goal of working capital management is to maximize short-term liquidity, which in turn is an essential resource for building and maintaining any business. As a rule, the higher the level of working capital, the more readily a business can expand and improve the efficiency of operations. The business can even function when there is a working capital deficit, but than it will not have the liquidity necessary for growth. Since, working capital is simply the difference between total current assets and total current liabilities, it can be effectively increased by any strategy that either maximizes the former (CA) or minimizes the latter (CL).

MODERN MANTRA — ZERO WORKING CAPITAL

It is said that in a perfect world the net working capital will be Zero. Zero or lower working capital is very much desirable—to save costs through lower operating capital requirements and operating efficiencies. Is a zero working capital achievable? No doubt the strategies and tactics employed to reduce or eliminate working capital can control significant costs and inefficiencies to improve financial and operating performance.

Reduction in inventories or receivables results in increase in cash flows. Moreover, investment in working capital cost money, so reducing the level of working capital saves interest and opportunity costs. With zero working capital—inventories disappear, so warehouses can be sold, labour and overhead costs are reduced, and chances of theft and obsolescence are minimized. Proponents of the zero working capital concept claims that a movement toward this goal generates cash, speeds up production, and helps businesses make timely deliveries and operate more efficiently.

- The investment freed from inventories or receivables reduces financing requirements on a permanent basis, or at least for that level of activity.
- Increase in accounts payable reduces financing requirements from other sources, provided the new level can be maintained.
- The investment freed from working capital creates a source of financing available for another more productive purpose.
- Return on Investments increase as the investment base decreases, and inventories and receivables are significant investments in almost all the businesses.

Working capital owes its existence to a large extent to inefficiency in the business system. Working capital is the investment a business firm makes in the inefficiencies of its processes and procedures. It also represents firm's investment in suppliers' inefficiencies, and customers' inefficiencies. Receivables owe their existence to extending credit and financing others, billing delays, returns to suppliers, delays in collection, uncollected discounts and rebates, etc. These factors generally represent timing and performance inefficiencies.

Inventories owe their existence to a variety of factors such as varying and unpredictable demand, bottlenecks in distribution, variances in forecasting, long lead times, unreliable supply, fluctuating pricing, lengthy production runs, etc. All of these factors reflect inefficiencies or buffers in the distribution process. Reducing the level of raw material and finished goods inventories can help reduce the investment in working capital. Of course, running out of raw material can cause costly disruptions to manufacturing process, and lack of finished goods in stock can cause lost sales and lose some customers to the competitors. But an accurate appraisal of investments in these areas may reveal the finance manager the ways to improve business efficiency and profitability. In a perfect world, we can say that inventory will be unnecessary, or at least very minimal inventory would be required. Inventories in general reflect inefficiency somewhere in the process.

Therefore, the investment in inefficiency is a significant untapped source of funds. Zero working capital can be the key focal point of a breakthrough strategy of improving process efficiencies. There can be huge benefits – savings in financing costs; reduction in the size of or eliminating warehouses; reducing costs of inventory shrinkage, damage, pilferage, and obsolescence; reducing the overhead associated with managing the investment in inefficiency; challenging all existing practices in credit and payables; and achieving economies through process improvement.

FACTORS INFLUENCING WORKING CAPITAL REQUIREMENTS

Following are the factors, in general, which affect working capital needs of a business firm.

(a) *Nature of Business:* Nature of a particular business influences the working capital requirements of a firm. For example, a service firm like a consultancy business has a short operating cycle as most of its business will be on a cash basis, therefore the requirement for working capital will also be lower. On the other hand, a manufacturing concern will have a longer operating cycle due to more investment in its current assets. Hence, the working capital requirement will be more.

(b) *Seasonality of Operations:* Factors such as seasonality of raw materials or of demand may require a high level of inventory to be maintained by the company. There are firms whose products are sold only during particular seasons. For example, coolers and air conditioners are sold more during the summer season. Similarly, industry norms of credit allowed to buyers determine the level of debtors of the company in the normal course of business. Therefore, the firms whose products demand is seasonal will have greater working capital requirements during peak seasons and lower requirements during slack seasons. The firms, which are not affected by variations in seasonal demands, have stable working capital requirements.

(c) *Level of Activity:* Inventories and receivables are normally expressed as a multiple of a day's production or sale. Hence, higher the level of activity, higher the quantum of inventory, receivables and thereby working capital requirement of the business. So the level of working capital is directly proportionate to the level of activity of the business. Usually the previous year's figures and the management projections for the year provide good indicators about the working capital level.

(d) *Market Conditions:* Market conditions, the level of competition in the market also influences the working capital requirements of a firm. A firm facing high competition cannot afford to neglect the level of current assets. A firm with high competition needs to maintain high reserve of cash and inventory to meet any unexpected level of demand. In a market where the number of sellers is large and competitions is intense, customers can easily switch over to competitor's products if their demands are not fulfilled. On the other hand, a firm which is enjoying monopoly in the market or where the number of sellers is small and the demand for the product is high, it can make its customers wait for its products or even it can demand advance money before processing their orders. Thus, it will have lesser requirement for raw material and cash reserves.

(e) *Supply Conditions:* The supply and availability of raw material and other consumables also affects working capital requirement. If the raw material's supply is timely and adequate, the firm can continue with a low inventory level. If, on the other hand, the supply of raw material is scarce, unpredictable or unavailable, the firm is required to maintain high levels of inventory to conduct operations throughout the year.

PROFITABILITY VS. LIQUIDITY

The primary goal of financial management is the maximisation of stockholder wealth, or in other terms, maximisation of the firm's profits. A business firm wants to be profitable, and at the same time it should be liquid in order to continue in business.

In order to maximize a firm's profits there is always a tradeoff between profitability and risk. The greater the risk incurred in a decision, the greater the anticipated profit demanded. The decision centers on whether the return on a specific investment is sufficient to justify the risk involved. In case of an individual also, this is the reason that some people invest in low risk or fixed income securities while others are willing to take more risk and invest in the stock market. Likewise, some firms are more willing than others to accept a high risk in order to achieve a high potential profit. The point is that in making business decisions the firm is faced with the tradeoff— Risk vs. Return.

Firms want to stay in business, so it should be no surprise that one of the goals of financial management is to guarantee financial viability. This goal is often measured in terms of liquidity (solvency). Liquidity measures the amount of resources a firm has that are cash or are quickly convertible to cash to meet the obligations the firm has in the near term. Generally the near-term, or current, means one year or less. Thus a firm is liquid if it has enough current resources to meet its current obligations as they become due for payment. Solvency is the same concept as liquidity, except it if for the long term rather than short term. Long-term simply means time period more than one year. Does the firm have enough cash generation potential over the long term to meet the major cash needs that will occur over this period? A firm must plan for adequate solvency well in advance because the potentially large amounts of cash involved may take a long period of planning to generate. It is not a good idea to be too conservative and attempt to have maximum liquidity or solvency.

Given that the goal of the firm is to make more money now and in the future, the financial manager must balance the need for liquidity with the need to supply funds for the firm to continue to grow and be fully invested and therefore profitable. Every rupee kept in a liquid form (such as cash, treasury bills, or money market instruments) is a rupee that could have been invested by the firm in some long term, higher yielding project or investment.

It must be kept in mind that profitability and liquidity are not synonymous. A firm can be profitable every year of its existence, yet it may go bankrupt. How this is possible? Usually, it is the result of rapid expansion of business and poor financial planning. Expansion and growth plans require outlay of substantial amounts of cash for fixed assets such as land, plant and machinery etc. moreover, the increased inventory levels are required to handle a growing sales volume. All this investment is done before the receipt of cash from customers. However, it does not lead to the conclusion that growing companies go bankrupt. But they do need to plan their solvency along with their growth and expansion programme. A key is to focus on long-term planning for cash needs. There are so many sources of finance exist. Funds can also be obtained from issuing of equity or bonds. A firm should continually perform cash flow projections to anticipate future cash needs. So, liquidity and solvency are crucial to the firm's long-term viability.

RISK-RETURN TRADE-OFF

The management of working capital involves risk-return trade-off. The net working capital positions of a firm can be improved by adding more current assets relative to its current liabilities. For example, a firm may hold larger levels of stock or more investments in marketable securities; this will increase the proportion of current assets of the firm. This can also be achieved by reducing current liabilities as compared to current assets, for example, by financing current assets using long-term sources of finance such as equity, bonds etc. rather than short-term borrowings.

If, for instance, a firm increases its net working capital by holding larger investments in current assets like marketable securities and inventories without changing the level of current liabilities. This will increase and improve the firm's liquidity position. It implies that in case of any cash crunch, the firm can use its additional marketable securities to meet unexpected shortfall in its cash flow. Moreover, the high level of inventory will minimize the chances of stoppages in production, and the loss of sales from inventory shortages. However, because of these extra investment in current assets, the firm will earn low returns, hence firm's profitability will reduce. On the opposite, if a firm reduces its net working capital by substituting a short-term source of finance such as commercial paper for long-term source such as bonds. It will increase the firm's profitability due to the reason a short-term source of finance carries a lower rate of interest. Moreover, when a short-term source of finance is used to finance seasonal working capital requirements the firm needs to pay the interest only for the seasonal period and not for the whole year when the seasonal demands were zero. In case of a long-term source of finance the firm incurs additional borrowing costs for the whole year which reduces overall profitability.

So, from the Risk-Return Trade Off we can derive the following inferences:

Large current assets (e.g. cash, marketable securities etc.) mean low profitability but mean low risk (high liquidity) and vice versa.

Large current liabilities (e.g. short-term bank loans) mean high profitability but mean high risk (low liquidity).

THE RETURN

Current liabilities provide a return to the firm, as they provide a flexible source of financing as compared to long-term liabilities. A finance manager can use current liabilities to match the timing of a firm's short-term financing needs. For example, if a firm finances its procurement of raw material which is for a three month period, with a three month maturity loan, it can provide substantial savings over a long-term loan.

The rationale is that the use of long-term borrowing will be for the whole year rather than for the period in which funds are required. This will increase the interest burden on the firm. This is another return associated with the working capital management. The other major return or advantage is the promptness, that is, short-term loans can be arranged quickly than long-term loans. This source also provides flexibility as short-term loans usually have fewer restrictions than long-term loans. Another merit of resorting to short term financing is low interest rates. Short-term interest rates are typically lower than long-term rates.

THE RISK

The return also brings with it equal amount of risk. The use of current liabilities in comparison to long-term borrowings invites a greater degree of illiquidity risk. Using short-term debt as a permanent source of financing brings the fixed interest burden for the firm. A short-term loan must be repaid on its maturity which increases the chances of default.

Another reason is the uncertainty of interest rates from year to year. Short-term interest rates fluctuate a great deal compared to long-term interest rates. A firm depending on the lender's perception about the firm's riskiness may get short term debt on low rates on a particular year and for the same reason on high rates another year. Whereas, in case of a long term debt the interest rate is fixed for the entire period of agreement. Moreover, during periods of tight credit markets, there may be chances of illiquidity risk if a firm has a heavy burden of short-term debt.

Therefore, using short-term financing over long-term financing has advantages and disadvantages. A firm chooses a Risk- Return Trade-off of Short-term Debt versus Long-term capital depending on its working capital policy.

WORKING CAPITAL POLICY

The working capital policy adopted by a firm depends on its objectives and goals. The objectives, in turn, are influenced by the type of business, general market conditions and economic trends. Often, the choice of objective presents a conflict between the goals of profitability and liquidity as discussed earlier. Working capital policies range between aggressive policies and conservative policies. The former increase profitability through holding low levels of cash and stocks, but run the risk of potential cash shortages and stock-outs. The latter provide greater flexibility, with higher levels of cash and stocks, which provide lower risk at the expense of reduced profitability.

Regardless of the policies adopted, improved management of working capital may have a significant impact on the level of requirement for external financing. Reductions in levels of WCR reduce the requirement for external financing and its associated costs. Maintenance of optimal, and therefore more manageable levels of WCR increase levels of efficiency and effectiveness and so additionally contribute to increased profitability and a reduction in the requirement for external financing.

A firm's working capital policy can be understood with the help of its two elements:

(a) Investment in current assets

(b) Working capital financing policy

The Risk-Return Trade-Off

Management	*Profitability*	*Liquidity*
More investment in marketable securities and inventories:	Lower	Higher
More use of short-term than long-term sources of finance:	Higher	Lower

(a) Investment in Current Assets

These policies are general strategies that firms may follow with regard to their overall investment in current assets.

(1) Flexible Policy: Under a flexible current asset investment policy (also known as Relaxed or Conservative Policy) a firm carries a relatively large amounts of cash, marketable securities, and inventories. Also sales are stimulated by a generous or liberal credit policy resulting in high levels of accounts receivables. This is a low risk strategy because the firm always has plenty of cash and inventory on hand. Moreover with high level of receivables, the chances of uncollectable debts also increase. This approach provides lowest risk and lowest expected return.

(2) Aggressive Policy: Under an Aggressive or Restrictive policy investment in current asset holdings such as cash, marketable securities, inventories, and receivables are minimized. This is a high-risk strategy because the firm tries to keep the minimum of cash and inventory. The return is high because less money is invested in low yielding assets. Therefore, this approach usually provides highest expected return and highest risk.

(3) Moderate Policy: A moderate policy for investment in current assets provides a mid way between the two extreme approaches. It strives to achieve a balance between flexible and aggressive current asset investment policies where the risk is moderate and potential returns are also moderate. A firm must hold enough working capital to conduct business operations. However, it is costly to hold working capital. Therefore, a firm should hold only as much working capital as it needs to continue business operations.

(b) Working Capital Financing Policy

Working capital or current asset financing policy answers the question — How will the current assets be financed? With long-term capital or short-term debt financing?

We have discussed earlier Risk- Return Trade-off of Short-term Debt versus Long-term capital in detail. Now let us understand the alternate policies available to a firm to finance different classes of current assets. Broadly, current assets can be classified as permanent or temporary.

PERMANENT AND TEMPORARY ASSETS

Assets can be regarded as Permanent and Temporary/Fluctuating as per investment. An asset will be permanent if the investment in the asset is for more than one year. Or in other words, permanent current assets are the current assets that the company needs to maintain throughout the entire year. It is to take care that the time period under consideration is the time to hold an investment in the asset, not the life of the asset. Temporary current assets are those current assets that are due to seasonal fluctuations. These assets will have investment for less than a year or in other words, these assets will be liquidated within a year but will not be replaced. So it is clear that some part of the firm's current assets is permanent and the remainder is temporary or fluctuating.

Following are the policies or general strategies that firms may follow with regard to how current assets are to be financed.

(a) Aggresive Financing Policy: Under this approach relatively high proportion of short-term debt is used as a permanent source of financing. The firm uses some short-term debt to finance some of its permanent level of current assets and even more short-term debt is raised during seasonal fluctuations. This approach is considered risky but it provides potential for high return.

(b) Conservative Financing Policy: Under this policy all the assets, fixed as well as current, are financed with long-term sources. Even some of the temporary current assets are also financed using long-term capital. When the firm has excess liquidity (cash), it invests in marketable securities but relies less on short-term debt during seasonal fluctuations. This is a low risk approach with low returns.

(c) Self-Liquidating Financing Policy: Self-Liquidating Financing Policy is also referred to as Maturity Matching or Hedging Approach. Under this policy, the maturity of the firm's assets is matched with the maturity of the firm's liabilities. This approach states that a sufficient level of liquidity should be maintained to meet the firm's maturing debts/borrowings on time. In other words, all long-term assets including the permanent current assets are financed with long-term sources of financing and temporary current assets are financed with short-term debt.

In this approach, cash inflows of an asset are matched with the maturity of the debt. For example, inventory should be financed with a short-term loan (current liability). The logic behind this principle is that the funds are required for a limited period and, when the time to repay the loan would come the firm will have cash inflow from the sale of the inventory in the shape of finished goods. On the other hand, if the firm resorts to a long-term source of finance, which means the firm will have the funds available even after the inventory is sold, that leads to excessive liquidity, which will earn no return (in case of idle cash) or low return (in case of investment in marketable securities) and the firm will have to bear the interest cost for the whole year. Therefore, the firm should finance the asset with a source of financing that matches the expected cash inflows from the asset. In nutshell, permanent assets are financed with permanent sources, and temporary assets are financed with temporary sources. The optimal financing policy involves the use of a mix of short-term and long-term sources of financing. The appropriate level of financing mix according to self-liquidating principle depends on the nature of the firm's needs for financing, i.e. whether the need is permanent or temporary.

WORKING CAPITAL MANAGEMENT IN MULTINATIONAL ENVIRONMENT

The principles and concepts of working capital management are same for domestic and multinational firms. The only practical problem faced by multinationals while managing their working capital is that they spend and receive money in different countries and there is always a difference between the exchange rates of different currencies. Moreover, a multinational company's assets are always valued in terms of foreign currencies. So, whenever there is a decline in the value of a foreign currency in relation to the value of domestic currency, the multinational company will lose. In other words, a multinational is always exposed to exchange rate risk. Though, this also helps sometimes when the value of a liability falls due to a fall in the value of foreign currency. It implies that a multinational will be concerned with evaluating its net position i.e. the difference between exposed assets and exposed liabilities for a particular time period and in each currency to which the firm has exchange risk exposure. In international environment, the problem of float is also more serious than in domestic operations. This is because of the loss of income on the funds tied up during the longer transfer process and their exposure to foreign exchange risk during the transfer period.

If a multinational is to manage its cash position and work against its foreign exchange exposure it needs good measures. The two major functions of multinational working capital management are optimizing cash flows and investing excess cash. These two functions, if performed properly, can lead to the efficient usage of funds.

A multinational firm invests in a portfolio of foreign currencies instead of just a single foreign currency. A portfolio of currencies reduces the possibility that the foreign investment may backfire because of depreciation in the currencies that make up the portfolio. If all funds are in an investment denominated in a single foreign currency, the possibility of that currency's substantial depreciation is relatively high as compared to the possibility of a substantial depreciation for an entire portfolio of currencies. There are three types of portfolio management techniques normally used by international cash managers. First, all excess funds of subsidiaries are remitted to the parent and then used to pay the parent's short-term debts. Second, multinational companies can centralize cash management in a third country and invest funds on marketable securities. Third, they can centralize cash management at headquarters with subsidiaries holding only minimum amount of cash for transaction purposes.

Multinationals sometimes maintains over-stocked inventory accounts, particularly the companies which rely on imported inventories. These companies buy inventories in advance and stockpile them till then there is a strong possibility for an imminent devaluation of a local currency. The other reason is the expectation that the host government will impose import restrictions.

In nutshell, multinational companies face a lot of external environmental constraints because countries have different tax laws, different financial markets, different regulations, and many other differences. So all advantages and techniques of international working capital management are subject to these constraints, such as regulatory, tax, foreign exchange, and other economic constraints. Multinational companies face these constraints because they operate across national borders. To determine the optimal amount of investment in various current asset accounts, the financial manager must consider all these constraints.

Chapter 3

WORKING CAPITAL FINANCING

(**Contents:** Introduction, Instruments For Financing Working Capital Needs: Commercial Paper (CP), Inter-Corporate Deposits, Accounts Receivable Financing, Spontaneous Financing, Inventory Loans, Bank Credit, Banking Policy For Working Capital Finance, Dahejia Committee Report, Tandon Committee Report, Chore Committee Report, Nayak Committee Report, Bank Credit — Current Scenario, Essentials For Bank Credit, Banking Procedure For Working Capital Financing.)

"A bank is a place where they lend you an umbrella in fair weather and ask for it back when it begins to rain."

— Robert Frost

INTRODUCTION

Almost all the business firms at one time or another realizes the need to raise capital. Apart from financing for investing in fixed assets, every business also requires funds on a continual basis for carrying on its operations. These include amounts expenses incurred for purchase of raw material, manufacturing, selling, and administration until such goods are sold and the monies realized. Business transactions are generally carried on credit with a number of days elapsing subsequent to the sale being effected for realization of proceeds. While part of the raw material may be purchased by credit, the business would still need to pay its employees, meet manufacturing and selling expenses (wages, power, supplies, transportation and communication) and the balance of its raw material purchases. This way, working capital refers to the source of financing required to by businesses on a continual basis for meeting these needs.

The availability and costs of this capital vary depending on the type of business and the stage of development in which the business finds itself at that time. If a new business firm experiences a need for short-term working capital during its first few years of operation, it can rely on equity or debt funds for working capital needs. If the firm is in existence for a long period of time then trade credit and bank loans can be good sources of short-term finance. Some business firms have enough cash reserves to fund seasonal working capital needs. However, this is very rare for a new business.

Factoring is another resource for short-term working capital financing. This type of financing is more expensive than conventional bank financing but is often used by new businesses.

Short-term finance can be availed for working capital from a wide range of financial intermediaries in many different forms. The credit can be Unsecured or Secured loan. Unsecured loans include all those sources that have as their security only the lender's faith in the ability of the borrower to repay the funds when due. The interest rate charged on secured short-term loans is typically higher than the interest rate on unsecured short-term loans. Typically, companies that require secured loans may not qualify for unsecured debt, and they are perceived as higher-risk borrowers by lenders. The presence of collateral does not change the risk of default; it provides a means to reduce losses if the borrower defaults. In general, lenders require security for less-creditworthy, higher-risk borrower firms. Since the negotiation and administration of these loans is more troublesome for the lender, the lender normally requires certain fees to be paid by the secured borrower. The higher rates on these secured short-term loans are attributable to the greater risk of default and the increased loan administration costs of these loans over the unsecured short-term loan. Secured loans involve the pledge of specific assets as collateral in the event the borrower defaults in payment of principal or interest. Commercial banks, finance companies, and factors are the primary suppliers of secured credit. The principal sources of collateral are accounts receivable and inventories.

INSTRUMENTS FOR FINANCING WORKING CAPITAL NEEDS

Major sources of short-term finance include accrued wages, taxes, trade credit, bank loans, commercial paper, Inter-corporate deposits etc. In order to raise capital, it is imperative that the finance manager understands the dynamics of the market in order to accurately assess the financing options available to the business at any given time. Following are the most common sources of short-term working capital financing.

COMMERCIAL PAPER (CP)

The Commercial Paper in India owes its growth to the Vaghul Committee appointed by RBI in September 1986. Initially minimum size of issue was restricted to Rs. 1 crore and the maturity period restricted to 91 days to 6 months. Subsequently the minimum amount was lowered to Rs. 25 lacs (now it is further reduced to 5 lacs) and the maturity period modified to 30 days to one year (now it is further reduced to 15 days) from the date of issue. CP can be issued in denominations of Rs.5 lacs or multiples thereof. The minimum amount invested by a single investor is at least Rs. 5 lacs.

In India, only the most creditworthy companies can issue commercial paper. Commercial paper is simply a promise to pay for short-term debt securities. It is an unsecured money market instrument issued in the form of a promissory note. In India, Commercial Paper was introduced to enable corporate borrowers with good credit standing to diversify their sources of short-term borrowings and to provide an additional instrument to investors. Issue of commercial paper became popular towards the late 1990 but remained essentially an instrument of working capital financing. Only highly rated corporate bodies, primary dealers, satellite dealers and financial institutions have been authorized to issue commercial papers.

The Reserve Bank of India amended the guidelines for issue of Commercial Paper in October 2000. Banks and financial institutions are prohibited from underwriting or co-accepting issues of Commercial Paper. Banks and FIs will, however, have the flexibility to fix working capital limits duly taking into account resource pattern of companies financing including CPs. As per the guidelines issued by RBI, a company is eligible to issue CP provided –

- Minimum tangible net worth as per the latest audited balance sheet should not be less than Rs. 4 crore.
- The working capital (fund-based) limit of the company from the banking system is not less than Rs. 4 crore and
- The borrowal account of the company is classified as a Standard Asset by the financing banks.

Tangible Net Worth means the paid-up capital plus free reserves (including the share premium account, capital and debentures redemption reserves and any other reserve not being created for repayment of any future liability or for depreciation in assets or for bad debts or reserve created by revaluation of assets) as per the latest audited financial reports of the company, as reduced by the amount of accumulated balance of loss, balance deferred revenue expenditure as also other intangible assets.

The minimum credit rating should be P-2 of Credit Rating Information Services of India Ltd. (CRISIL) or equivalent rating by other credit agency such as Investment Information and Credit Rating Agency of India Ltd. (ICRA), Credit Analysis and Research Ltd. (CARE), or Duff & Phelps Credit Rating India Pvt. Ltd. (DCR India). The issuer shall ensure at the time of issuing CPs that the rating obtained is current and has not fallen due for review.

The investor in CP may be any individual, bank, other corporate body registered or incorporated in India and unincorporated bodies, Non-Resident Indian and Foreign Institutional Investor. However, investment by FIIs would be within the limits set for their investments by Securities and Exchange Board of India (SEBI). At present the limit is 30 per cent set for their investments in debt instruments.

The aggregate amount of CP from an issuer shall be within the limit as approved by its Board of Directors. The total amount of CP proposed to be issued should be raised within a period of two weeks from the date on which the issuer opens the issue for subscription. Within 3 days of the completion of issue, a report must be submitted to Industrial and Export Credit Department (IECD), Reserve Bank of India through the Issuing and Paying Agent (IPA). Only a scheduled bank can act as an IPA for issuance of CP. Every issue of CP will be treated as a fresh issue and no issuer can have the issue underwritten or co-accepted.

Every issuer must appoint an IPA for issuance of CP. The issuer should disclose to the potential investors its financial position as per the standard market practice. After the exchange of deal confirmation between the investor and the issuer, issuing company shall issue physical certificates to the investor or arrange for crediting the CP to the investor's account with a depository. Investors shall be given a copy of IPA certificate to the effect that the issuer has a valid agreement with the IPA and documents are in order.

Issuers have to ensure that the guidelines and procedures laid down for CP issuance are strictly followed. Issuing and Paying Agent (IPA) which is a scheduled bank would ensure that issuer has the minimum credit rating as stipulated by the RBI and amount mobilised through issuance of CP is within the limit under the specified rating. The credit rating agency have the discretion to determine the validity period of the rating depending upon its evaluation about the strength of the issuer. Accordingly, CRA shall at the time of rating, clearly indicate the date when the rating is due for review. While the CRAs can decide the validity period of credit rating, CRAs would have to closely monitor the rating assigned to issuers vis-à-vis their track record at regular intervals and would be required to make its revision in the ratings public through its publications and website.

There are several advantages that accrue to the issuer of commercial paper. Commercial paper interest rates are generally lower than rates on bank loans and comparable sources of short-term financing. With commercial paper as a single source for all its short-term financing, the firm can satisfy its very large credit needs. Moreover, it enhances the reputation and prestige of the issuing firm because it is widely recognized that only the most creditworthy firms have access to the commercial paper market. Commercial paper as a short-term financing tool, however, involves high risk also. That is, the commercial paper market is highly rigid and do not provide any flexibility in terms of repayment.

INTER-CORPORATE DEPOSITS

Apart from CPs, companies also have access to another market called Inter-Corporate Deposits (ICD) market. An ICD is an unsecured loan extended by one corporate to another. This instrument of short-term finance involves movement of funds from funds-surplus companies to credit worthy corporate borrowers. The period of deposit varies from purely on call and to 180 days. This source is mostly used by those firms which do not have access to commercial paper because of low credit worthiness. Also the better-rated companies can borrow from the banking system and lend in the inter-corporate deposit market. As the cost of funds for a corporate is much higher than a bank, the rates in this market are higher than those in the other markets. ICD is an unsecured instrument, and hence the risk inherent is high. The ICD market is not well organised with very little information available publicly about transaction details.

A company cannot make any loan to any other body corporate, give guarantee or security in connection with any loan made by any person to another body corporate, or acquire, by subscription, purchase or in any other manner, securities in any other body corporate — exceeding 60 % of its paid up share capital and free reserves or 100 % of its free reserves, whichever is more, unless approved by a special resolution passed at a general meeting of members.

No loan can be made at a rate of interest lower than the bank rate prescribed by the Reserve Bank of India. A company which has defaulted in repaying public fixed deposits cannot make or give any investment/loan/guarantee/security unless the fixed deposit is fully repaid along with interest due as per the terms and conditions of the fixed deposit.

A register of such inter-corporate loans and investments must be maintained giving the relevant details.

The above provisions do not apply to any deposit/ guarantee / security made or given by–

- A banking company or an insurance company or a housing finance company in the ordinary course of its business or a company established with the object of financing industrial enterprises or providing infrastructure facilities
- A company whose principal business is the acquisition of shares, stocks, debentures or other securities
- A private company unless it is a subsidiary of a public company
- Investment made under Rights issue of securities
- Loan made by holding company to its wholly subsidiary company
- Guarantee or security given by a holding company for loan to its wholly owned subsidiary
- Acquisition of securities by a holding company in its wholly owned subsidiary

ACCOUNTS RECEIVABLE FINANCING

A firm's receivables can be termed as its most liquid assets and they serve as prime collateral for a secured loan. Two major modes of financing based on receivables are pledging and factoring.

(i) Pledging

A pledge of accounts receivable is the use of a firm's receivables to secure a short-term loan. The lender evaluates the quality of the accounts receivable, selects acceptable accounts, and files a lien on the collateral. After the selection of accounts, the lender determines the percentage advanced against receivables. It can range from 50 to 90 per cent of the face value of the acceptable receivables; this amount becomes the principal on the loan. Pledging receivables usually costs two to five per cent above the bank's prime lending rate. Finance companies usually charge an even higher rate.

The major advantage of pledging accounts receivable is the ease and flexibility it provides to the borrower. Moreover, financing is done on a continuous basis. The new receivables created through further credit sales becomes the collateral for the financing of new production. The only disadvantage associated with this method of financing is its high cost as compared with other sources of short-term credit.

(ii) Factoring[1]

Factoring accounts receivable is the outright sale to the factor or financial institution. A factor is a firm that acquires the receivables of other firms. The factor sets the conditions of the sale in a factoring agreement. The factor bears the risk of collection and services the accounts for a fee. The fee is stated as a per cent of the face value of all receivables factored usually from 1 per cent to 3 per cent. Normally factoring is done on a non-recourse basis (the factor accepts all credit risks), and the customer is usually notified that the account receivable has been sold. The factor firm typically does not make payment for factored accounts until the accounts have been collected or the credit terms have been met. If the firm wishes to receive immediate payment, it can borrow from the factor, using the factored accounts as collateral. Factoring can typically cost from 3 to 7 per cent above the prime rate including commissions and interest. This type of financing is provided by specialized financial institutions called factors. Some commercial banks and commercial finance companies also provide this service. The biggest advantage is immediate conversion of receivables into cash and also the known pattern of cash flows.

SPONTANEOUS FINANCING

The short term spontaneous financing is the financing that arises from the normal operating cycle. The two major sources of spontaneous financing are accounts payable and accrued expenses. Both of these sources are spontaneous, since their levels increase and decrease directly with increases or decreases in sales. If sales increase, the firm will purchase more new materials, resulting in higher accruals of these items. Neither accounts payable nor accruals have stated cost although accounts payable often have an unstated cost in cases where a cash discount is offered.

(i) Accrued Expenses

Almost all the business firms pay salaries and wages to their employees monthly. Accrued expenses are periodically recurring short-term liabilities such as wages accrued but not yet paid to employees and taxes owed but not yet paid. Therefore, firms accrue salaries and wages for a period usually a month, in essence, a loan from their employees. Similarly, firms generally make periodical income tax payments for their estimated tax liability. This means that the firm has the use of the tax amount it owes based on quarterly profits up through the end of the quarter.

---

1. This important source of funding the receivable is explained in detail in the Chapter Receivable Management.

The firm can use all the accruals it can since there is no actual cost involved. However, it has little control over the amount of accruals. In the same manner, business firms pay sales taxes and withholds income taxes for their employees. So longer the period, greater is the amount of financing for the firm.

(ii) Accounts Payable (Trade Credit)

Trade credit is a primary source of spontaneous financing as it arises spontaneously with the firm's purchases. Trade credit allows a firm to defer cash payments to its suppliers in exchange for its promise to pay them in the future. Using trade credit to purchase goods or services from suppliers creates an account payable. For trade credit, the firm needs only to place an order with its supplier of goods. The supplier depending on firm's credit rating grants the credit period and cash discount. The decision to extend trade credit to the purchasing firm is generally based on the supplier's credit policy. The amount of trade credit extended to the purchasing firm is based on supplier's estimate of the firm's creditworthiness, and its capacity to pay the bills. The purchasing firm pays for the goods as per the supplier's credit terms. Credit terms usually express the amount of the cash discount, the date of its expiration, and the due date. Trade discounts are generally listed on an invoice in the format: 2/10, Net 30. 2/10 indicates the amount of the discount offered and the number of days the firm has to make payment to avail that discount. Net 30 indicates when the full amount of the invoice (without the discount) is due if the trade discount is not taken. So, if payment is made within 10 days, a 2 per cent cash discount is allowed, otherwise, the entire amount is due in 30 days. Where the firm avails trade discounts the basic rule should be — Always make your payments on time, but never before they are due. In most of the cases the firm is better off to pay the bill early and take advantage of the trade discount. The cost of not taking the cash discount can be substantial.

The following is the calculation of cost of not availing the discount.

Suppose a firm makes purchases of Rs. 10,000 on credit and the terms of credit from the supplier are 2/10, net 30. If the firm wants to avail the 2% discount then the firm should pay on 10th day otherwise the payment is due on the 30th day after the purchase. If the firm takes the discount then it should pay Rs. 9800 (Rs. 10000-200) on the 10th day. So, if the firm does not take the discount, it is paying Rs. 200 interest on a 20 day loan of Rs. 9800. The periodic interest rate on this loan is as follows:

$$\text{Interest Rate} = \frac{\text{Discount percentage}}{100 - \text{Discount percentage}}$$

$$\text{Or } 2/98 = 2.04\%$$

Now, let us calculate the time period in terms of a year for which the credit has been taken, assuming 360 days in a year, as follows:

$$\text{Time Period} = \frac{360 \text{ days}}{\text{Credit period - Discount period}}$$

$$\text{Or } 360/(30 - 10) = 360/20 = 18$$

The annual cost (interest rate) of not taking the discount is

= Interest Rate ´ Time Period = 2.04% 18 = 36.7%.

36.7% a quite high interest rate, therefore, the firm should avail the discount option.

This way, trade credit can be termed as a short-term loan without interest. The amount of the loan is equal to the purchase price of the material the purchasing firm has purchased. The loan's maturity date is the date the firm is required to pay the supplier's bill. Trade credit is one of the easiest sources of short-term financing available to the firm. Moreover, trade credit is easily obtained and usually there are no formal agreements in obtaining the credit. No extra cost or interest is charged on this short-term loan, as long as the bill is paid as per supplier's terms. When a firm purchases on credit, it gets credit period in which it has to pay the dues. The firm can wait as long as possible to pay, so long as there are no penalties. Sometimes a firm might be able to get away with stretching accounts payable or deliberately paying late. However, this can create problems between the firm and its suppliers, even if there are no explicit penalties. Continued practice of deliberately paying late can lead to a loss of credit. A consistent payment history with the suppliers goes a long way in helping suppliers feel safe in extending trade credit. However, occasionally and for short periods, stretching accounts payable may offer the firm an emergency financing.

INVENTORY LOANS

For a manufacturing firm, inventory loans are a source of short-term secured credit. The amount of the loan that can be obtained depends on the marketability and life of the inventory. For a manufacturer, inventory is classified into one of three categories: Raw materials, work-in-progress and finished goods. Classification into one of these categories depends on the firm's business; what are raw materials for one firm may be finished goods for another. Inventory types have different levels of liquidity. Demand for raw materials and work-in-progress depends on the demand for finished goods. Raw materials such as grains, oil, chemicals etc. are excellent sources of collateral because of their marketability. But other items like work-in-process provide poor collateral because of their lack of liquidity.

Following are the most popular methods by which inventory can be used to secure financing.

(i) Floating Inventory Lines

Floating inventory lines are made by lenders and secured by a claim on inventory items. The interest charge on a floating lien is typically 3 to 5 per cent above the prime rate. Under this the borrower gives the lender a lien against all its inventories. From the view point of lender inventory provides a very weak collateral. The borrowing firm maintains the physical possession and control of the inventories. Therefore, lack of control over the inventory reduces the value of security to the lender.

(ii) Trust Receipt Inventory

Trust receipt inventory loans are often made by manufacturers' financing subsidiaries to their customers. Under this arrangement, merchandise is typically expensive, for example, automotive, industrial and consumer-durable equipments, and remains in the hands of the borrower. Moreover products such as automobiles, appliances, boats, etc. have to be displayed to be sold. The only way small firms can afford such displays is by borrowing money. The lender advances 80 to 100% of the cost of the salable inventory. Such loans are often secured by a note and a trust receipt. This trust receipt is the legal paper which is used for serial numbered merchandise. Inventory is serialized and cannot be sold without the lender's permission. Borrower retains physical control over the inventory. The interest charge is generally 2 per cent or more above the prime rate.

(iii) Warehouse Receipt Loan

A warehouse receipt loan is an arrangement whereby the lender receives control of the pledged collateral. The inventory may be retained by the borrower in the firm's warehouse with security administered by a field warehousing company. Or the inventory may be stored in a terminal warehouse located in the geographic vicinity of the borrower. Generally, less than 75 to 90 per cent of the collateral's value is advanced to the borrower. Banks also take commodities as security by lending money on a warehouse receipt.

BANK CREDIT

All over the world, bank credit is a major source of financing the working capital. Indian commercial banks have been making in larger measure, term finance to industry and providing investment banking services apart from setting up subsidiaries in such diverse areas as mutual funds securities trading and factoring. In addition to this, the development finance institutions (DFIs)[2] are increasingly getting into the areas of working capital finance and have also set up banking and mutual fund subsidiaries. The financing requirements of Indian corporate, whether from the DFIs or from the banks, are now being seen as an integrated operation. Non-banking financial companies (NBFCs) have proliferated in India in areas like consumer finance, hire purchase, equipment leasing and housing finance[3]. However, banking policies and practices in India are different from those prevalent in the developed countries. In India, for the banks to decide to lend funds for financing the working capital, a firm's creditworthiness is not judged by the strength of the current ratio and the net working capital. The major factor considered is the current assets charged in favour of the bank as security against borrowing. Moreover, this is also not followed strictly. Following are the financing arrangements provided by a bank for working capital financing in India:

---

2. After independence, India had only the traditional commercial banks. The banks in India were not keen to provide medium and long-term finance to industry and other sectors for their fixed asset formation. The banks were willing to fund basically the working capital requirements of the credit-worthy borrowers on the security of tangible assets. Since the government was keen to stimulate setting up of a wide range of new industrial units as also expansion /diversification of the existing units it decided to encourage setting up of financial intermediaries that provided term finance to projects in industry. Thus emerged a chain of national and state level development financial institutions (DFIs) for meeting requirements of medium and long-term finance of all range of industrial units, from the smallest to the very large ones. Reserve Bank of India and Government of India nurtured DFIs through various types of financial incentives and other supportive measures. The main objective was to provide long-term finance to the industry, which the then existing commercial banks were not interested to provide because of high risk.
3. Adapted from the Narasimhan Committee's recommendations — Second Report, 1997.

(i) Line of Credit (LOC)

A line of credit is an agreement between a commercial bank and a business that states the amount of short term borrowing the bank will make available to the firm over a given period of time. In a line of credit agreement, a bank may retain the right to revoke the line if any major changes occur in the firm's financial condition or operations. To ensure that the borrower will not default, frequently a line of credit requires the borrower to maintain a minimum balance in the bank throughout the loan period, called a compensating balance. In some cases, fees in lieu of balances may be negotiated. All this increases the effective cost of the loan to the borrower, unless a deposit balance equal to or greater than this balance requirement is ordinarily maintained in the bank. To ensure that money lent under the credit agreement is actually being used to finance working capital and not permanent asset acquisitions such as plant and equipment, banks require that the borrower have a zero loan balance for a certain number of days per year. This is called the annual cleanup period.

(ii) Revolving Credit

A revolving credit agreement is a guaranteed line of credit. Revolving credit is a special type of line of credit agreement in which the line of agreements usually extend from 1 to 5 years in duration. Under a line of credit agreement, a firm is not guaranteed that the bank will have funds available to lend upon demand, while under the more formal revolving credit agreement the availability of funds is guaranteed. Since the lender under the revolving credit agreement guarantees the availability of funds, the borrower pays a commitment fee for the unused portion of the line.

(iii) Bank Overdraft

The word overdraft means the act of overdrawing from a bank account. In other words, the account holder withdraws more money from a bank account than has been deposited in it. In the case of line of credit, a proper limit is sanctioned which normally is a certain percentage of the value of the commodities/debts pledged by the account holder with the Bank. Overdraft, on the other hand, is allowed against a host of other securities including financial instruments like shares, units of mutual funds, debentures, insurance policy etc.

(iv) Discounting of Bills

Bills of exchange are promissory notes issued for commercial transactions involving exchange of goods and services. Bills of exchange are negotiable instruments drawn by the seller (drawer) of the goods on the buyer (drawee) of the goods for the value of the goods delivered. These bills form a part of a company's banking limits and are discounted by the banks. Banks in turn rediscount bills with other banks. If the bill is payable at a future date and the seller needs money before the maturity of the bill then he may approach his bank for discounting the bill. The bank from the drawee will receive the maturity proceeds at the maturity date. If the bank needs fund before the maturity of the bill then it can rediscount the bill already discounted by it in the commercial bill rediscount market at the market linked discount rate.

BANKING POLICY FOR WORKING CAPITAL FINANCE

The Indian banking sector has come a long way from an era of stringent regulation to the present day deregulated and liberalised banking environment. The issue of computation of working capital financing has aroused considerable debate and attention over the past few decades. It is interesting to examine the development of working capital financing over a period, its new dimensions, the issues involved and the implications of the new pattern. For the first time in 1965, the need was felt for imposing some credit discipline on the large borrowers so as to prevent misuse of bank credit and to ensure a larger flow of credit to the industry. Consequently, the Credit Authorisation Scheme requiring commercial banks to obtain prior permission from the Reserve Bank (RBI) for extending working capital finance above a stipulated level was introduced.

In 1975, the working capital lending system was reviewed by the Tandon Committee and the Committee prescribed a specific structure for lending for working capital by commercial banks to bring consistency between the method of assessment and the post-sanction follow-up. The Committee formulated a consolidated approach by way of fixation of the Maximum Permissible Bank Finance (MPBF) by treating borrowings from different banks for working capital together and fixing limits in totality. Another important aspect was the introduction of a well-structured information system enabling smooth flow of information from borrowers to the financing banks through monthly, half-yearly and annual statements. Banks were earlier required to extend working capital to various categories of borrowers based on specific parameters laid down by the Reserve Bank for individual sectors as suggested by Tandon Committee. The Credit Authorisation Scheme (CAS) was introduced for very large quantum of working capital finance but it was only after a detailed scrutiny on several accounts that banks were permitted to extend a particular level of working capital to the industry. In due course, Credit Authorisation Scheme gave way to the Credit Monitoring Arrangement Scheme under which the banks were required to report the extent of credit given to large borrowal accounts, instead of forwarding the actual loan proposals.

Tandon Committee's recommendations reinforced by Chore Committee were implemented in all the Indian Banks and the Bank Credit became much more organised. However, from the industry's perspective the recommendations were very hard and strict. Since then there has been a strong demand from the Industry for movement from mandatory control to a voluntary market related control. The concept of Maximum Permissible Bank Finance (MPBF) introduced in 1975 on implementation of the recommendations of the Tandon Working Group to frame guidelines for follow-up of bank credit was liberalised over the years.

The committees headed by K. B. Chore in 1980 and S S Marathe in 1983, though did not make any structural changes, improved the efficiency of the system by stringent prescriptions for healthy industrial development and for overall economic development. However, by 1989, the need for a complete relaxation was felt and consequently the Reserve Bank replaced the credit authorisation scheme with the credit monitoring arrangement, taking away the requirement of pre-sanction approval and making post-sanction reporting compulsory. Another committee headed by Sh. P.R. Nayak known as Nayak Committee looked into the problems faced by Small Scale Industries due to the implementations of Tandon & Chore Committee recommendations.

From 1991 onwards, with the liberalisation of economy and reforms in the financial sector, RBI has given the freedom to the banks to work out their own norms for inventory and the earlier norms are now to be taken as guidelines and not a mandate. Further, beginning with the slack season credit policy of 1997-98, RBI has also given full freedom to all the banks to devise their own method of assessing the short term credit requirements of their clients and grant lines of credit accordingly. Most banks, however, continue to follow the methods and principle recommendations given by Tandon Committee report.

The financial and economic liberalisation and the process of integrating the Indian financial system with the global framework necessitated a relook at the contribution of bank lending to money market liquidity so as to avoid distortions and ensure stability. Accordingly, the loan delivery system was introduced to enable banks to plan their cash flow in a more realistic manner and reduce the maturity mismatches. The loan delivery system was also modified thrice by gradually tapering the cash credit component and increasing the term component to provide better liquidity leverage to banks. Finally, the entire system of following common norms for fixation of MPBF was taken away, giving greater freedom to banks to decide the quantum of finance, pattern, methodology and norms individually. The new system has wider implications and involves various issues. Bank credit to industry for working capital is having a different thrust. Companies are now getting greater manoeuvrability in deciding the pattern of assistance. The options available are many and the credit market for banks is going to be a buyer's market. A corporate borrower can approach a bank to structure a credit scheme to take advantage of the liquidity and interest differential.

Following is the brief summary of major recommendations given by Dahejia, Tandon, Chore and Nayak committees.

DAHEJIA COMMITTEE REPORT

After independence, banks encouraged industrial growth on large scale. For this first industrial policy resolution was framed in 1948 by the government. The banks used to extend the credit against the pledge of stocks. But in the late 1950s newer industries came into existence and banks began to assess the working capital requirements on the basis of their operating cycle. Banks allowed the borrowers to retain the physical custody of the stocks under pledge. This necessitated the assessment of borrowers' creditworthiness by the banks. All the assessments by banks were based on the future projections given by the borrowers. Moreover, banks used to make no attempts to verify whether the working capital extended previous year was justified in terms of actual sales achieved in the present year.

All the problems were expressed at the National Credit Council meeting held on July 24, 1968, in which the need to set up various committees to examine pertaining issues was felt. On October 11, 1968 a group was constituted to examine "the extent to which credit needs of industry and trade are likely to be inflated and how such trends could be checked". The committee was headed by Shri V. T. Dahejia, the then Chairman of the State Bank of India. The committee produced its report in September 1969. The committee held detailed discussions and examined the data collected by the RBI of medium and large-scale public limited companies for the period 1960-61 to 1966-67. The committee concluded that there had been inflation in the credit needs and diversion of short-term bank finance for bridging the long-term resources gap of industry and trade.

The committee pointed out that between 1961-62 and 1966-67, the short-term liabilities of 255 companies recorded a rise of Rs. 201 crores (of which bank credit accounted for Rs. 91 crores) as against a rise of Rs. 118 crores in their short- term assets; the excess of short-term liabilities amounting to Rs. 83 crores was utilised for financing the gap between long-term assets and long term liabilities of the companies during this period. Of the diversion of short-term sources of Rs. 83 crores, incremental gross fixed assets formation accounted for Rs. 59 crores, and the balance of Rs. 24 crores went to finance the growth in other non-current assets comprising loans and investments. The diversion of bank credit led to a deterioration in the current ratio of the 255 companies in the same period.

During the period from 1964 to 1966 the rise in bank credit to industry was substantially higher than the increase in value of industrial output. Many industrial units availed credit from banks over and above the increase in their production. Therefore, it can be concluded that in the absence of limits by banks on credit granting, industry was inclined to obtain short-term bank credit in excess of the amounts based on the growth in production.

The banking practice, prevalent at that time, of fixing credit limits for industrial borrowers was also varied and the banks were unlikely to prevent the emergence of excess demand for credit from certain borrowers. Over liberalisation of policies and practices during those years led to criticism in the banking sector. The banks were inclined to relate their credit limits to the security offered by the borrowers. The banks were not following any uniform method for prescribing margins and furthermore, the method of valuation of stocks was also not uniformly practiced.

It was observed that the banks were not concentrating on financing the short-term requirements of the industry rather only focusing on financing permanent assets. In order to prevent varied credit period practices and for utilization of resources of banks for productive purposes, it was considered that the credit period should not exceed 60 days and in special circumstances the maximum period could be 90 days. The government departments, if they fail to make payments within 90 days, should pay interest on due balances.

Due to the banking lending practices, certain types of credit facilities such as advanced against receivables could result in double or multiple financing of stocks. This could be eliminated only if due account was taken of the credit received on its purchases.

It was also observed that the relationship between the bank credit and growth of industrial output was getting weaker, due to the reason bank credit was being utilised for acquiring long-term fixed assets and for holding speculative inventories. The industrial inclination to obtain more short-term bank credit and other current liabilities for acquisition of non-current assets was due to the sluggish conditions in the capital market since 1962.

The lending system, it was observed, greatly assisted certain industrial units which heavily relied on short-term debt to finance their non-current investments. The working capital advances of banks were granted by way of cash credit limits which were repayable on demand. The system was found convenient in view of the emphasis placed by banks on the security aspect. These short-term advances though secured by current assets were not necessarily utilised for the intended purposes. The obvious result was that cash credit advances no longer remained short-term or self-liquidating.

A substantial part of the working capital advance was permanently required by the industrial units to carry on its operations. Therefore, it was necessary to judge the level of permanent working capital.

The study group suggested several remedial measures to prevent further diversion of bank credit for financing other than current investments or for non-productive purposes.

The measures suggested include the following:

(a) Credit applications should be appraised with reference to the total financial position of the borrower, both existing and projected, as revealed from cash flow analysis and forecasts submitted by borrower.

(b) Balances due in cash credit accounts should be treated as (i) 'hardcore' which is the minimum level of raw materials, finished goods and stores which the firm is required to maintain for a given level of production and (ii) and above that minimum component, short-term component will be the fluctuating part of the cash credit account.

The committee suggested that banks should finance the fluctuating or short-term component since it is credit required for financing current assets. The committee also recommended that where the firm's financial position is satisfactory, the hardcore component should be treated as a term loan and proper repayment schedule should be prepared. On the other hand, where the financial strength of the borrowing firm is not satisfactory or the size of the hardcore component is very large, then the firm can resort to additional issue of share capital, a debenture issue with a long maturity or the raising of long-term deposits and unsecured loans by the promoters. Where the bank is to finance the hardcore component on a formal term loan basis, the proposal must be appraised in detail by the bank.

The committee also suggested that banks should promote the practice of culminating credit sales by issue of bills. To reduce the scope for double or multiple financing of stocks, a borrower should route his entire business through one bank only. Further, banks, in the context of demand for industrial credit, should see the adequacy of inventory levels held by the various industries.

Dahejia Committee's recommendations could not produce anything concrete. However, banks tightened their system of appraisal. R.B.I also recommended that banks should analyse the funds flow statement of borrowers while extending working capital loans.

TANDON COMMITTEE REPORT

The Tandon Committee headed by Shri Prakash Tandon, the then Chairman of Punjab National Bank, was constituted by the RBI in July 1974 with eminent personalities drawn from leading banks, financial institutions and the industry with a view to study the overall structure of banks' finance for working capital and suggest ways for optimum utilisation of bank credit. This was the first elaborate attempt by the central bank to organise the bank credit. The report provided by the group is popularly known as Tandon Committee report. Most of the banks in India, even now, follow the methodology and recommendations given by the committee while assessing the credit needs of the corporate.

The committee viewed the bank credit as a tool of resource allocation in the economy, so there is a great need to define reasonable levels of inventories and receivable in each industry. Accordingly, the committee suggested inventory norms for 15 major industries, taking into account, company finance studies made by the RBI, process period in different industries, discussion with the industry experts and feedback received on the Interim Report of the committee.

The committee also suggested that the norms stipulated represent only the maximum level of holding inventory and receivables. If a company has managed with lesser inventories and receivables in the past, it should continue to do so. The norms do not entitle the company to take more credit. The norms were made applicable to all industrial borrowers, including small-scale industries with aggregate limits in excess of Rs. 10 lacs.

The Committee, however, felt that the norms are hard and rigid. Therefore, it recommended that deviations from norms may be permitted under certain circumstances for example, power cuts, strikes, unavoidable interruptions, transport delays and other bottlenecks etc. The committee identified the purpose of bank credit as supplementing the borrower's resources to carry on acceptable level of current assets. The committee implies that the level of current assets must be reasonable and based on certain norms; and a part of the credit required for financing current assets must be taken from long term sources. The major recommendations made by the group, covered the norms for inventory & receivables, different approaches to lending and overall supervision and control of bank credit. The committee suggested three alternatives (also known as methods of lending) for computing the maximum permissible level of bank borrowings:

First Method: Banks can compute the working capital gap (total current assets less current liabilities other than bank borrowings) known as (MPBF) Maximum Permissible Bank Finance and permit a maximum credit of 75 per cent of the working capital gap. The balance should be financed from long-term sources of funds. This approach was recommended only for very small business firms and where the credit requirements were not more than Rs. 10 lacs.

Second Method: Under this method, the borrower finances a minimum of 25% of total current assets out of long-term sources of funds i.e., owned funds plus long-term borrowings. A certain level of credit for purchases and other current liabilities will be available to fund the build up of current assets and the bank will provide the balance (MPBF). The total current liabilities inclusive of bank borrowings should not exceed 75% of current assets. RBI stipulated that the working capital needs of all borrowers having fund based credit facilities of more than Rs. 10 lacs should be calculated under this method.

Third Method: Under this method, the entire Core Current Assets should be financed from long term funds. The Core Current Assets has been defined by the committee as representing the absolute minimum level of raw materials, work in process, finished stock and stores which are in the pipeline to ensure continuity of production. Further, a minimum of 25% of the balance current assets (Total Current Assets less Core Current Assets) should be contributed out of the long-term funds plus term borrowings. However, this method was not accepted and not recommended.

WORKING CAPITAL COMPUTATION AS PRESCRIBED BY THE TANDON COMMITTEE

Working Capital Requirement (WCR) = Current Assets (CA) as per industry norms – Current Liabilities (CL)

Permissible Bank Financing (PBF) = WCR – Promoter's Margin Money (PMM)

As per First Method:

PMM = 25% of (CA – CL) and thereby PBF = 75% of (CA – CL)

As per Second Method:

PMM = 25% of CA and thereby PBF = 75% (CA) – CL

It is apparent that Second Method requires a higher level of PMM as compared to First Method. Second Method is generally adopted in case of bank financing. In cases of sick units where the promoter is unable to bring in PMM to the extent required under Second Method, the difference in PMM between First Method and Second Method may be provided as a Working Capital Term Loan repayable in instalments over a period of time.

The committee also recommended that the cash credit limits of the borrowers should be divided into two heads viz. a minimum level of working capital which is maintained throughout the year (permanent working capital) and the other part for variations (variable working capital) in the requirements exceeding this minimum level. This second part should be periodically reviewed to make adjustments in the requirements of the borrowers in tune with increase and decrease in the level of activity.

The Tandon committee emphasised need based credit, but it could not adequately provide for the exact criterion of judging the creditworthiness of the borrower. The committee recommended that the industry should be discouraged from accumulating excessive level of current assets and should maintain very lean inventory and receivable levels. The committee also laid down norms for investment in inventories and book debts, so that the borrowing companies should not cross the outer limits of reasonable requirements of working capital finance but it totally ignored that time prevalent banking practices of risky lending. Finally, it cannot be asserted that the committee's recommendations were practically implemented. However, on paper, the recommendation still serve the basis for working capital finance by banks to the industry.

CHORE COMMITTEE REPORT

In the year 1979, due to the non-implementation of one of the crucial recommendations of the Tandon Committee and other weaknesses in the Cash Credit Lending system, another committee was appointed by RBI to study the underlying problems. This committee was headed by Sh. K.B. Chore, then Additional Chief Officer, RBI and was named Chore Committee. The major objectives were to study and suggest:

(i) Amendments in the Cash Credit system to for better management of funds by the Bankers and

(ii) Alternative credit facilities to ensure better credit discipline and inter-relationship between credit and production.

The committee while concluding that the existing Cash Credit System was best suited to Indian conditions, made the following suggestions:

As per committee, all the borrowers having working capital limits more than Rs. 10 lacs should be treated by the second method of lending, suggested by Tandon Committee. However, RBI suggested that all borrowers with credit limits less than Rs. 50 lacs should be treated under the first method of lending, and the borrowers having credit limits over Rs. 50 lacs should be assessed under the second method of lending.

Borrowings for the shortfall in the working capital should be treated as a Working Capital Term Loan which should be repaid within a period of 5 years depending upon the cash flows of the borrowing business. The committee recommended that the Working Capital Term Loan should be charged two per cent higher interest rate in order to have faster recover of the loan. This suggestion was not accepted by RBI.

The chore committee suggested that the Tandon Committee's recommendation regarding the third method of lending was very rigid and there were difficulties in defining Chore Current Asset and due to the depress capital market conditions it was very difficult for borrowers to raise funds from long-term sources. RBI accepted this recommendation.

Receivable financing should be discouraged and instead bill limits should be sanctioned. At least 50% of the cash credit limit against raw materials to manufacturing units should be by way of drawee bills. However, this suggestion was not implemented due to procedural problems.

Banks should set separate limits for the regular and peak level requirements for industries having seasonal business.

Ad hoc limits or temporary accommodation in credit may be permitted as a separate one time account. RBI stipulated an additional one per cent interest on ad hoc limits.

The Committee simplified the periodic statements required to be submitted by borrowers as prescribed by the Tandon Committee. It introduced the system referred to as the Quarterly Information System, all borrowers with working capital limits over Rs. 50 lacs from the banking system would be required to furnish:

Form – I-a i.e. statement for the quarter indicating projected level of production, sales, current assets, liabilities, bank borrowings without the profitability projections and funds flow for the ensuing quarter.

Form – II represents actual versus projection for the same quarter

Form – III which represents a half yearly Profit & Loss and Fund Flow Statement.

Analysis of these statements reveals the utilisation of funds by the firm and the bank can easily ensure that credit has been used for financing the current assets. RBI have made it mandatory for banks to levy one per cent penal interest on the entire outstanding balances in the account for late submission of the quarterly information system forms. All borrowers having working capital limits of Rs. 10 lacs and above are required to submit a monthly statement indicating monthly, cumulative, figures of sales, production, current assets and current liabilities. Therefore, the banks obtain periodic information from the borrowing firms indicating profitability, sales volume, level of current assets, uses of funds etc. In addition to this, bank should also sought market information for better analysis of the borrower's profile and financial position.

NAYAK COMMITTEE REPORT

The Reserve Bank of India constituted a committee on 9th December 1991 under the chairmanship of Shri P.R. Nayak, then Deputy Governor to examine the difficulties confronting the small scale industries (SSI) in the country in the matter of securing finance. The representative of the SSI associations had earlier placed before the Governor, Reserve Bank of India, various problems, issues and the difficulties which the SSI sector had been facing. The Committee had a wide range of issues before it relating to institutional credit to the SSI sector. The objectives before the committee were:

(i) To examine the adequacy of institutional credit for the SSI sector with reference to the increase in the cost of raw materials and locking up of the available resources due to delay in the realisation of sale proceeds from large companies and Government agencies.

(ii) To examine the adequacy of institutional credit for term finance to the SSI sector and to examine the need for making any modifications in the norms prescribed by the Tandon/Chore Committee in respect of SSI units.

(iii) To examine whether any revision is required in the present RBI guidelines for the rehabilitation of sick SSI units.

(iv) In the light of the above, to suggest suitable arrangements for ensuring adequate flow of institutional credit for working capital and term finance to the small-scale industry.

In the development of our country, the Small Scale Industry has been playing a crucial role. The SSI sector provides the maximum employment after agriculture. As at the end of March 1991, the SSI sector provided employment to around 4.3 crore people of which traditional industries had the highest share of 57%. It accounts for more than 27% of the total exports of the country. Shorter gestation periods and low establishment costs are the distinguishing characteristics of the SSI units. The small-scale units are widely dispersed and therefore suited in building a geographically wider industrial base in the economy. They play a significant role in the programmes of rural upliftment and the removal of poverty. Further, they help to mobilise rural resources. The products of these industries meet a substantial part of the essential requirements of our rural and semi-urban areas. But SSI sector has its own problems in our country. Small scale industries have a distinct set of characteristics such as low bargaining power leading to problems of receivables and lower credit on purchases, poor financial strength, high level of variability due to dependence on local factors, etc. The SSI sector suffers from the limitations of inadequacies in infrastructure and technology. The major weakness of the SSI units is their low bargaining power which makes them dependent on large industries. Financially, they usually have a weak capital base, little access to the capital market resulting in a large reliance on borrowed funds and indigenous money lenders and a lack of managerial, organisational and financial skills. Credit institutions are rather hesitant to cater to the financial needs of the SSI Sector. Consequently, it was rightly argued that the industry norms on different current assets could not be adopted. Complaints were being voiced from time to time regarding the difficulties experienced by the small scale units in securing bank finance, particularly, for working capital purposes and these related not only to the quantum but also to the delays involved in the rules and procedures followed by bank branches in sanctioning or enhancing the quantum. The question of adequacy was addressed by the Tandon Committee and the Chore Committee respectively. The norms recommended by them as reasonable requirements and the methods of providing bank finance were accepted and made applicable. RBI issued a set of comprehensive guidelines to commercial banks in 1988 in the matter of financing the working capital requirements of SSI units. The Nayak Committee called the representatives of the SSI and of banks and noted the striking unanimity that existed on all sides that the guidelines were wholesome. But there was a widespread belief among the industry that the banks do not always follow these guidelines and that was the major headache for the SSI. The SSI associations alleged that the practice exists of sanctioning inadequate working capital and/or releasing such working capital to the SSI units in small amounts. Therefore, a sample study conducted by the RBI during 1989 also revealed that, even one year after the issue of the guidelines, the compliance at the field level was deficient in certain respects and that, in one-third of the branches surveyed, full working capital according to the instructions had not been sanctioned. The Nayak Committee considered the percentage of non-compliance too large to be overlooked and recommended as follows:

Banks should take immediate steps to ensure full adherence by all their branches to the RBI guidelines on financing of working capital requirements of SSI. RBI, as well as the banks themselves, should carry out special studies periodically on as large a sample of branches as possible, specifically, to ascertain the position regarding the Implementation of its guidelines.

SSI units are entitled to working capital of a minimum of 20 per cent of their projected sales turnover but not exceeding Rs. 100 lakh of their fund based needs.

The entire SSI sector (upto Rs. 60 lakh investment in plant and machinery) is entitled to priority sector lending of the banks. At least 40 per cent of the loans to the SSI have to be directed towards the cottage, KVIC (Khadi and Village Industries Commission) units, artisans and tiny industries or other such units subject to credit ceilings of upto Rs. 5 lakh.

State Financial Corporations (SFCs) will act as the principal financing agency for SSIs in 23 out of the 85 districts with significantly high industry density (each having more than 2,000 registered SSI units). They will take care of the working capital as well as the demand for term loans. The commercial banks will be the principal financing agency under the Single Window Scheme in the remaining districts. Commercial banks will also open specialised or dedicated branches in other areas of high small industry density.

An effective grievance redressal machinery will be established within each bank to take care of SSI problems.

The government announced a seven point action plan in 1995-96 Budget for the effective implementation of the Nayak committee report. This was done when it was found that the SSI sector was getting working capital worth 7.8 per cent of its turnover in 1995-96 down from 8.1 per cent is reported by the Nayak committee.

Village Industries and the smaller Tiny Industries with credit limits upto Rs. 1 lakh should have the first claim on the priority sector credit to the SSI, with an allocation built up from a notional 1989-90 base which should be at least 50% higher than the actual credit outstanding in March 1990 of about Rs. 2.800 crores.

Bank branches should give priority to those Village Industries and the smaller Tiny Industries which can use working capital efficiently, having established production successfully but unable to make further progress for lack of working capital. Close monitoring of the banks progress in this matter is necessary. RBI should make full use of the computerised credit planning and monitoring under the Service Area Approach in the years to come.

The new priority sector credit dispensation, when adopted, should fully provide for the working capital requirements of all tiny units up to credit limits of Rs. 10 lakhs, after first taking care of the working capital allocation made for village Industries and the smaller Tiny Industries with credit limits up to Rs.1 lakh. A specific allocation to the larger tiny units should be made by fixing their proportion of the credit to the total priority sector credit.

In regard to the larger SSI, the recommended minimum level of working capital bank finance at 20% of the output should be put on a firm footing by the provision of the required amount of credit by the commercial banks through an annual budgetary exercise. Besides, if the genuine need-based demand of the SSI sector as reflected in the budget requires diversion of a part of the resources flowing to the Medium and Large Industries sector, the same should be mandated by the top managements of banks. The working capital needs of the larger SSI should be fully met by the commercial banks and the Chief Executive of each bank shall ensure that this is done.

The Committee examined the demand for an availability of bank finance for the working capital requirements of the SSI sector during the 8th plan period. Based on the recommendations regarding the provision of working capital to the various segments of the SSI sector and also the past growth trends, the total incremental credit demand was estimated at Rs. 22,100 crores. As against this, the availability of resource for the sector was estimated at about Rs. 24,800 crores. Despite uncertainties due to recent new developments in the financial system, the Committee felt that the banks should manage to find the enhanced level of working capital resources needed by SSI. While the shortage of resources of the commercial banks could be one of the reasons for the various complaints voiced by the SSI sector, many of the difficulties brought to the Committee's notice by the SSI associations stemmed from the banks non-adherence to the RBI guidelines as also from the attitudinal orientation of the banks staff.

There should be frequent interaction between the banks staff and the SSI borrowers as a part of the training programmes. The confidential reporting on the banks staff should take into account their attitude towards the SSI borrowers and their achievements in lending to this sector. The branch managers should be vested with adequate discretionary powers which will enable them the grant ad hoc increases upto 10 per cent over the sanctioned limits to meet unforeseen contingencies, including increase in raw material/ input costs.

Where the borrower is unable to bring in the additional margin money immediately, banks should not insist on the additional margin to be brought in by the entrepreneur in one instalment at the time of granting 'ad hoc' increases in/enhancement of working capital limits to meet unforeseen contingencies. Such additional margin should be permitted to be built up within a reasonable period from future cash accruals.

Applications for fresh limits/enhancement existing limits which are not considered favourably by the appropriate sanctioning authority, should be referred to the next higher authority with all relevant particulars, and the latter should scrutinize each case and come to his own judgement. The final decision should be based on such review by the higher authority and should be taken within a reasonable time.

Four types of application forms may be evolved for use by SSIs on the basis of aggregate credit limits (a) not exceeding Rs. 50,000, (b) between Rs. 50,000 and Rs. 15 lakh, (c) between Rs. 15 lakhs and Rs. 25 lakhs and (d) above Rs. 25 lakhs.

Collateral security and/or third party guarantee should be dispensed with as a rule, irrespective of the amount of credit involved. Exceptions may be justified only in the case of larger advances of over Rs. 2 lakhs under noted circumstances such as where the technology is new and untried and the bank considers the lending risk to be higher than normal.

No applications for advances should be rejected merely for want of collateral security.

Undesirable and unhealthy practices such as the insistence by some banks on compulsory deposit mobilisation by the unit as a basis for the sanction of credit to SSI units must be prevented through the issue of unambiguous guidelines.

The bank should prepare a budget in respect of working capital required by SSIs well before the year begins. Such budgeting should cover (a) functioning (healthy) units which already have borrowing limit with the banks, (b) new units/units whose proposals are under appraisal, and (c) sick units under nursing and also sick units found viable and for which rehabilitation programmes are under preparation. The budgeting exercise should begin at the level of the borrowing units and the branches financing them. It is essential that the unit level working capital budget should be accepted by the unit itself and once the budget is so prepared, it should not be modified by the bank unilaterally. In finalising the budgets of individual units, working capital at around 25 per cent of output should be considered as the minimum requirement in cases where inventory norms as per the Tandon Committee recommendations are not applicable or not available. In regard to the larger units with aggregate credit limits of over Rs. 10 lakhs, the budget will follow the prescribed inventory norms, wherever such norms are available. The working capital budget prepared by the bank branches should form the basis on which resources should be allocated to the SSI sector by the top managements of banks.

Banks should advise RBI of the budgets so prepared and the resources allocated there against. If the top management has not been able to fully support the ground-level budgets, RBI should be apprised of the fact and the reasons therefore. RBI should accept the bank's allocation for the budgeted working capital to SSI or suggest suitable inter-se changes in allocation. RBI should, however, provide refinance for working capital to the extent the banks budget.

To facilitate timely decisions on credit proposals by eliminating delays inherent in the consideration of proposals by successive tiers in the hierarchy, a committee approach will be helpful in which decisions are taken by the competent authority after a structured discussion with the branch manager and also the intervening levels. Along with the procedural changes suggested, it is important to create a more open system which will foster mutual confidence between the banks and the SSI entrepreneurs.

ASSESSMENT OF WORKING CAPITAL FINANCING AS PER NAYAK COMMITTEE

The Nayak Committee simplified norms for computation of working capital bank financing at 20% of the projected annual turnover. However, in case of units which are non-capital intensive such as hotels, etc. banks often assess requirements both on the Nayak Committee norms as well as the working cycle norms and take the lower of the two figures. The method of assessment is applicable in case of SSIs, with working capital requirement of less than Rs. 5 crores. In case of other industries, with working capital requirement of less than Rs. 1 crore. The quantum of working capital bank financing will be 20% of the projected annual turnover subject to promoter's contribution of a margin of 5% of the projected annual turnover i.e. 20% of the total fund requirement that has been estimated at 25% of the projected annual turnover.

BANK CREDIT — CURRENT SCENARIO

Consistent with the policy of liberalization, greater operational freedom was provided to banks and RBI withdrew the prescription of Maximum Permissible Bank Finance. Banks are now free to determine the working capital requirements according to their risk perception of the borrower and his credit needs; the only requirement which continues to this day is that the bank should lay down with the approval of their Boards transparent policy and guidelines for credit dispensation for each broad category of economic activity. Banks are also governed by exposure norms relating to single borrowers/group of borrowers and other prudential norms which have been laid down by the RBI with global practices. Similarly, the mandatory norms relating to consortium/multiple/syndicate lending were also withdrawn so much so the banks could be free to adopt the route and quantum of credit in a mutually acceptable manner.

The formula based calculation of working capital requirement, as suggested by Tandon and Nayak Committees, has been subjected to much debate over the past few decades. The advantage of such computation has been that it removes discretion of the bank officials which is a common case in the public sector banks. Thus, this uniformity reduces the scope for accusation of bias. However, the strongest argument against the MPBF lending has been that it does not take into account the variations arising out of location, relative bargaining of the enterprise and other reasons, which could vary its need for working capital. Even though the banker could understand the problem, it was not possible to act on it due to the norms. Further, this ensured that banks never needed to develop credit appraisal skills and lent to all. Further, the method has also been criticized as being more appropriate for the era where credit was rationed out. Banks today are capable of undertaking better assessment of the requirements and welcome the idea of offering higher limits to worthy and established units in order to survive in the competition from other banks. In 1997, the RBI permitted banks to evolve their own norms for assessment of the working capital requirements of their borrowers.

Another method for computation of working capital is based on the Cash Flow and other financial statements. Cash flow based computation of working capital requirement has been recommended by the RBI for assessment of working capital requirement permitting the banks to evolve their own norms for such assessment. The reason for this has been that cash flow factors in the past trends, takes into account the company specific factors and is based on mutual discussion between the banker and the borrower thereby increasing its acceptability. Also, large companies have adopted cash budgeting systems for managing their cash flows and hence such a system does not impose additional requirements on the industry. Cash flow is the most realistic means of assessing the operations of an enterprise. Drawing up cash flow statements (monthly or quarterly) for the past few years clearly indicate the seasonal and secular trend in utilization of working capital. The projections drawn up by the entrepreneur may then be jointly discussed with the banker as modified in light of the past performance and the banker's opinions. The peak cash deficit is ascertained from the cash budgets. The promoter's share (margin money) for such requirement maybe mutually arrived at by the banker and the borrower with the balance requirement forming the Bank financed part of Working Capital.

Cash flow system is extremely relevant in case of the seasonal industries to assess the peak credit requirement and in case of large companies (working capital requirements above Rs. 10 crores). However the reluctance to provide the cash budgets and disclosure of additional information to the banks, has led to even larger companies not using the Cash Budget method of assessing Working Capital. Consequently, Cash Budget method is currently prevalent mainly in case of seasonal industries, construction sector as well as other entities whose operations are linked to projects.

Though, presently the norms for computation of working capital have been liberalized, PSU banks continue to adopt the formula based norms to assess working capital. This is on account of the public sector bank's practice of following norm based lending which protects them from any accusation of bias in lending. Or in other words we can conclude from this that in most cases, industries get some credit but not according to their working capital requirement.

Over the past few years, the fear of NPAs (Non-Performing Assets), enquiries on bad loans, prudential norms for asset classification, capital adequacy norms, competition, technology upgradation and entry of new players has made banks credit averse to take additional credit exposure. This is especially so in case of new projects where the promoter does not have a track record. In such circumstances banks are increasingly resorting to investing in risk-free government debt and avoiding taking high industrial lending. The problem has been more acute in the small-scale sector. The SSI sector had witnessed a high level of directed lending in the past decade most of which turned bad thereby putting off the banks from further credit to the SSI sector.

Now, the banks are facing tough competition from private banks. The existing infrastructure in public sector banks is quite insufficient to meet the challenges ahead. The private sector and foreign banks are providing credit and support to industry in a big way. Private sector and foreign banks have acquired the necessary skills and support either from their sponsors abroad or by sending their personnel abroad. These banks are faster, customer friendly and attempt to understand the borrower's business and fund requirements, while structuring the transaction. They work through correspondent branches to extend their reach and offer customized solutions including cash management, demand loans against assignment of immediate committed payments and branches banking and banking through the Internet. Under these competitive circumstances, public sector banks are finding it difficult to structure innovative loan products and compete with foreign and private sector banks unless they immediately take steps to acquire this expertise and train their personnel to meet the emerging challenges.

ESSENTIALS FOR BANK CREDIT

The methods for computation of working capital requirement have led to much debate and attention over the past few decades. A directed credit approach was adopted by the Reserve Bank of ensuring the flow of credit to the priority sectors for fulfilment of the growth objectives laid down by the planners. Consequently, the quantum of bank credit required for achieving the requisite growth in Industry was to be assessed. The committees such as the Tandon Committee and the Chore Committee, as discussed earlier, were constituted and studied the problem at length. Norms were fixed regarding the quantum of various current assets for different industries (as multiples of the average daily output) and the Maximum Permissible Bank Financing (MPBF) was capped at a certain percentage of the working capital requirement thus arrived at.

Based on the level of activity decided and the unit cost and sales price projections, the banks calculate at the annual sales and cost of production. The quantum of current assets (CA) in the form of Raw Materials, Work-in-progress, Finished goods and Receivables is estimated as a multiple of the average daily turnover. The multiple for each of the current assets is determined generally based on the industry norms. The current liabilities (CL) in the form of credit availed by the business from its creditors or on its manufacturing expenses are deducted from the current assets (CA) to arrive at the Working Capital Requirement (WCR).

The financing limits are granted based on assessment of the working capital requirement. The assessment factors include various characteristics such as the nature of industry, industry norms, actual level of activity for the previous year and the projected level of activity for the subsequent year to arrive at the working capital requirement. The bank financing limit is thereafter decided after factoring in margins on the different types of current assets forming part of the working capital.

The Bank Financing Limit is fixed on an annual basis. However, since such limit is provided to meet specific requirements, utilizing the limits is subjected to the Drawing Power, which is decided on a monthly/ quarterly basis.

The bank financing is the minimum of the following two:

Bank Financing Limit which is determined on an annual basis based on an assessment of the current year's projections and the actuals for the previous year.

Drawing Power which is linked to the quantum of current assets and current liabilities of the business with appropriate margins. It is fixed on a monthly or quarterly basis depending on the submission of monthly or Quarterly Information System statements indicating the position of the stock statement, receivables, Work-in-Progress, payables, etc. Therefore, Max. Permissible Bank Credit is equal to Bank Credit Limit or Drawing Power whichever is less.

Commercial banks measure the risk of business loans with reference to five principal considerations: cash flow, liquidity, leverage, collateral and the quality of management.

(i) Cash Flow

A bank is primarily concerned with whether or not the business will generate sufficient cash flow to service the loan under consideration. A cash flow ratio can be determined by dividing EBIT (Earnings before interest and taxes) by the Interest paid on the loan, or by dividing net income by the principal payments. Acceptable ratios vary with the type of industry involved, but the minimum ratio is about 1.2 to 1. This minimum might be acceptable for a business such as a grocery store which has a consistent and dependable cash flow. Much higher ratios would be required for high-tech manufacturing firms.

New firms have no historical basis for cash-flow determination, so banks place a high reliance on projected cash flow. These projections must be realistic to ensure that the loan officer gives the loan proposal due consideration.

(ii) Liquidity

Liquidity refers to the amount of cash-on-hand or the amount of available assets which can be quickly converted to cash. A business needs enough available cash to carry on the business's day-to-day operations as well as make its loan payments. The bank wants to see that there is sufficient liquidity so that in the normal course of business, the firm will not go under as a result of its debt obligations. Liquidity can be determined by dividing current assets by current liabilities. A more conservative measure is determined by dividing liquid current assets (current assets minus inventories) by current liabilities.

(iii) Leverage

Leverage refers to the amount of debt carried by the business. The leverage of a firm is determined by dividing the business's total liabilities by its net worth. A low amount of leverage would be a ratio of about 1 to 1. This would be a firm which is well capitalized and would be considered a good risk. Higher ratios may be acceptable, as high as 3 to 1 or 4 to 1, if the firm has strong cash flow or sufficient collateral.

To determine whether the cash flow and liquidity of a business will be sufficient to service the debt as well as finance the firm's day-to-day operations, the bank will typically request the following:

- Business financial statements, which include the income statements and balance sheets for the previous three years;
- Interim business financial statement, showing the most recent income and balance sheets, dated no older than 45 days;
- Business debt schedule, which must be dated the same as the interim financial statement and show all liabilities listed on the interim statement; and
- A projections worksheet, showing the expected monthly income and expense forecasts for one year after the signing of the loan agreement.

(iv) Collateral

Banks require sufficient collateral to secure debt financing. In terms of quality of collateral, the bank looks for collateral that can be easily converted into debt repayment in the event of default. Banks accept collateral for security on the basis of a percentage of the value of the assets. Generally, banks accept 75% of real estate's value as security, 50% for equipment, 50% to 80% for receivables, and 20% to 50% for inventories. Banks usually require personal guarantees from the business principals.

To determine the firm's collateral position, usually a bank requires:

- a schedule of collateral, which shows all collateral to be used as security for the loan, including all present liens on the assets; and
- personal financial statements of the business principals.

(v) Quality of Management

A bank wants to be certain that the business owners or managers know enough about the industry and the operation of the business to ensure a successful enterprise. The bank usually looks for educational experience in the field and/or resume experience and actual practical experience in the industry and the operation of a business.

To assess the quality of management and experience of those engaged in the operation of the business, a bank requires:

- Personal histories of the business principals and hired managers showing education, work and management experience.
- A history of the business, showing the date it was established, the nature of the business, the types of products and services, customer profile, key customers, major competitors, major past accomplishments, future plans for growth and expansion, and how this loan will benefit the company; and
- Corporate bylaws or partnership agreement and an approved resolution for borrowing on behalf of the firm.

BANKING PROCEDURE FOR WORKING CAPITAL FINANCING

Banks exercise extreme caution in lending to first time applicants starting up their business. A first time applicant would be asked for collateral in the form of land, building or residential property. This would be in addition to a second charge on the fixed assets of the enterprise. Following is the usual banking procedure to avail working capital finance:

(i) Submission of Application

The application for working capital funding requires a covering letter containing a request for sanction of working capital limits. The following documents are required to be enclosed alongwith:

- Detailed Project Report containing the detailed financial projections of operations for the next 5 years.
- A copy of Memorandum and Articles of Association of the firm.
- Copies of incorporation documents, in case of a company.
- Statutory approvals obtained/ applied for such as for power, water, pollution control, environment clearance and approvals from other agencies and departments concerned with the nature of the business.
- Other relevant documents – Letters of intent/ confirmed orders from prospective buyers.
- Networth statement of promoters.

In case of the larger loans (above Rs. 5 crore), the projections are generally submitted in the format prescribed by Reserve Bank of India.

(ii) Initial Sanction

The timeframe for sanction depends upon the time taken for submission of necessary documents and the processing time taken by the bank. Most of the large banks have specialized SSI branches at the industrial concentrations in the country. These branches are headed by senior executives with sanctioning power of five to six crores of rupees at the branch level. In such instances, delays for processing the applications at the bank are limited. In other cases, such processing may take one to two months time for according initial sanction to the project. The private sector banks are generally faster in according such approval. The significance of this initial in-principle sanction of working capital is that such sanction is necessary for obtaining term funding from the financial institutions.

(iii) Final Sanction

The final sanction of the request for working capital is based on a thorough appraisal of the Detailed Project Report (DPR). The traditional banks generally have specified formats for submission of the DPR. The usual coverage of the DPR includes:

- Overview of the business.
- Background of promoters.
- Details of products to be manufactured, manufacturing process and raw material etc.

- Market overview and competition, sensitivity analysis for finished goods prices, raw material costs etc.
- Detailed financial projections covering the Balance Sheet, Profit and Loss Account, Funds Flow Statement and the Financial Ratios.

The timeframe for the final sanction in cases where all the requirements have already been submitted by the borrowing unit is three months from the submission of the application. Then there are Post sanction requirements which requires completion of documentation creating a charge in favour of the bank. This may include a charge on assets related to the business and charge on collateral offered, if any. In case of the assets of the business already being mortgaged with the term lending institution, a second or third charge maybe created in favour of the bank. The financing facilities sanctioned can thereafter be availed by the borrower.

(iv) Follow-up and Review

Working capital financing is extended for the current asset build up of a business, which is linked to its activity level. These assets are mobile such as inventory and also easily convertible into cash. At best, the banks have a second charge on the fixed assets of the enterprise and without the power of seizure, which is available to the state financial institutions, realizing money from the security is time consuming. Hence, banks pay extremely high importance to the monitoring and follow-up of the loan.

The system of a current account through which all the transactions are routed acts as an in-built check on the operations of the borrower. By studying the current account transactions in detail, the bank is able to make an assessment of the business. In addition to this, the banks also undertake other forms of monitoring. These include the Stock Statements collected on a monthly basis from the borrower and Quarterly Operating Statement giving details of the operations for the quarter.

In addition to these checks, banks often employ methods such as Stock Audit and Branch Level Inspection.

- Stock Audit is done by independent firms of chartered accountants. This involves visits to the storage areas of the borrower, inspection and scrutiny of the stock statements at the spot. Crosschecking these with the statements given by the borrower provides a means of check.
- Branch Inspection is conducted by the internal auditor or bank staff. In case of larger loans, consortium meetings in which the operations of the unit are jointly reviewed are also undertaken.

Review of limits is also undertaken on an annual basis. In cases where a request for enhancement of limits is made by the borrower during the year, such request is processed based on the stock statements and quarterly operative limits etc. In case of temporary need, an ad hoc limit of upto 25% of the existing limits could be granted on request. In case of highly seasonal industry such as sugar or tea, RBI have indicated that fixation of limits will not follow the Tandon Committee pattern but will be based on projected monthly cash budgets, the limits corresponding to the projected peak cash deficit.

Chapter 4

CASH MANAGEMENT

(**Contents:** Introduction, Finance Manager's Role, Cash: Meaning and Nature, Reasons for holding cash, Functions of cash management, Cash Conversion Cycle, Cash Conversion Cycle & Operating cycle, Cash Management System a) Acceleration of Receipts - Float, Components of a Float, How to measure a Float? Does float work, today? Speeding up collections - Lockbox System, Recent developments, Establishment of a lockbox, When a lockbox system is beneficial? b) Slowing Down Disbursements - Zero Balance Accounts, Controlled Disbursement, Electronic Funds Transfer (EFT). Cash Management in Multinational Environment: Process Management of Cash Forecasts, Cash Pooling, Software Requirements.)

First secure an independent income, then practice virtue.

— Greek Proverb

INTRODUCTION

Cash management refers to the practices and techniques designed to accelerate and control collections, ensure prompt deposit of receipts, improve control over disbursement methods, and eliminate idle cash balances. In general, the cash management function involves the effective and efficient use of cash to maximize cash flow at minimum cost. The concept of cash management as a separate and vital function of corporate financial management has developed into a complex discipline.

In today's financial environment, electronic delivery and payment systems are becoming increasingly important because of increased competition and the demand for more efficient and convenient capabilities. A significant number of transactions and amounts of funds can be moved electronically from one place to another almost instantaneously. Consequently, the opportunities presented can pose significant risks to a business firm. Such threats include internal and external fraud, theft, and unauthorized manipulation of financial data. Therefore, one can easily observe the rapid transition from the most basic and traditional principles to now complex strategies dominated by the technology and globalization, but the basic goal is same — the efficient utilization of cash in a way which is consistent with the overall strategic objectives of a business unit. Companies do not fail because they are insolvent rather they fail because they become illiquid. Just as water is the lifeblood of human survival, liquidity is fundamental to corporate vitality. The finance executive must focus on precise working capital management as a critical component of Financial Management.

FINANCE MANAGER'S ROLE

One of the most important responsibilities of a finance manager is the ability to understand the cash requirements of the business firm. Preparation of payroll bill, expenses for procurement of inventory, taxes etc. are also some of the tasks accomplished by the finance manager. A finance manager must understand that the area of cash management and forecasting is an art as well as a science, based on common sense and logic combined with a good understanding of business's financial statements.

In order for a cash management system to work well, finance manager with cash management responsibility must also have appropriate delegated authority over the collection, disbursement and investment of cash. Without such authority, he will not be able to deliver the desired performance. If a manager has broad cash management responsibilities, then he may also need authority over the methods of generating and collecting cash receipts, the timing and method of cash payments and the investment of surplus cash balances.

Incentives are a fundamental component of any accountability relationship as they motivate managers to achieve performance targets. Performance targets may be clearly specified, but if managers receive no recognition for good performance, or face no penalty for poor performance, there is a little incentive for them to achieve targets. Good management of cash is one major element of a manager's performance and in many cases directly linked to the personal remuneration of the manager. Although this linkage is not always desirable, as cash management is only one component of performance, and other components such as the manager's responsibilities for the production of outputs may be more important. Cash management targets may be incorporated in the general performance expectations of firm, and a manager may be assessed and rewarded in relation to overall performance across a number of areas.

CASH: MEANING AND NATURE

Cash is the basic unit of economic exchange. Cash may be currency or the right to draw currency. Cash includes cash items such as currency notes, coins, bank balances and other depository receipts. Cash provides flexibility and carries minimal risk in the short term. Since cash is immediately negotiable, it has the highest inherent risk of all assets. The amount of cash held varies from organisation to organisation, depending on the anticipated needs of funds. Cash is a non-earning asset which is required for many purposes, but by itself, it earns nothing. Therefore, excessive cash balances can have an adverse effect on the earnings of the firm. As such, an opportunity cost associated with maintaining cash balances exists because these funds could be invested elsewhere to provide a better overall return to the business firm. Excessive balances may also reflect ineffective administration of the firm's resources by management. Conversely, account balances that are too low could leave the firm in a vulnerable position from an available funds standpoint. The risks and costs of holding this asset must be adequately managed to ensure the safety and soundness of the firm. The objective of cash management is to "keep the investment in cash as low as possible while still operating the firm's activities efficiently and effectively."[1] Consequently, it involves balancing the opportunity costs of holding cash against the benefits of saving the time and transaction costs associated with selling securities or other assets every time cash is needed.

REASONS FOR HOLDING CASH

Well known economist John Maynard Keynes gave three major reasons to explain why firms hold cash. The three reasons are — for the purpose of making transactions, for the purpose of precaution, and for the purpose of speculation. All three of these reasons stem from the need of firms to possess liquidity.

Thus, motives for holding liquid assets are:

1. Transactions motive – to make routine payments
2. Precautionary motive – to protect the firm against being unable to satisfy unexpected demands for cash.
3. Speculative motive – to take advantage of favourable market conditions

Let us dwell on the motives for holding cash further:

1. Transaction Motive

Transactions balances allow the firm to make payments that arise in the ordinary course of doing business. Business firms primarily holds cash to satisfy the transaction needs. For example, cash is collected from sales and new financing and disbursed as wages, salaries, trade debts, taxes, and dividends. Firms are in existence to create

---

1. Corporate Finance by Stephen Ross, Randolf Westerfield, and Jeffrey Jaffe, 5th Ed. Irwin Mcgraw Hill, Singapore, 1999.

products or provide services. Providing of services and creating of products results in the need for cash inflows and outflows. Firms hold cash in order to satisfy the cash inflow and cash outflow needs that they have.

2. Precaution Motive

Precautionary balances provide a buffer stock of liquid assets that can be drawn down if unexpected demands for cash arise. So, holding cash as a precaution serves as an emergency fund for a firm. If expected cash inflows are not received as expected cash held on a precautionary basis could be used to satisfy short-term obligations that the cash inflow may have been bench marked for.

3. Speculation Motive

Speculative balances permit the firm to take advantage of future profit making situations.

Economist Keynes described this reason for holding cash as creating the ability for a firm to take advantage of special opportunities that if acted upon quickly will favour the firm e.g., changes of interest rates. Another example can be purchasing extra inventory at a discount that is greater than the carrying costs of holding the inventory.

Other Reasons for Holding Cash

- Cash is also maintained for compensating balances. Compensating balances are the bank balances that a firm must maintain to compensate the bank for services rendered or for granting a loan. A minimum required compensating balance at banks providing credit service to the firm may impose a lower limit on the level of cash a firm holds.
- Cash is desirable because it offers more liquidity than other interest bearing securities provide.
- Suppliers frequently offer trade discounts for making payments early. From a financing viewpoint, the cost of not taking these discounts is very high, so firms should always have enough cash on hand to take advantage of cash discounts.
- An adequate supply of cash helps keep the firm's current and quick ratios high enough to maintain a good credit rating.
- An adequate supply of cash helps ensure that the firm can face seasonal and cyclical downturns.

FUNCTIONS OF CASH MANAGEMENT

Cash is just like any other raw material required to continue the production process. If a firm keeps too little funds in the bank, it will need to make repeated sales of securities every time it has to make some payment. This incurs high transaction costs. On the other hand, if the firm keeps excessive cash in the bank it loses the opportunity to earn interest. Moreover, there is a cost to holding too much cash, i.e. the interest foregone. Therefore, the finance manager will want to hold cash up to the point where marginal value of liquidity is equal to the value of interest foregone. Cash management is concerned with striking a sensible balance between the two.

A cash management system in an organisation not only strives for optimal cash balances but also implements processes and procedures to speed up the collection and delay the disbursement (payment) of cash. An effective cash management system requires an ability to forecast cash needs based on a company's collection and disbursement patterns, while also taking into account seasonal shifts in the business activity and any capital expenditures that are planned.

1. Eliminating Idle Cash

Every rupee held as cash rather than used to augment revenues or decrease expenditures represents a lost opportunity. Funds that are not needed to cover expected transactions can be invested to generate a flow of funds or to buy back outstanding debt. Minimizing idle cash balances requires accurate information about expected receipts and likely disbursements.

The finance manager must minimize cash on the balance sheet as part of a successful working capital programme. Unless cash can earn more than its cost, unused cash negatively impacts the balance sheet. Idle cash also increases a firm's asset base. The combination of a low yield on idle cash and an increased asset base negatively impacts Return on Assets (ROA). The challenge is to determine the right amount of cash to hold.

2. Depositing Collections

Having funds in-hand is better than having accounts receivable. The cash is easier to convert immediately into value or goods. A receivable, an item to be converted in the future, often is subject to a transaction delay or a depreciation of value. Once funds are due from the receivables or from investments, they should be converted to cash-in-hand immediately and deposited in the firm's account as soon as possible.

3. Facilitating Payments

Prepayments for goods or services, unless required by the contractual arrangements with the supplier should be avoided. Some payments are to be made on a specified or legal date, such as taxes, debt redemption etc. For such payments, there is no cash management decision. For other payments, such as inventory payments, discretion in timing is possible. Suppliers of inventory face the same cash management needs, they also want to accelerate collections. The suppliers offer discounts and incentives for timely payments. The business firm can avail discount by making payment on time. The firm must maintain adequate cash balances that will permit it to meet the disbursal needs that occur in the course of doing business.

CASH CONVERSION CYCLE

Business firms vary widely in size and also in their ability to manage their working capital, so there exists a need for an overall measure of effectiveness. A firm's objective should be to minimize working capital subject to the constraint that it has sufficient funds to support the firm's operations. Minimizing working capital is accomplished by speeding up the collection of cash from sales, increasing inventory turnover, and slowing down the disbursement of cash. We can incorporate all of these factors in a single measure called the Cash Conversion Cycle. The cash conversion cycle is the length of time between when the firm makes payments or invests in the manufacturing of inventory, and when it receives cash inflows, or realizes a cash return from its investment in production. Or in other words, cash conversion cycle is the time period (number of days) between when the firm makes payment (cash outflow) and when it receives payments (cash inflow). Cash conversion cycle measures the number of days in which cash is tied up in assets. Cash conversion cycle in a manufacturing firm involves the following events:

- Procurement of raw materials on credit (Creation of accounts payable)
- Labour converts materials to finished products (Accrued wages and other expenses)
- Finished products sold on credit (Creation of accounts Receivable)

The cash conversion cycle is a tool that can be used as a guideline for liquidity. It combines widely used financial ratios calculated with financial statement data. Cash conversion cycle is composed of:

1. Inventory Conversion Period
2. Receivables Collection Period
3. Average Payment Period

All these measures can be computed as follows:

1. Inventory Conversion Period

The inventory conversion period is the average length of time required to convert materials into finished goods and then to sell those goods. It is the amount of time the product remains in inventory in various stages of completion. The inventory conversion period is calculated by dividing inventory by the cost of goods sold per day.

$$\textbf{Inventory Conversion Period} = \frac{\text{Inventory}}{\dfrac{\text{Cost of goods sold}}{360}}$$

Here, 360 refer to the number of days in a year.

2. Receivable Collection Period

The receivables collection period is the average length of time required to convert the firms receivables into cash i.e., to collect cash following a sale. The receivables collection period also is called the Days Sales Outstanding (DSO), and it is calculated by dividing accounts receivable by the average credit sales per day.

$$\textbf{Receivable Collection Period} = \frac{\text{Receivables}}{\dfrac{\text{Sales}}{360}}$$

3. Average Payment Period

Average Payment Period or Payables Payment Period is the average length of time between the purchase of raw materials and labour and the payment of cash for them. It is computed by dividing accounts payable by the daily credit purchases.

$$\text{Average Payment Period} = \frac{\text{Accounts payable}}{\dfrac{\text{Cost of goods sold}}{360}}$$

Therefore, cash conversion cycle = average receivables collection period + average inventory processing period – average payment period:

The major objective of cash management is to shorten cash conversion cycle and it should be accomplished without increasing costs or depressing sales. This improves profits because the longer the cash conversion cycle, the greater is the need for external financing, and such financing has a high cost. Note that the accounts payable period, or the credit offered by suppliers, provides some financing for the working capital cycle, but longer the cash conversion cycle, the larger is the investment in working capital. Thus, cash conversion cycle can be shortened by:

(1) Reducing the inventory conversion period by processing and selling goods more quickly.

(2) Reducing the receivables collection period by speeding up collections.

(3) Lengthening the average payment period by slowing down the payments.

CASH CONVERSION CYCLE AND OPERATING CYCLE

Sometimes operating cycle and cash conversion cycle are assumed to be one and the same concept. But a firm's operating cycle differ from its cash conversion cycle. Let us understand how cash conversion cycle is different from operating cycle. A business's operating cycle begins with the purchase of inventory which is turned into products and sold. The sale results in a receivable that becomes cash when collected. The cash is used to purchase more inventory starting the cycle again. The term operating cycle refers to both the sequence of events and the time required to operate it once.

It is calculated by adding the Accounts Receivable days (Receivable Collection Period) to the Inventory days (Inventory Conversion Period).

So, Operating Cycle = Inventory conversion period + Receivable collection period

The cash conversion cycle is the operating cycle in days less the payables deferral period, which is the time between receiving and paying for inventory. In simple terms, the cash conversion cycle is the number of days in the firm's Operating Cycle (OC) minus the Average Payment Period (APP) for inputs to production.

Therefore, CCC = Operating Cycle – Average Payment Period

The cash conversion cycle takes into account the time at which payment is made for raw materials; this spontaneous form of financing, partially or fully, offsets the need for financing.

A positive cash conversion cycle requires the firm to use non-spontaneous financing (bank lines, secured financing arrangements etc.) to support the cash conversion cycle. A negative cash conversion cycle may be favourable, indicating that spontaneous financing exceeds the operating cycle (APP>OC). However, a negative cash conversion cycle may indicate that a firm has stretched its average payment period to an unreasonable length. Non-manufacturing firms are more likely than manufacturing firms to have a negative cash conversion cycle, as they can often carry smaller, faster moving inventory and often sell their products for cash. With a negative cash conversion cycle, excess spontaneous financing can be used for other aspects of the business such as fixed assets. Thus, a firm should try to minimize its cash conversion cycle without losing sales or its ability to purchase on credit.

CASH MANAGEMENT SYSTEM

The basic premise of sound cash management is to ensure that cash inflows (sources of funds) and outflows (uses of funds) are effectively controlled and utilized. To effectively control cash flow, firms must implement adequate cash management techniques to expedite cash collections and cheque clearing in order to access and use the funds. Firms must also develop cost-effective disbursement mechanisms for transferring funds. The management is ultimately responsible for selecting the best collection and payment mechanisms as well as adopting appropriate strategies, operating policies and procedures, and audit requirements. In some cases, firms may deploy other financial institutions and organisations for cash management related services that can be performed more economically or efficiently. Such services include transfer and payment of funds, collection and concentration of funds, sweep account services, information reporting, and so on.

A cash management system in any business organisation achieves its objectives by (a) Accelerating the Receipts and (b) Slowing down the disbursements.

(a) Acceleration of Receipts

An important function of the cash management system is the prompt collection of funds. This process involves speeding up the conversion of receipts into available funds. By minimizing the delay time associated with collection of accounts receivable and extending the time period on the accounts payable side, firms can more effectively manage cash. Hence, firms should effectively develop a system to collect payments from customers.

Cash acceleration and deceleration techniques revolve around the concept of float. Float is the difference between the balance shown in the firm's account books and the balance on the bank's books. Before discussing the major elements of a cash management system, let us understand how float affects the overall collection and disbursement process.

FLOAT

In simple words, Float is the difference between the bank balance and the book balance of cash. When a customer mails a cheque, this does not mean that the funds are immediately available for the firm's use. It must go through the mail. It must be deposited in the firm's bank account, which must then send it to the customer's bank. Finally the customer's bank transfers funds to the firm's bank, and finally funds are actually available for use. The same reasoning is true when the firm writes a cheque. So, time between the moment the customer writes the cheque and the time the bank cashes the cheque — there is a difference in the firm's book balance and the balance the bank shows for the firm's account. That difference is float. Therefore, Float is the difference between the balance in a firm's cheque book and the firm's balance on the bank records.

This float can be positive or negative.

If bank balance > book balance (e.g. writing a cheque reduces book cash before bank cash)

It implies a positive (disbursement) float.

If bank balance < book balance (e.g. receiving and depositing a cheque increases book cash before bank cash)

It implies negative (collection) float.

Net Float = Disbursement Float + Collection Float

Float management seeks to speed up the collection and slow down the disbursement of cash. Speeding up of collection process amounts to minimizing collection float, the delay between the time when cash goes into a firm's books and the time when the cash appears in the firm's bank account. Delaying the disbursement of cash means maximizing disbursement float, the time that elapses between when a payment decreases book cash and when the payment amount is actually deducted from a bank account. Both types of float are driven primarily by three forms of processing delays: the time it takes for a payment to travel through the postal system (mail float), the time required for in-house processing of a payment (processing float), and the time required for the banking system to process and clear a payment (availability float). Efficient Cash Management generates positive net float. Basically a firm's net float is a function of its ability to speed up collections and cheques received and slow down disbursements and cheques written.

The reduction in collection float will result in:

(1) Increased usable funds that are released for company use and

(2) Increased returns produced on these freed-up balances.

COMPONENTS OF FLOAT

(a) Mail Float: It refers to the funds that have been mailed by a payer but are not yet received by the payee. This represents funds which are not usable to the firm because of the time necessary for a customer's remittance cheque to travel through the mails to a company collection center.

(b) Processing Float: Processing float represents funds tied up due to the time needed for the company to process the remittance cheques and get them ready for deposit in a demand deposit account.

(c) Availability Float: Availability float refers to the time lag required for a deposited cheque to clear through the commercial banking system and become usable funds for the use by the firm.

The objective before the finance manager is to minimize collection float and maximize disbursement float. Now, it is clear that for a business firm the Float can be of two types:

1. Collection Float and
2. Disbursement/Payment Float

1. Collection Float

Collection float is the time which elapses between the time a payer deducts a payment from its accounts ledger and the time when the payee actually receives the funds in actual form.

The collection float usually, consists of Mail float, Processing float, and Availability float.

Collection Float

Customer mails the cheque	Company receives the cheque	Company deposits the cheque	Bank processes and clears the cheque
— Mail Float —	— Processing Float —		— Availability Float —

2. Disbursement/Payment Float

Disbursement float this refers to funds available in the firm's demand deposit account due to the time needed for a payment cheque to clear through the banking system. Or in other words, it is the lapse between the time when a firm deducts a payment from its accounts ledger and the time when the funds are actually withdrawn from its bank account.

Disbursement/Payment Float

Company mails the cheque to Supplier	Supplier receives the cheque	Supplier deposits the cheque	Bank processes and credits Supplier' account
— Mail Float —	— Processing Float —		— Availability Float —

Let us understand the concept of collection and disbursement floats with the help of examples.

Example: Suppose a firm issues cheques of Rs. 5,000 on an average each day, and it takes 6 days for the cheques to be deducted from its bank account. The firm's books will, on average, show Rs. 30,000 less than the balance at the bank. This difference is called disbursement float – the value of the cheques written but not deducted from its account yet. This is the positive type of float, from the firm's point of view.

Suppose also that the firm receives an average of Rs. 5,000 in cheques each day, and that it takes only 4 days for them to be deposited and credited to its bank account. This will result in a Rs. 20,000 collections float. Collections float is the value of the cheques received but not yet credited to the firm's account. This is the negative type of float, from the firm's point of view.

In total, the firm's net float is the difference between the Rs. 30,000 positive disbursement float and the Rs. 20,000 negative collections float, or Rs. 10,000 (positive). This means that the firm's cheque book balance is Rs. 10,000 less than the balance at the bank.

The firm should strive to reduce collections float to a minimum through an efficient collection and clearing process. If it is efficient enough, the firm could actually have a *negative* balance on its own books, but a *positive* balance at the bank.

HOW TO MEASURE A FLOAT?

Float is usually measured in 'Rupee Days' and is a function of the transaction's rupee amount and the number of days of delay. So, float can be calculated by multiplying the payment amount by the number of days it is delayed. It is simply a means of quantifying the efficiencies or inefficiencies of the cash cycle (cash coming in and going out) and focusing on opportunities and costs. A firm benefits from shortening all types of float associated with cash inflows and lengthening all types of float associated with cash outflows.

Example: Suppose a payment of Rs. 20,000 is delayed for 5 days. The value of float which will be in 'Rupee Days' is as follows:

Float = Payment value × Delayed days

= 20,000 × 5 = Rs. 100,000 days.

Average Daily Float

Average daily float can be computed by dividing the float value with the number of days of delay. Let us take the previous example to calculate average daily float. It will be:

= 100000/5 = Rs. 20000 days.

This is the case of one individual payment; in the same manner other payment's float can be calculated and summed up to get a total average daily float of the firm.

Cost of Float

Cost of float is the opportunity cost of the cash which was not available with the firm due to mail, processing or availability delay. It is calculated by multiplying Average daily float by Opportunity cost of cash.

Cost of float = Average daily float × opportunity cost

Example: In the previous example Average daily float was Rs. 20,000 and say, the opportunity cost is 24 per cent per annum.

Annual cost of float = 20,000 × 24%

= Rs. 4,800.

and Monthly cost of float = 20,000 × 0.24/12

= Rs. 400

Or alternatively,

Monthly cost of float = Annual cost of float/12

= Rs. 4800/12 = Rs. 400

DOES FLOAT WORK, TODAY?

Today, the technology is working against the Float. Now, in this IT age there is a shorter span between the time a cheque is deposited and the time it is cleared. In other words, the days of playing the float are fading away.

The float is that lapse in time between when a cheque is deposited into an account and when the money becomes actually available. The float for paper cheques is between two and six days. Banks use this time to verify the legitimacy of a cheque. In the meantime, the bank earns interest on dormant cheques.

Let us understand how the paper cheque float works: Once a cheque is deposited into an account, it is routed automatically from the recipient's bank to the cheque writer's bank. This can take up to six working days. During this time, the cheque is sent to clearing bank for clearance, and then sent back to the recipient's bank. Along the way, several occurrences can add more days to the clearance process: The cheque writer's bank can refuse to honour the cheque because the account does not have enough money, the cheque may appear to be forged or the signature may be unsatisfactory. The length of time it takes for a cheque to clear depends upon where the cheque is going and how the cheque writer's bank decides to get it there.

In the western countries where the banking system and banking habits of people are very much developed, a group of neighbouring banks that consistently present many cheques to each other find it convenient to organize a regular cheque exchange. They mutually agree to accept cheque presentment at a central location. This system simply cuts down the float time.

Regardless of the shortcuts, banks usually make money available on local cheques within two banking days of deposit. The time allowance may be longer for deposits made by new account holders or with out-of-state cheques. Money on cheques drawn on out-of-state banks is available within six banking days. In reality, most cheques clear through the system in two to three days. Quite often it is the exceptional cheque that is held; due to a new account where the bank does not know the customer or if it involves a large amount.

As online banking and electronic bill payments have become more popular; payments made online usually clear by the end of the day. Debit card transactions are instantaneous because point-of-sale transactions are cleared at the time of purchase. More and more firms are requiring payment by wire or by automatic electronic debit. For such payments, float is reduced to zero. So, it seems that playing with float is now loosing its significance. Rapid developments in the area of electronic payment systems will have a large impact on float management, but indications are that these developments will take place slowly, at least in a country like India. The other factor in favour of float can be the cost aspect. The cost of processing an electronic payment is currently higher than the costs for a paper-based payment. This is especially true in the case of India where banking system and banking habits of people are not, yet, very well developed and easily accessible.

Speeding Up Collections

- Invoicing customers as quickly as possible.
- Taking immediate action when a customer delays the payment.
- Rewarding customers for making early payment by offering a discount.
- Imposing a finance charge on customers that are delinquent.
- Evaluating the financial soundness of customers before extending credit.
- Accepting credit cards or post dated cheques for payment.
- Issuing monthly statements to remind customers of amounts owed.
- Placing collection centers near customers.

Now, we will discuss some techniques for speeding up collections:

LOCKBOX SYSTEM

In a lockbox system, a firm collects payments through one or more locations and transfers available funds to a commercial bank. Lockboxes are post office boxes rented by the firm at one or more locations near its customers. A nearby bank collects payments made to that address on behalf of the firm, deposits them, and sends a record of deposit to the collecting firm same day. This record of deposit can be a paper photocopy or a computer file which can be transferred online. The economic benefit of using a lockbox is a trade-off between reducing collection float and paying fees to a lockbox processor over and above internal processing costs. This is the most widely used and effective tool available for accelerating the collection of receivables. Under a lockbox system, usually a Post Office Box is established at the Post Office, specifically for the firm. Customers are directed to send their remittances to the P.O. Box instead of sending them to the firm's head office. Several times a daily, the local bank collects the contents of the post office box and deposits the cheques into an account for the company. The bank informs the firm of the receipts each day. The lockbox system allows incoming payments to bypass corporate head office and come directly to the bank. This process results in reducing mail, processing, and collection float.

The major *advantages* of a lockbox facility are as follows:

- Rapid conversion of receivables into cash.
- Saves mailing time as customers deposit cheques into local post office directly.
- Reduces costs associated with the manual preparation of daily deposits.
- Company's processing time (i.e. time spent on receiving cheques, ledger entries, then depositing into the bank) is also saved.
- Facilitates critical credits and funds management decisions by providing detailed receivables and deposit information same day.
- Cheques are usually drawn on local banks so it reduces the availability float.
- Provides an audit trail for easier research of payment inquiries.
- Reduces uncertainty attached with traditional postage system. In India, still, ordinary post is not very reliable.
- Provides early knowledge of dishonest cheques.

RECENT DEVELOPMENTS

Recent innovations in the information technology have improved the concept of lockbox even more. Earlier the bank used to provide photocopies of the receivables received. Modern banks today have evolved from paper photocopies, to microfilm, and now, to digital document imaging. Although in India this is not common, but the technology is available with big leading commercial and private banks. Banks now have high speed cheque imaging (scanning) systems to provide a digital image of the cheques and the supporting documents. A company can receive anywhere from hundreds of cheques to thousands of cheques each business day. Depending on the level of banking services chosen, the documents can be delivered as hardcopies or in digital format. Often these digital cheque and document images are delivered to the client company on a CD-ROM (Compact Disc Read Only Memory). A CD-ROM can hold approximately 20,000 images, or roughly the equivalent of a four-drawer file cabinet. This CD-ROM technology provides fast access to the transaction documents and a digital record of the images. However, it creates search, file, and storage issues for the company. Some banks also offer on-line access to the cheques, documents and resulting deposit transactions. This on-line technology allows fast access to recent cheques and supporting documents, however, it creates archival, security, and control issues for a company. Typically, images are maintained on-line by the banks for a limited period of time, i.e. 30, 60, or 90 days, and then are delivered to the company on CD-ROM.

On the payable side, banks may also send scanned front and back images of the company's cancelled cheques rather than returning the actual paper instrument. This also helps speed the account reconciliation process and reduces the storage burden. While these new procedures are now a vast improvement over the previous trail of paper documents, integration with an internal document imaging system by the companies immensely improves the process. This application of technology can have an immediate and profound effect on the cash management and remittance processing of virtually any company.

ESTABLISHMENT OF A LOCKBOX

The establishment and maintenance of an efficient collection system involves many elements. While pricing, service quality, and other information needs are important, the primary consideration in almost every lockbox decision remains to minimize float. So, the essence of all lockbox decisions is the estimation of mail and availability float. In order to accurately estimate float, lockbox study depends on surveys of mail times and on bank availability schedules. It is of the utmost importance that these two separate sources of information be considered and dealt with together in order to closely approximate potential lockbox performance.

A lockbox study identifies the optimum number of lockbox sites for a company to have, the best locations for these sites, the most efficient assignment of customers to the selected sites and the amount of float in the lockbox system. The study also can be used to evaluate the current performance of an existing lockbox system or fine tune an existing system by reassigning customers among lockbox sites.

Data and computer models have been developed over the years to help finance managers identify the most favourable number and location of lockbox sites. They are used to plan investment strategies, forecast cash flows, and locate lockbox and disbursement facilities. However, there is not a single best way for companies to pursue a lockbox study. Each analysis must be carefully designed and executed to meet the individual circumstances of each company. Special care must be taken to choose the appropriate sample period and sample size, the appropriate modelling technology and assumptions, and the correct interpretation of results. As already noted, the primary consideration in every lockbox decision is minimizing float, the amount of time funds are in the collection process. When evaluating float it is critical to consider only total float (mail time plus availability) rather than drawing conclusions based on either mail time or on funds availability alone.

Managers should thoroughly understand the lockbox processing environment of current and prospective service providers, in which ways it is consistent or inconsistent with assumptions made in the analysis, and what impact the inconsistencies will have. Once a system is in place, it should be monitored for float performance, as well as for the timeliness and accuracy of processing. The account analysis, bank statement, end point analysis and daily balance reports can be used to track some fairly simple indicators of float trends within a bank.

WHEN A LOCKBOX SYSTEM IS BENEFICIAL?

The benefits from lockbox are not cost free. Bank charges for each cheque processed through the system. Then there are annual charges for a lockbox. The benefits derived from the lockbox system must exceed the operating costs of the lockbox. Therefore, when the benefits derived from this system are greater than the cost incurred only then it is beneficial to have a lockbox collection system. Companies having small average size of their receipts should avoid a lockbox system.

Let us understand how to calculate the costs and benefits of a specific lockbox system:

Example: Suppose the number of average daily receipts = 100

And average amount of receipt = Rs. 5,000

Let the saving in mailing and processing time = 1 day

Annual charges for the lockbox = Rs. 3,000

Bank's service charges = Rs. 30,000

Annual interest rate =10%

So, lockbox will increase the company's cash balance by

= 100 receipts × 5,000 average amount per receipt × 1 day saving

= Rs. 500,000

Now, annual interest saving = Rs. 500,000 × 10%

= **Rs. 50,000**

The annual cost of operating lockbox = Rs. 3,000 (annual charges) + Rs. 30,000 (bank charges)

= **Rs. 33,000**

Clearly, benefits in terms of saving from the interest income is greater than the cost incurred, therefore, it is beneficial to have lockbox arrangement for collection. Moreover, company's internal time on processing and depositing cheques is saved.

(b) Slowing Down Disbursement

Cash management system also includes the design and operation of efficient and effective payment mechanisms. Types of payments may range from the purchase of raw materials to the payment of debt. The payment of accounts is an important part of a cash management system. Payments should be made on time, neither early nor late. Early payments deprive the firm of the opportunity to earn interest on those funds. Late payments may result in the firm incurring penalties or loss of goodwill. Efficient payment mechanisms may lead to considerable savings. Funds can also be saved by delaying the payments until they are due. We can delay payments by:

(1) Mailing cheques from locations not close to customers. This will increase the mail time or mail float.

(2) Disbursing cheques from a remote bank. This will increase the time required for the payment to clear the bank i.e. availability float.

(3) Purchasing with credit cards so that the time required for making payment is much longer. By using a credit card, one receives a bill at the end of the month payable in thirty days. This creates more processing time or processing float.

By increasing the float times within disbursements, we have the use of cash for several more days. This is a source of spontaneous financing and we can measure our cash savings. Various disbursement techniques are available for firms to effectively manage the disbursement process.

ZERO BALANCE ACCOUNTS

Under this system of cash disbursement, a firm does not keep any cash balance in the bank account. Cash is transferred only when the cheque is presented for the payment to the bank. So, a Zero Balance Account is a disbursement account on which cheques are written even though the balance in the account is zero. Therefore, a Zero balance account is a bank accounts with a zero balance in which only an amount sufficient to cover a day's cheques is deposited. Idle cash balances are thus minimized. A transfer of funds from the firm's master account covers the payments. Funding of the ZBA account is automatic and involves only an accounting entry by the bank. Credits and debits are posted just before the close of business when a credit from the master account is posted to bring the balance back to zero. If there is a credit balance in the ZBA account, the ZBA will be debited and a credit made to the master account. Cash provides flexibility and carries minimal risk in the short term. The amount of cash held will vary from organisation to organisation, depending on anticipated needs.

CONTROLLED DISBURSEMENT

Where a company is not able to access Zero Balance Account, another method known as controlled disbursement can be used. Controlled disbursement is the strategic determination of mailing points and bank accounts to lengthen mail and clearing floats. In this system, the required cash (estimates based on forecasts and other payment information) is deposited with the bank everyday in the morning. Of course the actual amount required for payment cannot be judged with hundred per cent accuracy. So there remains always the chance of errors in the projections. To hedge this risk, a permanent stock of cash is kept with the bank. The stock of cash is also projected considering minimum and maximum size of payments to be made during the day.

ELECTRONIC FUNDS TRANSFER (EFT)

Like collection systems, disbursements can also be made electronically. Funds operated by wire transfers are moved almost instantaneously, thereby reducing float time. But this is a costly way to disburse funds compared to cheques and drafts transactions.

The popular modes of funds transfer at present are demand draft, mail transfer and telegraphic transfer. The demand draft facility is paper based. The remitter, after purchasing demand draft from a bank branch, dispatches the same by post/courier to the beneficiary. The beneficiary, in turn, lodges the draft to his/her bank for collection and clearing. The time taken for completing the process is about 10 days. In the case of telegraphic transfer, fund reaches the beneficiary either on the same day or the next; but both the remitter and the beneficiary would have to be account holders of the same bank. If they are customers of different banks, a good deal of paper processing is required. On the other hand, EFT system is an inter-bank oriented system. RBI acts as an intermediary between the remitting bank and the receiving bank and effects inter-bank funds transfer. The customers of banks can request their respective branches to remit funds to the designated customers irrespective of bank affiliation of the beneficiary.

The Reserve Bank of India has taken up solid measures to the establishment of an integrated payment and settlement system in the country. A number of initiatives have either already been implemented or are in an advanced stage on the drawing board. Identification and classification of the Systemetically Important Payment System (SIPS) have been done and various measures have been initiated to facilitate real time or near real time large value inter-bank funds transfer in secured environment. EFT as a method of payment has been recently introduced by Reserve Bank of India (RBI)[1] to help banks offering their customers money transfer service from account to account of any bank branch to any other bank branch. EFT facilitates transfer of funds electronically within and across cities and between branches of a bank and across banks. EFT is operated by RBI, and is available for funds transferred across major cities in the country. The Reserve Bank's EFT facility was extended in 1999-2000 to encompass 12 other scheduled commercial banks besides the 27 public sector banks. This facility is available from 2500 bank branches located in 500 centres. With effect from October 1, 2001, large value transactions up to Rs. 2 crore have been permitted under EFT. Average monthly transactions under EFT has increased from 100 valued at Rs. 5 lakh in 1998-99 to 600 valued at Rs. 9 crore in 1999-2000.

Funds transfer is possible from any bank branch to other bank branch - both inter-city and intra-city. Although the system is designed primarily for inter-bank funds transfer, intra-bank funds transfer (money transfer between the branches of the same bank) is also possible. Let us understand how it works. The remitter fills in the EFT form giving the particulars of the beneficiary (city, bank, branch, beneficiary's name, account type and account number) and authorises the branch to remit a specified amount to the beneficiary by debiting the remitter's account. The remitting branch prepares a schedule and sends the duplicate of the EFT form to its Service branch for EFT data preparation. If the branch has a computer system, data preparation is done at the branch level in the specified format. The Service branch prepares the EFT data file by using a software provided by RBI and transmits the same to the local RBI (National Clearing Cell). The RBI at the remitting centre consolidates the files received from all banks, sorts the transactions city-wise and prepares vouchers for debiting the remitting banks on the same day itself. Thereafter, bank-wise remittance data files are transmitted to banks. Bank-wise vouchers are also prepared for crediting the receiving banks' accounts the next morning. Next morning the receiving banks at the destination centres process the remittance files transmitted by RBI and forward credit reports to the destination branches for crediting the beneficiaries' accounts.

It is not necessary for all branches to have computer systems. Branches can send the remittance details to their service branch in paper format. The Service branch will make data entry and transmit the funds transfer information electronically to local NCC. But, if a branch has computer facility, it can transmit funds transfer information electronically to its service branch either on a floppy or through a network. This would minimise the data entry work at the service branch.

The acceleration in the pace of computerisation in the Indian banking industry in recent years has facilitated the orderly development of modern payment and settlement systems in a secure manner. The thrust is placed on commercially important centres which account for 65 per cent of banking business in terms of value. At present, there are about 6,103 fully computerised branches among public sector banks across the country. The switchover from cash based transactions to paper based transactions is gathering momentum with the banking business on the rise. The value of transactions put through cheque clearances as a proportion to GDP is estimated to have reached over 402 per cent in 1999-2000 as against 352 per cent in 1998-99. The rise in cheque clearances was partly reflective of the operation of MICR clearing of cheques at more centres than the traditional four metropolitan centres. MICR clearing has been operational in 12 cities in 1999-2000 as against 10 cities in 1998-1999. The daily average value of cheques processed in clearing operations in the four metropolitan cities has gone up to Rs. 19,679 crore reflecting in part the installation of modern S/390 systems, and the rising trend in daily turnovers in the principal segments of the financial markets, namely the call money market, the gilt market and the equity market. The electronic clearing services (ECS) are offered at 15 of the offices of the Reserve Bank across the country with debit services available at the six major centres. At the end of 1999-2000, there were 26 ECS debit users and 171 ECS credit users. The number of ECS transactions has gone up from 4.3 million valued at Rs. 67.37 crore for credits and from 5.2 lakh transactions valued at Rs. 181.77 crore for debits in 1998-99 to 6.9 million valued at

Rs. 934.45 crore for credits and to 8.4 lakh transactions valued at Rs. 301.87 crore for debits in 1999-2000.

CASH MANAGEMENT IN MULTINATIONAL ENVIRONMENT

Today, in most multinational companies, cash management is organized centrally. The major goal is to concentrate overall group liquidity as much as is possible and reasonable. Ideally this pooling is done across national borders and banks. In a broader sense, cash management comprises the organisation of the process of all incoming and outgoing payments in the most efficient way. To achieve this, organisations need, on the one hand, instruments like bank policy and cash pooling, and, on the other hand, software intelligence. In reality the right mix of organisational and software intelligence probably leads to the best result.

One major instrument to improve the efficiency of cash management is the bank policy of a multinational company. The major problem here is the degree of complexity the finance manager has to cope with. The more bank accounts that are involved in cash management, the more complex and challenging is the cash concentration process. Concentration of bank business to a limited number of banks consequently leads to less number of bank accounts. This implies higher transparency of liquidity and gives good opportunities for successful price negotiations with banks.

PROCESS MANAGEMENT OF CASH FORECASTS

It is crucial for the liquidity management to get a short term forecast with best quality. This information problem is especially difficult to handle in the case of cash pools because one normally needs to integrate information from more than one company. The quality of cash pooling can be measured by the gap between the forecasted and the realized cash position of the company. The smaller the difference between projections and reality, the higher is the efficiency of cash management.

Regarding the forecast of cash inflows, one must keep in mind the whole process, from the order, to the invoice, right up to the payments. A proper database for the medium term forecast is required in the accounting system. From there, via reports, the maturity structure of all orders and invoices can be drawn. For the short-term horizon, the manager can work with advices and suggestions from banks. Cash outflows and payments are known to the manager well in advance. The longer horizon can be covered by using the information from the purchase process.

The easiest way to get information about future cash inflows and outflows from all other cash pool participants is the use of computer based worksheets such as MS- Excel etc. These must be completed on a regular basis and can be automatically imported into the treasury software. Alternatively the participants can directly key in expected cash flow data into the treasury software. This requires a direct access of all related companies to the system.

A logical further step in cash management is the organisation of the payments in a centralised way. Such concepts are labeled as Payment Factory. From one place all payments for all connected subsidiaries of a multinational company can be managed. This includes single payments as well as mass payments. If the payments are managed using treasury software, a key issue is the database system. This system must be able to cope with a mass of transactions. For the cash management and the disposition of cash flows a payment factory leads to substantially better quality of forecast.

CASH POOLING

Cash pooling is the standard instrument for efficient cash management. There are two basic concepts available: Notional Pooling and Zero Balancing Approach.

The notional pooling is organised as interest compensation across the participating bank accounts. Alternatively, the zero balancing approach requires physical concentration of all cash flows on one concentration account. The latter approach is the most used concept today. An ongoing challenge for cash pools are situations when liquidity has to be concentrated across borders and banks. With respect to this, a lot of opportunities arose after the introduction of the Euro. The new currency made cross border pooling simpler than ever before. Many companies make use of this. Two concepts can be distinguished.

(a) Cash Pooling Within one Bank or Banking Group

This structure requires bank accounts of all participating subsidiaries to be within one bank or banking group. Due to central bank requirements and other issues in each country in Euroland, a prepooling is done first. The result of the different prepoolings is sent to the master concentration account of the parent company. The advantage of this solution is that there are normally no technical problems because the data formats within one bank or banking group are standardized and the technical platform is harmonized. A conflict can be that you need to convince all affiliates to make use of the cash pool which requires acceptance of the pooling bank.

(b) Cash Pooling Across Different Banks by use of an Oerlay Bank

The assumption here is that all subsidiaries within one country work with the same/ local bank and pool their funds to this bank. The result of these pooling of local banks in different countries is then concentrated on the master concentration account of the parent company at an overlay bank. This pooling across different banks or bank groups is possible in Euroland but requires a lot of synchronization of data formats which causes difficulties. As all information from all banks must be electronically integrated in a treasury software, the data formats must be synchronized and stable over time. The advantage of this approach is the probable high acceptance of the local banks at the level of the subsidiaries.

SOFTWARE REQUIREMENTS

The minimum set-up for efficient liquidity management includes a cash management system with an interface to an electronic banking system. Ideally, the cash management software is part of an integrated treasury software. This allows the efficient linking of liquidity management with the process of settlement and accounting of transactions. The necessary links between banks, treasury software and accounting system can be realized via interfaces.

Chapter 5

CASH FORECASTING

(**Contents:** Introduction, Cash Forecast, Forecast Period, Basis of Forecast, Financial Statements, Sales Forecast, Accounts Receivable Collection Patterns, Disbursement Patterns, Benefits of forecasting, Problems in forecasting, Cash forecasting techniques, (1) Projected receipts and disbursements approach, (2) Balance Sheet Approach, (3) Per cent of Sales Approach, (4) Statistical Techniques: (a) Time Series Techniques, (b) Moving Average Techniques, (c) Exponential Smoothing, (d) Regression Techniques Budgeting, Cash budget.)

"As far as the laws of mathematics refer to reality, they are not certain; and as far as they are certain, they do not refer to reality".

— Albert Einstein

INTRODUCTION

Cash is the lifeblood of a company and is fundamental to its very existence. Anyone who controls people, material and services or makes decisions affecting resources has an impact on the cash position of the organisation. Managers must understand how their decisions on investment, operations and financing lead to specific cash flow movements within the business system. These decisions, in one form or another affect the company's ability to pay its bills, obtain credit from suppliers and extend credit to its customers. A part of management's job is to maintain an appropriate balance between the inflows and outflows of cash. The main task of a cash management system is to ensure that the right amount of cash is available, at the right time, at the lowest possible cost. Cash management systems at the whole of firm level need to consolidate a range of information relating to production and sales, loan repayment schedules, asset sales, transfer payments and firm's operating flows and capital requirements. Cash management systems also need to interface with debt management systems to ensure that current interest and principal obligations can be met. Cash flow from receivables is the critical component in working capital management, and the ability to forecast cash inflow is critical. Credit and collections departments now have increased responsibilities to increase their efficiency, eliminate cash flow bottlenecks and to report the ever-changing patterns of payments from customers. This information helps finance organisations to plan for cash management efficiently across all operations.

Accurate forecasting of cash flows ensures that a firm has sufficient cash to satisfy its obligations at any point of time. This avoids unanticipated shortfalls in the amount of cash and the high interest cost associated with emergency borrowing. Although firms usually have overdraft facilities with a bank, these overdraft facilities may be relatively expensive. Accurate forecasting also enables the cash inflows and outflows of firms to be offset against each other, thus reducing the overall amount of borrowing required to meet cash requirements. Where overall surplus balances are identified, accurate forecasting enables the large investment for longer period than would otherwise be possible. Effective management of cash flow is thus the key to business success and survival.

There are many advantages that come from the regular use of cash forecasting. Some of the more common are listed below:

- Anticipating Short-term Financing Needs
- Financing Seasonal Business Fluctuations
- Planning Debt Reductions
- Planning Capital Expenditures
- Taking Advantage of Cash Discounts
- Planning Inventory Purchases
- Evaluating/Designing Credit Policies
- Planning Long-term Financing
- Increasing Investment Income

The preparation of a cash forecast does not revolve around a major strategic decision rather it is required to determine how day-to-day operations will be performed. This process is called planning for short-term cash needs.

The overall objective is to prepare a cash flow forecast that is accurate enough to determine cash sufficiency. As a general rule, it is more difficult to predict cash receipts than cash disbursements. When estimates about receipts and disbursements are made future expected values are estimated. A cash forecast is a presentation of cash results based upon assumptions about conditions and events expected to exist or occur during the forecast period. So, the major points to remember are as follows:

1. The time period or forecast period for making cash forecast must be defined.
2. Certain estimates about what is going to happen must be made and documented to project the cash result. Estimates must have some logical foundation.
3. A cash forecast must be prepared in written form. It should be complete and understandable.
4. Concrete actions based upon the estimates must be taken to ensure the relevance of cash forecast.

FORECAST PERIOD

A cash forecast is always prepared with reference to some time period e.g. a week, a month, a quarter etc. There are no rules of thumb for determining the length of the forecast period. However, as a general rule, it should be long enough to show the effect of management policies, yet short enough so that estimates can be made with reasonable accuracy. The length of the budget period also depends on the type of business, the duration of operating cycle, the ease or difficulty of forecasting future market conditions etc. Normally, the time period for the purpose of forecasting and budgeting is divided as follows:

Long-term Plans — For more than a year

Medium-term Plans — For one month to one year

Short-term Plans — For one day to one month

Most of the forecasting efforts are concerned with the preparation of medium-term category such as a three-month forecast. This forecast is quite common because it is close enough to the current business position to allow most of the variables to be predicted with reasonable accuracy.

On the basis of successful preparation of medium term forecast, longer range plans and the forecasts are prepared projecting at least one year ahead. Longer-range plans are prepared in the form of the capital-expenditure budget. These plans detail the business's plans for acquiring fixed assets, renovation and modernization, or for projects over five years, ten years, or even longer period. These plans cannot be as detailed as the annual cash budget, but they take into consideration major deciding factors such as sales, long-term capital expenditure, new product development, research and development programmes etc. Long-range budgets help companies in anticipating future hurdles and preparing for them. Short-range budgets do not enable this. On the other hand, long-range forecasts are less reliable as predictions for the long-term are not very certain.

Whereas short-range forecasts have the advantage of accuracy in budgeted figures relating to the future events. The other more desirable reason, for the very short-term forecast, is to take advantage of excess cash balances by making very short-term, highly liquid investments. To do this estimates about the cash needs and excess balances are required for the short-term periods. The more common reason for very short-term forecasts is to try to make an inadequate amount of cash stretch to cover required disbursements. It is always helpful to know what is expected to be received and what is expected to clear the bank on a daily basis, but too often short-term analyses are attempts to manage with inadequate cash, rather than an attempt to maximize investment return on cash.

USE OF A COMPUTER

With the aid of a computer and suitable software, a mathematical model can be used to prepare cash flow projections and project short term financing requirements for a business. The use of a computer-based model reduces the burden of carrying out numerous repetitive calculations and simplifies the presentation of results. A computer-based model can be constructed using a spreadsheet or can be acquired a ready-made package. A cash flow model can be used to compile forecasts, assess possible funding requirements and explore the likely financial consequences of alternative strategies. Used effectively, a model can help prevent major planning errors, anticipate problems, identify opportunities to improve cash flow or provide a basis for negotiating short-term funding from a bank. Generally, when seeking external funding, the time horizon covered by a set of projections should be equal to or greater than the period for which the funding is needed. The greater the amount of funding required and the longer the financing period, the more comprehensive must be the supporting projections and plan. A computer model for short-term bank planning uses assumptions on sales, costs, credit, funding etc. to produce monthly cash flow projections for up to a year ahead. The initial assumptions can be readily altered to evaluate alternative scenarios. For example, a model can be used to explore the degree to which future sales can be increased while having bank financing within pre-determined limits; to assess the effects on cash flow of varying level of sales, costs or credit terms; or to determine the likely short-term funding requirements for a business. Once assumptions on sales, expenses payments etc. have been established, a model can be used to produce the cash flow projections which, in turn, indicate the likely future cash balances or banking requirements. However, the quality of these projections will be completely determined by the standard and reliability of the underlying assumptions. For example, if forecasts for sales, working capital or costs are unrealistic or inadequately made, then the value of the model's output is greatly reduced. An impressive set of projections is of no use if it is not supported by experience or research and is just based on speculation only. In fact, it will be very damaging and can even destroy the business.

BASIS OF FORECASTING

There are several factors such as market trends, economic factors, growth of population, consumption pattern, industrial production, national income, government, and economic and industrial policy that are considered while making financial forecasts.

Based on these parameters, the future sales for the company are forecasted, on the basis of which, projected profit and loss account and the balance sheet are prepared. These projected financial statements help in guiding the organisation's activity towards its future objectives.

To begin the process of making and updating the own cash forecasts there are certain requirements for accurate estimates. Following provides for the basis for cash forecast:

1. Financial Statements.
2. Sales Forecast.
3. Accounts Receivable Collection Patterns.
4. Payment Patterns for Inventories, Expenses, Wages etc.

1. Financial Statements

Financial statements — Profit & Loss Account and a Balance Sheet are required for any financial forecast. It does not matter whether the statements are prepared in-house or by an outside source, such as a CA or an auditing firm. The important thing is that the statements are accurate, consistent, and timely. For a finance manager, it is important to be comfortable with the financial statements and able to read and understand them without undue difficulty.

He must be able to understand the revenues, costs, and expenses and to analyse the types of transactions that make up each account on the Profit & Loss Account. Likewise, with respect to the balance sheet, he must know how to verify each individual asset and liability to its supporting documents in the office. A strong understanding of the financial statements leads to a meaningful cash forecast.

Percentage Profit & Loss Account which shows each account as a percentage of total revenue is also useful for the analysis. All these percentages are very important because in some instances they become the basis of the projections.

Another important financial statement is cash flow statement. The Cash Flow Statement explains how changes in liquidity have occurred during the past year. The measure of liquidity is either cash or working capital, and is the bottom line of the statement showing the net change in that item. The Cash Flow Statement shows how cash flows in and out of the business. In other words, it describes the cash flow that has occurred in the past. It is an important tool for cash flow management. The primary purpose of the cash flow statement is to provide information about a company's cash inflows and outflows. Moreover, it provides information about the investing and financing activities of the company. Information reported in the statement, when used with other financial statements provides the analyst with insights about the company's ability to generate future cash flows. Cash Flow Statement is discussed in detail in the last section of this chapter.

2. Sales Forecast

Financial Forecasting describes the process by which a firm foresees and prepares for the future. The forecasting process provides the means for a firm to express its goals and priorities and to ensure that they are internally consistent. It also assists the firm in identifying the asset requirements and needs for external financing. The foundation upon which a cash forecast is built is the sales forecast. To project accurate sales, an organised process is required. The sales or revenues should be divided into logical categories that have similar characteristics and variables. These categories should be analysed over the last three years or more. Also, the specific variables that will affect each category of the sales or revenues for the forecast period should be listed and analysed. This will involve a very thorough process that will consider several factors. Some of them are — Price of the product, customer demographics, production capacity and supply of the product, promotional plans and budgets, market conditions etc. Some research in trade and economic publications about factors concerning the industry, the customers, the product, the geographical region, etc must be conducted. All this information will give the manager a wider picture to make better decisions. Analysis of all these variables will answer many of the most basic questions to ensure successful operation.

The manager must understand the relationship of the costs and expenses to the sales forecast. The end product for the sales forecast is a document that lists sales, by category, for each month of the forecast period. It is imperative that the forecast be done monthly to provide the proper foundation for the monthly costs and expenses projections. The sales forecast sets the expected level of business that the firm plans to conduct during the forecast period. Therefore, all of the costs and expenses will be affected. In other words, if the firm relies on a poorly made sales forecast, it will end up with an inaccurate or incomplete cash forecast.

3. Accounts Receivable Collection Patterns

If the significant portion of the firm's sale of its product or service is on credit, proper analysis of the collections from accounts receivable is must in order to produce accurate cash forecast. The manager should set up a worksheet, either on paper or on the computer, and should try to analyse several months of credit sales and collections. He should set up column headings across the top for months and list transactions down the worksheet. This should be exercised for each month's sales. Also, the time gap between the credit sales and the ultimate collection of the cash for the transaction must be considered and evaluated.

4. Disbursement Patterns

Behaviour of payments and expenses also requires equal consideration. Although, this is not a difficult task, but requires a fair amount of detail work. For a manufacturing firm, following are the major categories of expenditures:

- Payment for raw materials etc.
- Operating Expense
- Payroll
- Payment for loans and advances
- Interim dividend
- Taxes

The objective here is to develop information that reveals the monthly cash payments for each of these major head of expenses. Some expenses will have a regular percentage relationship based upon monthly sales. Others will be fixed in amount, such as rent or wages payments. It is the responsibility of the finance manager to become sufficiently familiar with each expenditure head to be able to project the future with confidence.

With the help of sales forecast, disbursement pattern can be projected which is related to the level of sales. With the help of monthly Profit & Loss Accounts with percentages, or in the absence of these, Profit & Loss Accounts can be used to calculate the percentages by simply dividing each expense item by net sales. Profit & Loss Account provides the various expense headings necessary for the monthly expense projections.

BENEFITS OF FORECASTING

Financial forecasting provides the following benefits to the organisation: -

- Management is compelled to anticipate the problems likely to arise in the course of achieving forecasted targets and therefore it is well prepared to meet them.
- Financial forecasting enables control of income and expenditure
- It acts as a tool for monitoring and periodic evaluation of managerial policies and decisions.
- It facilitates optimal allocation of resources for maximisation of profit.
- It facilitates coordination and decentralisation of tasks while still retaining control. It helps identify weaknesses and deficiencies during the process of achieving targets.
- It gives a sense of direction to organisational activities.
- It provides systematic and disciplined solutions to problems.

DANGERS OF FORECASTING

When preparing cash flow projections, the financial manager must be aware of the following dangers and problems of forecasting:

- Over-estimation of sales forecasts.
- Under-estimation of costs and delays likely to be encountered.
- Ignoring past trends or performances by debtors.
- Unduly optimistic assumptions about the availability of bank loans, credit, grants etc.
- Using financial forecasting as a substitute for business planning.
- Future cannot be predicted with complete accuracy and therefore, forecasting cannot be precise.
- Management should avoid the mistake of putting too many expectations on the forecasting, since they all may not always be fulfilled.
- Responsibility must be matched with control. Costs that should be considered uncontrollable may not necessarily be treated as such in evaluating individual performance, resulting in discontent and de-motivation.

The above mentioned problems can arise as the result of a lack of foresight or knowledge, or because of excessive optimism. They can lead to under-estimation of the cash and other resources required to sustain or develop a business. When forecasting bank requirements and preparing cash flow projections, realistic views should always be taken about future prospects. There is often merit in compiling 'worst case' projections to complement most likely or best forecasts and to accept that the worst case might occur and to plan accordingly. Computer based forecasting models offer extensive facilities for doing sensitivity analysis.

Preparing a set of forecasts and projections is only a means to an end. Once plans or projections have been approved or in the process of being implemented, they should be regularly updated and compared with the results being achieved.

CASH FORECASTING TECHNIQUES

Cash forecasting is a process that most companies recognise as an integral part of the cash management system but some companies find it difficult to use cash forecasting process. The reasons for this are numerous. Some companies do not know how to develop an effective cash forecasting process. Others lack required resources to manage the process. Sometimes obstacles to the forecasting process are blamed. These include complex cash management structures, decentralised operations and scattered information systems. These factors discourage companies from devoting the necessary time and effort to forecasting.

A number of fundamental forecasting techniques are available that can be used with a computer software in order to create an effective, yet manageable cash forecasting process. These techniques can be used independently, or in combination, to provide effective forecasting. Before selecting an approach and designing the process, it is important to define how the forecast will be used. Some companies are only interested in projecting book cash balances at specific points in time, usually coinciding with financial statement dates. Other companies want to project bank cash balances on a daily basis, so as to facilitate more effective liquidity management decisions i.e. positioning of debt/investment maturities. An occasional firm may choose to forecast cash for both purposes. While a number of forecasting techniques would work under each of these scenarios, certain techniques are better suited for daily forecasting, and others for predicting balance sheet cash levels. Accordingly, once the purpose of the forecast is defined, the choice of technique can be made.

Following are some of the popular cash forecasting techniques:

(1) Projected receipts and disbursements approach

(2) Projected balance sheet approach

(3) Per cent of sales approach

(4) Statistical techniques

While each of the three methodologies has unique qualities, they all share a number of common characteristics. All rely on historical data as a key input to the forecasting process. They all utilise variables representing inflows and outflows as the basis for determining the cash availability. All require consistency and discipline in how they are managed and executed. All require a rigorous process of review and assessment to ensure continuous improvement in forecast accuracy (through forecast to actual comparisons). All three methods rely on high quality raw data. Regardless of the method, each technique is only as accurate as the accurate raw data input is used. Many forecasting processes fail because of the popular principle – 'garbage in, garbage out'. Finally, if applied properly and consistently, each method provides accurate results.

1. Projected Receipts and Disbursements Approach

One of the most common methods used to forecast cash is the receipts and disbursements approach. The approach follows a simple process of constructing a timeline depicting known and estimated cash inflows and outflows. This can be easily maintained using common spreadsheet software e.g. MS-Excel. The timeline may represent any period – a week, a month, a year. This approach requires a detailed understanding of all the types of cash inflows and outflows, which in aggregate comprise an organisation's bank cash balances. Common inflows consist of cash receipts, bank deposits, lockbox collections, electronic transfers, foreign exchange receipts, investment interest, refunds, etc. Cash outflows represent any outgoing payments – payroll, accounts payable, investment activity, etc. Once all of the cash flow categories are identified, they should be divided between known transactions (scheduled to be paid/received on a specific date for a specific amount), and unknown in terms of timing and/or amount. The known transaction is entered into the timeline spreadsheet. The unknown financial transactions must be estimated. There are a variety of methods that can be used to estimate the unknown transactions, ranging from simple averaging to statistical estimation through regression or time series models.

Once the unknown variables are adjusted and projected, they too are dropped into the time line spreadsheet and the forecast is completed. The receipts and disbursement forecasting technique offers users the ability to project cash balances on a daily basis. This level of forecast detail aids the liquidity management process and helps basic cash management and planning. Better financial decisions can be made with regard to the timing of debt/investment maturities, cash transfers, cash repatriation, and other cash related activities. Depending upon the extent of variability in the data, the approach may require more work to establish and maintain than some other techniques. When first establishing the process, this approach relies more heavily on consistent, historical data.

Actual to forecast review and comparisons require more time, given the higher number of variables involved. However, when set up and maintained properly, this technique is capable of producing very accurate results that can be continuously improved through ongoing forecast to actual comparisons.

2. Balance Sheet Approach

The balance sheet approach is a forecasting method based on the fundamental accounting principal "Assets = Liabilities + Shareholders' Funds". A Pro Forma Balance Sheet is prepared using knowledge of past balance sheet items e.g. inventory, accounts receivables, accounts payable, etc. and future expectations. All items in the pro forma balance sheet are populated except cash item. The cash figure is used to bring the equation into balance (i.e. Assets = Liabilities + Shareholders' Funds). As this represents 'book' cash in the financial statements, it does not reflect cash in the bank accounts, or available cash. Timing and reconcilement differences explain the variance between book and bank cash balances. This method of forecasting has proved very effective particularly for firms interested in estimating cash balances at balance sheet dates.

As a result of the consistency required by Generally Accepted Accounting Principles, a firm's balance sheet usually remains fairly constant from one period to the next. To the extent that balance sheet items must be estimated, significant historical data exists on which projections can be based. Almost all the major items experience change from one period to the next. The items that usually vary the most are inventory, accounts receivable and accounts payable. These components are forecasted using budgeted levels or ratio analysis (days sales outstanding, inventory turnover, days payables outstanding etc.). The balance sheet approach offers a mechanism for projecting cash at specific dates. The technique also makes variance analysis very simple, since a standard format is used by both the forecast and the actual balance sheet. However, this technique is not feasible for companies desiring to project cash levels on a daily basis. This technique will not be useful for new organisations with no track record, as it requires consistency to be effective.

3. Per cent of Sales Approach

The principal force behind the forecasting process is generally the Sales Forecast. Since most financial statement accounts are related to sales, the forecasting process can help the firm assess the increase in assets (both current and fixed), which will be needed to support the forecasted sales level. Similarly, the external financing which will be needed to pay for the forecasted increase in assets can be determined. A business firm also has to think about its capital mix, cash requirements, dividend policy etc. The forecasting process allows the firm to determine if its forecasted sales growth rate is consistent with its other objectives and policies.

Per cent of firm's sales approach is the most common method for making future cash projections. It forecasts the Balance Sheet and Profit & Loss Account by assuming that most accounts maintain a fixed proportion of Sales. The per cent of sales approach involves estimating the level of an expense, asset, or liability for a future period as a per cent of the sales forecast. The percentage used can come from the most recent financial statements as a per cent of current sales, from an average computed over several years, from the judgment of the analyst, or from some combination of these sources. Traditional financial forecasting takes the sales forecast as a given variable and makes projections of its impact on the firm's various expenses, assets, and liabilities. This approach of financial forecasting provides reasonable estimates of a firm's financing requirements only where asset requirements and financing sources can be accurately forecast as a constant per cent of sales.

Although this method of cash forecasting is not precise and detailed but it is quite simple and easy to use. This offers a relatively low-cost approximation of the firm's financing needs for a future period.

4. Statistical Techniques

There are numerous methods of forecasting that can be classified as 'statistical techniques.' Following is the detail of most commonly used statistical techniques.

(a) Time Series Techniques: Time series techniques focus on predicting or measuring a response in a variable over some span of time. Time series data is often described as being a compilation of four primary component series: long term trend, cyclical effect, seasonality, and random variation (noise). The trend represents the general direction of the data. Cyclical effect is a wavelike upward or downward movement around the trend that is often the result of long term influences such as demand for the product. Seasonality represents upward or downward shifts in the data at recurring points in time e.g. increased sales of product in the peak season. Smaller, unexplained variations in the data are defined as random variation or 'noise'.

Time series adjustment techniques are valuable in forecasting as they provide a means to smooth or remove some of the effects that may otherwise distorts the meaning of the data under review e.g. seasonality or pronounced trends. The most common adjustment techniques rely on moving averages to accomplish the required smoothing.

(b) Moving Average Techniques: Moving average techniques simply compute a mean average of a defined number of historical data elements in a time series. The averaging range shifts by one period each time the average calculation is performed, thus explaining why the technique is called 'moving average'.

A more elaborate technique, the Ratio to moving average method, applies a two step moving average process to smooth the data, and then produce seasonal indices for each recurring time element. Once seasonally adjusted/smoothed, the data is projected using simple mean averages or other basic forecasting techniques. The forecasted results are then multiplied by the respective seasonal index to reintroduce the seasonal component to the forecast. This technique is simple to use and is extremely effective in adjusting for seasonality.

(c) Exponential Smoothing: Exponential smoothing is a forecasting technique that allows the analyst to apply a smoothing factor to determine how much importance to place on past forecast versus actual results, in determining the next forecast value. First and second order differences apply moving averages to the differences and 'differences of differences' in time series data to smooth pronounced trends. For example, June data would be compared to May data, and May to April, etc. to identify first order differences. These differences can then be compared to each other. Through a simple formula, second order differences are averaged and used in projecting forecast values.

(d) Regression Techniques: A variety of regression techniques are available to help define the relationship between independent variables and the dependent variable i.e. cash. These techniques range from basic linear regression models to multiple regression techniques. Most can be performed using basic spreadsheet software e.g. MS Excel. The value of these techniques come from the statistical measures available to define confidence levels and to measure data correlation. These tools are powerful and accurate. However, they require an understanding of statistical methods. Whether a business firm requires projections to enhance liquidity management decisions, or it needs to project a balance sheet position at a future date, forecasting techniques are easy to follow. Using basic techniques and simple tools, very effective forecasting models can be developed and maintained.

BUDGETING

A budget is a financial plan. It is a plan to achieve the goals of the company during a specific time period. Budgeting perform following major functions for a business firm:

- Budgets provide a plan of action or a set of guidelines.
- Budgets indicate the amount and timing of the firm's needs for future financing.
- Budgets allocate resources to various activities and influence the process of business strategy formulation.
- Budgets provide the basis for taking corrective action if the future events do not go as per plans.
- Budgets set standards and acts as yardsticks that give a direction to the business plans.
- Budgets provide the basis for measurement of performance. With the help of budgets, management can evaluate the performance of those responsible for carrying out the plans.

A budget provides a plan of action or a set of guidelines. It sets deadlines for departmental objectives as well as standards for performance measurement. These standards or targets give a direction to the activities of the business. Budgeting allocates resources to various activities and influences the process of business strategy formulation.

Budgeting facilitates coordination of the various activities performed by different departments such as purchasing, production and marketing in a manner that ensures maximisation of organisational profit.

The budgets of individual departments act as performance standards. At the end of the budgeting period, the actual departmental performance is compared to the targets set by the budget. Thus, deviations from these targets are identified to evaluate performance and suitable action is taken where necessary. Budgeting facilitates reliable and accurate measurement of performance besides aiding in cost control.

DIFFERENCE BETWEEN BUDGETING AND FORECASTING

Budgeting and forecasting are, usually, termed as one and the same thing. In the above discussion also both the terms are used interchangeably. However, it is important to make clear the thin difference between the two terms.

Forecasting involves estimating future events and analysing their implications on the budget. Forecasting is an integral part of budgeting. Budgeting on the other hand, involves preparing budgets and using them as the basis for control. A budget is like a financial plan. Forecasts are not plans but predictions of the future, which are required as an important prerequisite to the budget process. A forecast is not a budget but a prediction of future environments, events, and outcomes. Forecasting usually relies on the analysis of past data to identify patterns used to describe it. Patterns may then be extrapolated into the future to prepare a forecast. Forecasting involves estimating future events and analysing their implications on the budget. Forecasting is an integral part of budgeting process. Budgeting is an important tool for financial planning and control in the organisation. Budgeting involves preparing budgets and using them as the basis for control. Moreover, forecasting may be done for various purposes such as future business conditions, identifying future opportunities etc. These estimates are not included in the budgeting process. Moreover, within the organisation, forecasting may be done for various purposes such as future business conditions, identifying future opportunities etc. These estimates are not included in the budgeting process.

CASH BUDGET

The preparation of a cash budget is an important management task. A cash budget can protect a company from being unprepared for seasonal fluctuations in cash flow or prepare a company to take advantage of unexpected quantity discounts from suppliers.

A cash budget is a management plan for the most important factor of a company's existence i.e. its cash position. A company's cash position determines how suppliers will be paid, how a banker will respond to a loan request, how the company will expand, how and how much dividends can be paid etc. A cash budget is an operational tool which show patterns of monthly receipts, payments and repayment of outstanding credit over the period of a year. Cash on hand at the beginning of each month is incremented by collections from accounts receivable, and reduced by various disbursements for that salaries, utilities and purchases, giving cash on hand at the end of the month. This end of month cash on hand is compared to an optimum cash balance planned by management, that is considered at an adequately safe level to avoid possible default, yet not excessive to avoid idle cash that earns no return. If there is excess cash beyond the target minimum cash balance, it can be used to repay an outstanding credit line or other debt, or it can be placed in marketable securities. If the balance is short of the planned minimum, this tells management how much credit must be obtained from its bank. Thus, the cash budget is used as a tool to determine month by month the amounts that need to be borrowed, and how the borrowed amounts will be repaid. Many business firms find it helpful to prepare cash budgets and to analyse any variances between the budgeted and actual amounts on a monthly basis. This enables a business to stay on top of any unexpected cash uses.

Budgeting exercise also establishes a basis for internal audit by regularly evaluating departmental results. The budget process should ensure that scarce resources are allocated in an optimal way, and so enable expenditure to be controlled. Management is forced to plan ahead so that long-term goals are achieved. The budget provides a yardstick for performance rather than solely rely on past years comparisons. Areas of efficiency and inefficiency are identified through reporting of variances, and variance analysis prompts remedial action. The budget process should identify the people responsible for items of cost and revenue so that areas of responsibility are clearly defined. The preparation of a cash budget requires a manager to make forecasts about all the different aspects of the company and its operating environment. A cash budget cannot be prepared in a vacuum. Before and during the budgeting process, finance manager must consult with line managers, suppliers, and key personnel to make the best forecast possible. The budget preparation process has become easier with the introduction of powerful IT resources; it has also resulted in more accuracy required within the estimates and also within a shorter timeframe. The preparation of budgets for planning and control purposes needs the involvement of people to provide realistic plans and the motivation for performance targets to be achieved.

The final budget should not be accepted until the projected financial position of the business has been reviewed in terms of the adequacy of funding. Risk analysis and risk assessment is essential to be carried out on each of the uncertain areas of the budget, to determine any requirement for additional funding and safeguard the future of the business. Additional funding may be obtained by way of extended overdraft facilities, loans or additional share capital. The appropriate funding decision may be made and matched with the type of activity for which funding is required. For example, major capital expenditure projects cannot be funded by an overdraft, but with longer-term sources of finance.

A sample cash budget is given at the end of this section.

ADVANTAGES OF BUDGETING

The budgeting process provides the following benefits to the organisation: -

- Management is compelled to anticipate the obstacles likely to arise in the course of achieving budgeted targets and is thus well prepared to meet them.
- Budgeting enables control of income and expenditure
- It acts as a tool for monitoring and periodic evaluation of managerial policies and decisions.
- It facilitates optimal allocation of resources for maximisation of profit.
- It facilitates coordination and decentralisation of tasks while still retaining control. It helps identify weaknesses and deficiencies during the process of achieving targets.
- It gives a sense of direction to organisational activities.
- It provides systematic and disciplined solutions to problems.

LIMITATIONS OF BUDGETING

The following limitations of budgeting should be given consideration along with its benefits: -

- Budgeting is based on forecasting. So, if the forecasts fail, budgeting also fails.
- A budget in not an independent variable. While making budgets, overlooking industry performance norms, competitors' response and avoiding generally accepted financial ratios and guidelines makes budgets useless.
- Giving insufficient consideration to working capital requirements leads to misleading and wrong budgets.
- Ignoring historic trends or performances at company, sectoral and national levels makes budgeting ineffective.
- Successful implementation of the budget requires cooperation and coordination among the different functional managers.

CASH BUDGET

(For three months ending March 31, 20XX)

	January		*February*		*March*	
	Budget	*Actual*	*Budget*	*Actual*	*Budget*	*Actual*
Expected Cash Receipts:						
1. Cash sales						
2. Collections on Accounts Receivable						
3. Other income						
4. Total cash Receipts						
Expected Cash Payments:						
5. Raw materials						
6. Payroll						
7. Other factory Expenses (Including Maintenance)						
8. Advertising						
9. Selling expense						
10. Administrative Expense (Including Salary of owner Manager)						
11. New plant and Equipment						
12. Other payments (Taxes including Estimated Income Tax; Repayment of Loans; Interest; Etc.)						
13. Total Cash Payments						
14. Expected Cash Balance Beginning of the Month						
15. Cash increase or Decrease (item 4 minus item 13)						
16. Expected cash Balance at end of Month (item 14 plus item 15)						
17. Desired working Cash Balance						
18. Short term loans Needed (item 17 minus item 16 if item 17 is larger)						
19. Cash available for Dividends Capital Cash Expenditures and/or Short Investments (item 16 minus item 17 if item 16 is larger)						
Capital Cash:						
20. Cash Available (item 19 after deducting Dividends Etc.)						
21. Desired Capital Cash (item 11 New Plant Equipment)						
22. Long Term Loans Needed (item 21 less item 20 if item 21 is larger)						

- Budgets some times represents unachievable and difficult targets to meet which demoralizes the team members.
- The budget is merely a financial tool, which provides general guidelines to management but cannot take the place of management's experience and foresightedness.

The budget process is developed to allow companies to better understanding where they were standing, where they are currently standing, and how they can get where they want to go. Significant number of large companies such as Ericsson, Volvo, General Electrical, SKF and others, have abandoned the traditional practice of budgeting. The reasons is that budgets are frequently late, based on trade-offs, take too long to develop, take too many organisational resources and fail to measure the all the critical variables that make organisations successful in today's fast paced business world. But it does not mean that budgeting process does not have its place and function. The large companies may want to use some of the better alternatives which are available today which provide 'what if' analysis and change the budgeting process into a strategic planning tool rather than doing an annual routine exercise.

CASH FLOW MANAGEMENT

Cash flow management is the process of monitoring, analyzing, and adjusting business's cash flows. The most important aspect of cash flow management is avoiding extended cash shortages, caused by a time gap between cash inflows and outflows. A firm cannot stay in business if it is not able to pay its bills on time. Therefore, a cash flow analysis is required on a regular basis so that it can take the necessary steps to meet cash flow problems. Today, even in the large business organisations cash is not as readily available as it was before, so companies are looking into ways to gain better visibility into future cash flows and to monitor it for better planning. There is a growing need for companies to forecast more accurately because in addition to tightened cash flow, there is an increasing need for timely forecasts as market conditions have become volatile. One of the best ways to manage cash in the business is to fully understand cash flow patterns. This helps a firm in avoiding cash deficiencies as well as excessive idle cash balances.

Moreover, cash flow analysis is needed:

1. To ensure that the cash balance always remains above the desired minimum level

2. To predict when cash levels will rise sufficiently above the minimum level to facilitate investment of idle balances.

CASH FLOW CONCEPTS

In its simplest form, cash flow is the movement of money in and out of the business. It can be described as the process in which a business uses cash to generate goods or services for the sale to its customers, collects the cash from the sales, and then completes this cycle all over again.

CASH INFLOWS

Cash Inflows are the movement of money into the business. Inflows are most likely from the sale of goods or services to the customers. If credit is extended to its customers, then an inflow occurs as the firm collects on the customers' accounts. Normally, the main sources of cash inflows to a business are receipts from sales, increases in bank loans, proceeds of share issues and asset disposals, and other income such as interest earned.

CASH OUTFLOWS

Cash Outflows are the movement of money out of the business. Outflows are generally the result of paying expenses. If the business involves reselling goods, then its largest outflow will be for the purchase of inventory. A manufacturing business's largest outflows is for the purchases of raw materials and other components needed for the manufacturing of the final product. Salaries and wages to staff, capital and interest repayments for loans, dividends, taxation, capital expenditure, purchasing fixed assets, and paying accounts payable are also cash outflows.

NET CASH FLOW

Net Cash Flow is the difference between the inflows and outflows within a given period. A projected cumulative positive net cash flow over several periods highlights the capacity of a business to generate surplus cash and, in the same manner, a cumulative negative cash flow indicates the amount of additional cash required to sustain the business. Cash flow planning entails forecasting and tabulating all significant cash inflows relating to sales, new loans, interest received etc. and then analyzing in detail the timing of expected payments relating to suppliers, wages, other expenses, capital expenditure, loan repayments, dividends, tax, interest payments etc. The difference between the cash in- and out-flows within a given period indicates the net cash flow. When this net cash flow is added to or subtracted from opening bank balances, any likely short-term bank funding requirements can be ascertained.

FREE CASH FLOWS

Some financial analysts give much importance to a concept of cash flow called 'Free Cash Flow'. The cash is considered free if it can be used for any desirable purpose. The larger is the amount, the more a firm has flexibility and investment strength because it can use the money immediately to take advantage of an opportunity. The accumulation of free cash comes from free cash flows which are calculated as cash flow from operations, less capital expenditure for ongoing production needs and payment of dividends. Free cash may be accumulating in liquidity but it is not intended to be used for financing working capital requirements. Instead, it is used for long-term purposes such as capital budgeting expenditure on assets, mergers, acquisitions etc.

CASH FLOW VS. PROFITABILITY

When planning the short or long term financing requirements of a business, it is more important to analyse the likely cash requirements than to project future profitability. While profit is a vital indicator of the performance of a business but the generation of a profit does not necessarily guarantee its growth and development. Sales and costs and, therefore, profits do not necessarily coincide with their associated cash inflows and outflows. Though, a sale may have been secured and goods delivered, the related payment may be deferred as a result of giving credit to the customer. At the same time, timely payments must be made to suppliers, staff, rebuild depleted stocks, purchase new equipments etc. The net result is that cash receipts often lag cash payments and, though profits may be reported, the business may experience a short-term cash shortfall. It is worth keeping in mind that more businesses fail for lack of cash than for want of profit. For this reason it is much more essential to manage cash flows than to project likely profits.

Therefore, profit and cash flow are two entirely different concepts. The concept of profit is somewhat narrow, and only looks at income and expenses at a certain point in time. Cash flow, on the other hand, is more dynamic. It is concerned with the movement of money in and out of a business. Moreover, it is concerned with the time at which the movement of the money takes place.

Profits can be converted into actual cash flow by using the following formula. If a business is keeping its books of accounts on the accrual method of accounting, it will have to make some adjustments to determine its actual cash flow. These adjustments are necessary because certain accrual accounting transactions are taken into account to determine accrual net profit, even though these expenses do not currently require a cash outlay. To convert accrual profit to cash flow profit, a balance sheet for the beginning and end of the period under examination is required.

Net Profit

+ Depreciation

– Increases (+ Decreases) in Accounts Receivable

– Increases (+ Decreases) in Inventories

+ Increases (- Decreases) in Accounts Payable

– Decreases (+ Increases) in Bank Loans

= **Net Cash Flow**

Cash flow is the cycle of cash inflows and cash outflows that determines a firm's solvency position. Cash flow analysis is the study of the cycle of firm's cash inflows and outflows, with the purpose of maintaining an adequate cash flow for the business, and to provide the basis for cash flow management. Cash flow analysis involves examining the components of the business that affect cash flow, such as accounts receivable, inventory, accounts payable, and credit terms. By performing a cash flow analysis on these separate components, a firm can more easily identify cash flow problems and find ways to improve cash flow.

A business must establish what is the minimum cash balance required. Next step is to analyse whether the plans and expected actions will maintain the minimum required balance. If a firm is able to manage successfully and keep sufficient positive balances in the accounts, then it can make plans to use idle cash balances as short-term investments for additional profits. Therefore, an analysis is required to ensure that a business do not spend more cash than it has or expects to have. Sound cash flow management also answers several questions, such as how long can we invest idle cash, when will it be necessary to borrow cash, and when can we purchase new capital assets. There are several simple and complex methods of preparing a cash flow analysis. The most effective and useful tool for cash flow analysis is the preparation of Cash Flow Statement.

CASH FLOW STATEMENT

In a business in a perfect world there is no time gap between a cash inflow and a cash outflow. But in real world, cash outflows and inflows occur at different times, and never actually occur together. Usually, cash inflows lag behind the cash outflows, leaving the business short of cash. This shortage is termed as cash flow gap. The cash flow gap represents an excessive outflow of cash that may not be covered by a cash inflow for a definite period of time say a few weeks, few months, or even few years. Managing the cash flow allows a firm to bridge the cash flow gap. It does this by examining the different items that affect the cash flow of the business.

The cash flow statement provides information regarding a company's cash receipts and cash payments. The statement complements the Profit & Loss Account and Balance Sheet. Over the life of a company, total net profits or income and net cash inflow will equal. However, as discussed earlier, income determination is based on accrual accounting, profits and cash flows are rarely equal in an annual accounting period.

All companies provide the cash flow statements as part of their financial statements, but cash flow can also be calculated as net income plus depreciation and other non-cash items. Proper cash flow levels vary from industry to industry. The importance of cash flow to the short-term credit is based on a simple fact, *trade obligations are satisfied with cash not profit.* It is possible for a firm to be very profitable but at the same time may not be able to service its obligations. Even a profitable company (in the accounting books) can be in a financial crunch if there is not enough cash on hand to meet current payments.

A company not generating the same amount of cash as competitors is bound to lose out when there are difficult times. Short-term liquidity can also be achieved by deferring payments of current obligations, however, company's ability to generate cash flow through the deferred payments of current liabilities will be exhausted. This statement is useful for decision making because it provides relevant and reliable information for predicting future cash flows.

The cash flow statement is an important analytical tool that the trade creditor can use to determine if a customer is able to generate sufficient cash to meet its trade obligations. The ability of a company to adapt during a period of financial adversity, to obtain financing, and generate adequate amounts of cash for specific purposes are very important factors in the review process. Using the cash flow statement in the credit analysis process can help users evaluate a customer's solvency, liquidity position, and its financial flexibility.

In the cash flow statement, c*ash receipts and payments are classified as operating, investing and financing activities.* The cash flow statement explains the change during the period in cash and cash equivalents. Cash includes currency on hand and demand deposits. Cash equivalents are short-term, highly liquid investments that are readily convertible to cash. The cash flow statement must summarize the cash flows so that net cash provided or used by each of the three types of activities is reported. Beginning and ending cash must be reconciled based on the net effect of these activities.

CASH FLOW FROM OPERATING ACTIVITIES

The statement provides information about the cash generated from a company's primary operating activities. A company's operating activities include the transactions associated with the company's primary products or services. Operating activities that generate cash inflows include customer collections from sales of products or services, receipts of interest, dividends and other operating cash receipts. Operating activities that create cash outflows include payments to suppliers, payments to employees, interest payments, payment of income taxes and other operating cash payments.

CASH FLOWS FROM INVESTING ACTIVITIES

This area lists all the cash used or provided by the purchase and sale of income-producing assets. Investing activities include giving loans and advances, collection from those loans and advances, buying and selling productive assets that are expected to generate revenues over long periods, and buying and selling securities not classified as cash equivalents. Cash inflows generated by investing activities include sales of fixed assets such as property, plant, equipments, sales of debt/equity instruments and the collection of loans.

CASH FLOWS FROM FINANCING ACTIVITIES

This section measures the flow of cash between a firm and its owners and creditors. Financing activities include borrowing and repaying funds from creditors, obtaining resources from owners and providing both types of suppliers of funds, a return on their investments. The return on investment is provided in the form of dividends and interest. If the firm uses debt or equity to expand its operations, it is disclosed in the financing activities. Also, if the firm uses cash to retire debt, it appears in the statement. Negative numbers can mean the company is servicing debt but can also mean the company is making dividend payments and share buyback, which is good news for investors.

PREPARING THE CASH FLOW STATEMENT

The balance sheet gives a one-time snapshot of a company's assets and liabilities. The Profit & Loss Account indicates the business's profitability during a certain period. The cash flow statement differs from these other financial statements because it acts as a kind of company's cashbook that reconciles the other two statements. The cash flow statement records the company's actual cash transactions during the period. It exposes the reality that all those revenues disclosed in the Profit & Loss Account may not have been actually collected. At the same time, all the expenses the company accrued may not have been paid. For the preparation of cash flow statement, information is obtained from the Profit & Loss Account or Income Statement for the year and comparative Balance Sheets for the last two years. Net income is adjusted for deferrals and accruals. The purpose of these adjustments is to convert the accrual basis Profit & Loss Account to cash flows.

The cash flow statement is divided into three sections: operating, investing and financing activities. There are two methods of calculating and reporting the net cash flow from operating activities. The *direct method* reports gross cash inflows and gross outflows from operating activities. The *indirect method* reconciles net income with net cash flow from operating activities by adjusting net income for deferrals, accruals, and items that effect investing and financing cash flows. Both indirect and direct methods yield same figures for net cash flow from operating activities because the underlying accounting concepts are the same.

ABC Co.
Profit & Loss Account
For the year ended
December 31, 20XX

Sales
Cost of Goods Sold
Gross Profit
Office Expenses
Depreciation and Amortization
Operating Profit
Other Income (Expense)
Gain on the Sale of Equipment
Interest Expense

Net Income

A practical approach for preparing the statement of cash flows is to first determine the net increase in cash and cash equivalents for the period. This amount serves as a control figure, the net cash inflow or outflow must agree with the net change in the cash account on the comparative balance sheets. The Profit & Loss Account data from the current year and the balance sheets from the prior two years are combined on the Cash Flow Worksheet.

ABC Co.

Cash Flow Worksheet

Comparative Balance Sheets	*Last Year*	*Current Year*	*Account Balance Change*	*Cash Inflow/ Outflow*	*Activity Type*
Assets					
Cash				Control	Cash
Accounts Receivable			Decrease/Increase	Inflow/Outflow	Operating
Inventories			Decrease/Increase	Inflow/Outflow	Operating
Plant and Equipment			Decrease/Increase	Inflow/Outflow	Investing
Depreciation			Decrease/Increase	Outflow/Inflow	Operating
Land			Decrease/Increase	Inflow/Outflow	Investing
Total Assets					
Liabilities					
Accounts Payable			Decrease/Increase	Outflow/Inflow	Operating
Salaries Payable			Decrease/Increase	Outflow/Inflow	Operating
Bonds Payable			Decrease/Increase	Outflow/Inflow	Financing
Premium on Bonds Payable			Decrease/Increase	Outflow/Inflow	Financing
Common Stock			Decrease/Increase	Outflow/Inflow	Financing
Retained Earnings			Decrease/Increase	Outflow/Inflow	Operating

Total Liabilities

Next, the change in each balance sheet account is calculated and the change is, determined if it is a cash inflow or outflow, and the activity that the account should be included in. The change in account balances is reflected in the Account Balance Change column of the worksheet. It is calculated by subtracting the prior year account balance from the current year balance. After calculating the account balance change, it is important to determine if the balance change is an inflow or an outflow of cash. The table states that a decrease in an asset balance and an increase in a liability or equity account are cash inflows. The opposite is true for increases in an asset balance or a decrease in a liability or equity account, which results in a cash outflow.

Table 1

CASH EFFECTS OF BALANCE SHEET ACCOUNT CHANGES

Cash Inflow	*Cash Outflow*
A Decrease in an Asset Account	An Increase in an Asset Account
An Increase in a Liability Account	A Decrease in a Liability Account
An Increase in an Equity Account	A Decrease in an Equity Account

CASH FLOWS FROM OPERATING ACTIVITIES

Generally accepted accounting procedures require that the operating activities section of the cash flow statement should be prepared first. This section measures the cash used or provided by a company's normal operations. It shows the company's ability to generate consistently positive cash flow from operations.

There are two methods of presentation of the statement of cash flows — Direct Method and Indirect Method. Both the methods affect cash flows from operating activities only i.e. cash flows from investing and financing activities remain the same. The direct method presents cash flows from operating activities by listing all cash inflow received (e.g. from sales) and all cash outflows paid out (e.g. salaries, purchases, taxes etc.). The indirect method starts with operating income as shown in the income statement, then a reconciliation adds back non-cash expenses and revenues and subtracts cash used to increase working capital components (or adds back in case of working capital decrease). In the direct method the reconciliation is presented below the statement of cash flow itself.

Table 2

CASH FLOWS BY ACTIVITIES

	Operating Activities	Investing Activities	Financing Activities
Inflows of Cash	Collections from Customers	Collection on Loans	Issuance of long-term Debt
	Interest Income	Sale of Debt Instruments	Issuance of Equity Securities
	Dividends Receipts	Sale of Equity Instruments	
	Other Operating Cash Receipts	Sale of Productive Assets	
Outflows of Cash	Payments to Suppliers	Purchase of Productive Assets	Payment of Dividends
	Payments to Employees	Purchase of Debt Instruments	Acquisition of an Entity's Own Equity Securities
	Interest Payments	Purchase of Equity Instruments	Repayment of Amounts Borrowed
	Payment of Income Taxes	Making Loans	
	Other Operating Cash Payments		

DIRECT METHOD

Under the Direct Method the following sources of operating cash inflows and outflows are reported:

- Cash collected from customers, lessees, licensees, and similar parties
- Interest and dividends received
- Any other operating cash receipts
- Cash paid to employees
- Cash paid to suppliers of goods and services
- Interest paid
- Income taxes paid
- Any other operating cash payments

It is important to note that we are using financial statements that were created using accrual accounting and we are converting these statements into cash accounting. Net income (accrual accounting) and net cash flow (cash accounting) can never be the same because of non-cash transactions that impact the performance of a business. For example, depreciation expense is a non-cash expense which appears on the Profit & Loss Account under accrual accounting but is not part of net cash flow. With the help of Table III, and data from the Profit & Loss Account and the Cash Flow Worksheet, Cash Flows from Operating Activities can be calculated.

Table 3

CASH FLOWS FROM OPERATING ACTIVITIES (DIRECT METHOD)

ABC Co.

Cash Flow Statement

For the Year Ended December 31, 20XX

Cash Flows from Operating Activities (Direct Method)	
Cash Collections from Customers	Rs.
Cash Payments to Suppliers	
Cash Payments for Salaries	
Cash Payments to Employees	
Cash Payments for Interest, Taxes etc.	
Net Cash Provided by Operating Activities	

INDIRECT METHOD

The second method that can be used to calculate the Cash Flows from Operating Activities is referred to as the Indirect Method. Using the Indirect Method, cash flows from Operating Activities are reported by adjusting net income for revenues, expenses, gains, and losses that appear on the Profit & Loss Account but do not have an effect on cash.

Using Table 4 as a guide, and Table 1 and Table 5 to determine if the change is an inflow or outflow, we can extract data from the Profit & Loss Account and Cash Flow Worksheet to prepare the Cash Flows from Operating Activities using the Indirect Method.

Net Income
Adjustments to reconcile net income to netcash provided by operating activities
+ Depreciation
– Amortization of Bond Premium
+ Amortization of Bond Discount
– Gain on Sale of Equipment
+ Loss on Sale of Equipment
+ Decrease in Accounts Receivable
– Increase in Accounts Receivable
+ Decrease in Inventory
– Increase in Inventory
– Decrease in Accounts Payable
+ Increase in Accounts Payable
– Decrease in Accrued Expenses
+ Increase in Accrued Expenses
+ Decrease in Prepaid Expenses
– Increase in Prepaid Expenses
– Decrease in Taxes Payable
+ Increase in Taxes Payable

Table 4

CASH FLOWS FROM OPERATING ACTIVITIES USING (INDIRECT METHOD)

Cash Collections from Customers	Sales - increase (+ decrease) in Accounts Receivable + increase (- decrease) in Deferred Revenue
Cash Payments to Suppliers	Cost of Goods Sold + increase (- decrease) in Inventory increase (+ decrease) in Accounts Payable
Cash Payments for Salaries	Salary expense - increase (+ decrease) in Accrued Salaries Payable
Cash Payments for Other Operating Expenses	Other Operating Expenses - Depreciation and Amortization Expense for Period + increase (- decrease) in Prepaid Expenses -increase (+ decrease) in Accrued Operating Expenses
Cash Revenue fromInterest	Interest Revenue - increase (+ decrease) in Interest Receivable
Cash Paid for Interest	Interest Expense - increase (+ decrease) in Accrued Interest Payable
Cash Revenue from Dividends	Investment Income - increase (+ decrease) in Investment Account
Cash Paid for Taxes	Tax Expense - increase (+ decrease) in Accrued Taxes Payable - decrease (+ increase) in Prepaid Tax

Table 5

CASH EFFECTS OF PROFIT AND LOSS ACCOUNT CHANGES

Cash Inflow	Cash Outflow
Revenue Accounts are Sources of Cash	Expense Accounts are Uses of Cash

RECONCILING THE CASH ACCOUNT

To complete the statement of cash flow, the operating, investing and financing activities are combined into one statement. The final step is to reconcile the cash account. The beginning cash balance less the ending cash balance is control amount.

The primary purpose of the cash flow statement is to provide information about a company's cash inflows and outflows. A secondary purpose is to provide information about the investing and financing activities of the company. Information reported in the statement, when used with other financial statements provides the analyst with insights about the company's ability to generate future cash flows. When cash flow statement is a projection of future activity, the analyst can see clearly how the increase in fixed assets and working capital necessary for expansion is going to be carried out by using some cash from operations and some from new funding sources. For instance, if a sales promotion is planned and additional production is necessary, but no increase in plant and equipment and no increase in inventory appear in a pro forma statement of cash flows, the analyst can conclude that management expectations are unrealistic hence, no expenditure should be incurred to support the sales promotion. The statement also helps the analyst understand the differences between a company's income flows and cash flows. The information provided by the cash flow statement also helps assess a company's ability to pay its debts and to meet its external financing needs.

LIMITATIONS OF CASH FLOW STATEMENT

Cash flow statement has its limitations too. For example, cash flow does not reveal the profit earned or lost during a particular period. Cash flow also does not indicate the overall financial health of the company. Though, the statement of cash flow gives a good indication of what the company is doing with its cash and from where cash is being generated, but these do not directly reflect true financial condition. The cash flow statement does not account for liabilities and assets, which are recorded in the balance sheet. Accounts receivable and accounts payable, each of which can be very large for a company, are also not reflected in the cash flow statement. In other words, it is a compressed version of the company's cashbook that includes a few other items, like the financing section, which tells the amount of money the company spent or collected from the repurchase or sale of stock, the amount of issuance or retirement of debt, and the amount the company paid out in dividends. In conclusion, interpreting the cash flow statement is not a very easy and simple task. Analysing the cash flow together with the other statements gives a glimpse into the short-term financial position of a company.

ABC Co.

Statement of Cash Flows
For the Year Ended December 31, 20XX

Cash Flows from Operating Activities	Rs.	
Cash Collections from Customers		
Cash Payments to Suppliers		
Cash Payments for Salaries		
Cash Payments to Employees		
Cash Payments for Interest, Taxes etc.		
Net Cash Provided by Operating Activities		Rs.
Cash Flows from Investing Activities	Rs.	
Sale of Fixed Assets		
Sale of Shares, Debentures of other firms		
Purchase of Fixed Assets		
Purchase of Shares, Debentures of other firms		
Net Cash Provided by Investing Activities.		Rs.
Cash Flows from Financing Activities	Rs.	
Issues of Shares		
Issue of Debentures, loans, bonds etc.		
Payment of Dividends		
Payment of Bond, Loan or borrowed money		
Payment of Interest on borrowed money		
Net Cash From Financing Activities		
Net Increase (Decrease) in Cash		
Cash at Beginning of Year		
Cash at End of Year		

Chapter 6

RECEIVABLE MANAGEMENT

(**Contents:** Introduction, Components of Receivable Management: 1. Credit Policy - Reasons for Credit Policy, Formulation of a Credit Policy, 2. Credit Analysis - Consumer/Individual Credit, Trade/Commercial Credit, Five C's of Credit, 3. Collection Policy - Collection Analysis Tools, Collection Process, Principles of Collection, Financing Receivables: Factoring, Cost of Factoring, Benefits of Factoring, Process of Factoring, Factoring Problems In India.)

"If you don't ask, you don't get."
— *Mahatma Gandhi*

INTRODUCTION

A receivable is any claim for money, goods, or services which have been earned or paid for but not yet received. Accounts receivable are usually non-written promises to pay for goods or services, normally extended for 30 to 60 days, and represent usually 'open accounts[1].' Accounts Receivable are assets for the business firm. If a sale is made on credit, a corresponding receivable account is created on the day of that sale. The accounts receivable balance is the total money owed to the company by customers as a result of sales. A business firm extends credit to its customers so that the firm may not loose any sale. At the same time, it avoids long overdue accounts so that the capital is not tied up and there are fewer chances of debtors becoming bad. A big receivable balance can also mean that the company is having problems collecting the money it is owed. Moreover, if the receivable balance is piling up too quickly and as a result many collections are still outstanding, the company may be holding on to older receivables that should probably be written off. Therefore, in the business world, the way in which an organisation manages its accounts receivable has significant implications for its financial health and long-term survival. This creates an imperative to ensure the management of receivables is both efficient and effective. The practices used in common business processes such as accounts receivable management have universal application and are not industry specific. In this regard there are lessons to be learned by other firms from the practices followed by organisations for which accounts receivable is a core business process.

COMPONENTS OF RECEIVABLE MANAGEMENT

Accounts receivable that is, the money owed by the customers/debtors as a result of sales made on credit for which payment has not yet been received are a major element in working capital for most companies. Managing accounts receivable is a critical element of the overall cash flow management function and one that can be very costly and time-consuming. Effective management of accounts receivable presents important opportunities for a firm to achieve strategic advantage through improvements in customer service, cash management and reductions in costs.

The management of accounts receivable can be broken down into:

1. Credit Policy and Terms of Sale
2. Credit Analysis
3. Collection Policy

Although the credit granting procedure and collection policy are laid down in the credit policy but they require separate discussion as a part of receivable management function. That is why they are dealt with in detail as separate heads in this chapter.

Credit policies covers the questions concerning terms of credit, credit limits, cash discounts etc. Credit analysis gives the answer to the question: To whom should credit be given and how much? Collection policies are to ensure the money owed is collected. Some accounts receivable will be paid on time, some after the date due, and others that

1. An open account or open-end credit, is credit extended by the selling company under a plan in which there is no formal documentation of the sale transactions and the selling company sends a regular statement to notify its customers of their outstanding credit amounts.

will never be paid at all. While these variables are not completely within the company's control, they can be controlled to some extent through the company's collection policy. While most companies have these policies, some do not. And whether or not they exist at a company, an increase in business can put tremendous pressure on those departments that are responsible for granting credit and collecting money when due or overdue.

Now, let us discuss these variables in detail.

1. Credit Policy and Terms of Sale

A policy is a general course of action developed for recurring situations, designed to achieve established objectives. A policy must express a general course of action. It can be supplemented, however, with some procedures that can guide routine functions. A credit policy document is a key component of the accounts receivable function and needs to cover all aspects of credit sales and debt collection practices.

Credit policy is nothing more than the firm's policy on granting and collecting credit. The major elements concerning the credit function of the firm are credit period, credit standards, collection policy, and discounts. The credit period is the length of time for which credit is extended. If the credit period is lengthened, sales will generally increase, as well accounts receivable. This will increase the financing needs and possibly increase bad debt losses. A shortening of the credit period will have the opposite effect.

Credit standards determine the minimum financial strength required to become a good credit for the firm. When a firm tightens its credit standards, it sells on credit more selectively. This way, it will likely sell less and certainly will make fewer credit sales. Profit may be affected in either direction. The optimal credit standards equate the incremental costs of credit to the incremental profits on increased sales.

The collection policy is the procedure for collecting accounts receivable. A change in collection policy will affect sales, day's sales outstanding, bad debt losses, and the percentage of customers taking discounts.

Credit terms are statements of the credit period and any discounts offered for timely payment. A less stringent credit policy in terms of the credit period stimulates sales. Credit terms are usually stated in the following form: 2/10, net 30. This means a 2 per cent discount will apply if the account is paid within 10 days, otherwise the account must be paid within 30 days. Cash discounts are often used to encourage early payment and to attract customers by effectively lowering prices. The larger cash discount will probably induce more sales, but they will likely be from customers who pay bills quickly. Further, some of the current customers who do not take the discount may be induced to start paying earlier. The effect of this would be to reduce accounts receivable and increase in profits.

A business firm is not required to accept the credit policies employed by its competitors, but the optimal credit policy cannot be determined without considering competitors' credit policies. A firm's credit policy has an important influence on its volume of sales, and thus on its profitability. A credit policy should be:

- Written in simple language so that it is understandable by staff and customers;
- Accessible to all staff who are required to administer it; and

- Made available to customers in summary form.
- Kept up to date. This means it should be reviewed at regular intervals so that consideration can be given to incorporating new practices or initiatives, and be endorsed by executive management.

In addition to this, a business firm should establish a financial threshold under which it is uneconomical to pursue recovery action and set down criteria against which a debt might be considered for waiver.

A firm should have a well expressed and written credit policy for the following reasons:

(i) Efficiency: The responsibility of managing receivables is a serious undertaking. It involves limiting bad debts and improving cash flow. With outstanding receivables often being a firm's major asset, it is obvious that a reasoned and structured approach to credit management is necessary. One can see that developing a policy is more than a necessity. It is an opportunity to improve the efficiency of the entire organisation.

(ii) Clarity of Objectives: A policy assures a degree of consistency among departments. By writing down what is expected, the functional departments of the company (whether marketing, production, or finance) will realize that they have a common set of goals. Conversely, a written policy can delineate each department's functions so that duplication of effort and needless friction are avoided.

(iii) Improved Customer Relations: It provides for a consistent approach among customers. Decision-making becomes a logical function based on pre-determined parameters. This simplifies the decision process and yields a sense of fairness that will improve customer relations.

(iv) Aid to Top Management: It can provide some recognition of the credit department as a separate entity, one which is worthy of providing input into the overall strategy of the firm. This allows the department to be an important resource to top management.

(v) No Ambiguity: Credit policies differ in both length and content. Some are as short as several paragraphs, while others can go on for many pages. A detailed policy leaves little room for doubt. Procedures are spelled out, and employees need only refer to their manual to know how to perform. There will be no confusion between departments, and consistency will reign. On the other hand, a long and excessively detailed policy can limit employee creativity or empowerment. New ideas on how to work in a changing world will be superseded by a set of omniscient regulations. Also, a huge volume of rules can be overwhelming. Too many written regulations can actually get in the way of productivity. Therefore, it presents a question of balance.

The question of companies having policies with differing contents is worth mentioning. This can result from many factors which may include the competitiveness of industry, the location, profit margins, company's goals for market share, the company's own cash requirements, production needs, or the size and culture of firm. It is a truth that many policies can be designed, and each one may be correct for a particular firm.

Formulation of a Credit Policy

New customers represent an opportunity for increased sales and profits. However, certain procedures must be followed before a prudent credit decision can be made. It is important for the management to furnish a clearly defined statement of what is desired of the credit department. Through this communication, a credit policy can provide the framework for consistent credit decisions directed toward attaining company goals. In order to write a policy, following are the questions that a business firm must answer:

- What is its mission and its goal?
- Who has specific credit responsibilities?
- How is credit evaluated?
- How is collection handled?
- What are the terms of sale?

Once the above mentioned questions are answered, they can be put together in the format of a policy. Several potential answers can be offered for each question, and a firm should choose one that meets its requirements. It should be kept in mind that there is no right or wrong answer, whatever the firm chooses should reflect the solutions to its problems. Implementations of a credit policy, also requires support from top management as well as from different functional areas. The policy should be advantageous to all of the departments of a firm. Other areas which must be considered while developing a credit policy include company's views on reporting, ethics, quality, training, deductions, and credit interchange with other professionals. Let us discuss the major questions and concerns for a credit policy.

(a) Mission and Goals: The most important part of a policy is defining credit department's mission. This mission must coincide with the firm's overall direction. The credit policy does not require constant revision because mission and goals of a firm will not change frequently. It is important to note, however, that this should not be treated as a mechanism to ignore goal setting. Instead, written goals should be established in a separate memorandum so the entire organisation understands its aims.

(b) Credit Responsibility: Fixing responsibilities in the credit policy that spells out the specific roles and duties of the credit and collections staff streamlines operations, prevents redundancy, and improves productivity. Each position created in the department should have a clear job description. All this properly defines the role and authority of each individual who relates to credit. Duplication of effort is avoided and inter-departmental conflict can be avoided. Another important approach, recognizes a team concept within the organisation. There is nothing wrong with sharing responsibility and authority as long as it is properly defined within the policy.

(c) Credit Evaluation: The process of assessing credit risk and determining credit limits is critical to receivable management and should be detailed in the credit and collections policy. For credit evaluation, the credit manager should consider the following sources:

- Credit agency reports
- Financial statements

- Credit references
- Public records
- Other facts obtained from the applicant

Establishing regular credit evaluation as part of the credit policy allows the firm to monitor any changes in the risk level of its receivable portfolio. It can then adjust credit and collection policy accordingly. Specifically, if the portfolio is becoming riskier than the management's risk perception, it can review credit policy and tighten its collection plan. Depending on the size and complexity of the organisation, credit evaluation may involve a varying degree of detail. The credit department should review larger limits on a periodic basis. Moreover, it should keep the option open to revise limits based on changing levels of creditworthiness of its debtors. The department receives referrals of all orders that would place an account over its limit, and credit personnel may release additional orders if higher credit is justified.

A different approach is to list some details in the policy itself. This may lend itself to a smaller organisation where orders are for a lower rupee volume. For example: The sales representative will obtain a credit application from each customer. This will contain a bank reference and some trade references. After calling references, the Credit Department will determine if a customer has demonstrated the ability to pay bills in a prompt manner. If so, a credit limit will be assigned. This credit limit should not exceed the highest extension reported by references. What is important is to establish a consistent procedure so all potential customers are treated equally.

(d) Collection Efforts: The credit department is responsible for performing collection activity. Letters and/or accounts statements may be supplemented with telephone collection calls. Sales personnel are also advised of particular problems. In some cases, credit personnel will visit customers. If appropriate payment arrangements cannot be made, the credit department may withhold further delivery. The credit manager determines if an account is not collectable by the above means. Uncollectable accounts usually include bankruptcies, assignments to creditors, and customers that do not respond to normal collection activities. In such cases, the accounts will be referred to collection agencies or attorneys.

Under a different approach, in a business firm, the credit department monitors all collections for the company. The department provides sales representatives with a weekly list of customers whose accounts are due. The sales representative makes customer contacts and advises of results. If delinquency still exists after the wait of some additional days, orders are withheld.

(e) Terms of Credit Sale: Including the terms of sale in the credit policy sets up guidelines that allow for quick, consistent decision making at the time of sale, and when determining when the account falls due.

While terms may vary among a company's product lines, having a written policy dealing with terms of sale issues is essential. Any exception to the established terms must be based on competitive practices and generate a satisfactory return on investment.

It is important to have no confusion about when the bills are due. For some businesses, this is not a difficult problem. They have a homogeneous product line with consistent set of terms. Thus, their policy may be relatively simple. For other companies, however, the problem may be more complex and critical. Some companies have many product lines with varying sets of terms. Other firms offer special seasonal dating. Finally, others may react to competitive practices and grant individual customers special arrangements. These firms may choose to address the issue within their policy or with individual procedures.

(f) Other Factors: Other factors could include management's perception about ethics, legality, quality, industry customs, reporting, personnel, credit interchange and professional organisations, systems, deductions, returned cheques, collection mechanisms, record retention etc. The items that have not been anticipated earlier may be included in this list.

Finally, we must remember that a policy is not a static document. It should be reviewed periodically to reflect changing circumstances.

2. Credit Analysis

Many potential credit problems can be eliminated before they happen through investigation and prudent judgement when granting credit to customers. The need for sound judgement is particularly critical since credit extension policies should be neither too liberal nor too restrictive. Liberal credit policies invite excessive receivables and bad (uncollectible) debts while overly restrictive policies cause lost sales. Thorough investigation of credit requests protects a business from the fraudulent applicant who has no intention of paying as well as the applicant who is extremely slow in paying. The accounts receivable function must ensure the full and timely collection of payment from the customer base, thereby streamlining the sales-to-cash cycle. The management of accounts receivable maintains this critical balance between strong customer relationships and tight cash inflow management. The primary objective of accounts receivable is to collect dues and to assist in meeting cash flow requirements. An effective accounts receivable function can assist in achieving the desired cash flow outcome through the timely collection of outstanding debts.

Credit limits are a means through which the credit manager may delegate authority for credit responsibility, while at the same time retaining the degree of control necessary to protect the company from excessive losses. A well-established credit guideline may also prove to cheque reckless buying on the part of an over optimistic buyer. The ultimate responsibility for the establishment of a new customer account rests with the credit executive. It is essential to set guidelines for performing the necessary procedure. If new customer orders are to be pre-screened for credit approval, it is necessary to describe in a procedural document for the benefit of sales and credit personnel what the parameters are for new account acceptance.

The basic source of information for decisions on credit extensions is the credit application. Credit application may come from an Individual Customer or it may be a Trade/Commercial application. Credit extended to an individual is also known as Consumer credit.

There are three major factors to consider in evaluating a credit applicant.

- Applicant's ability to pay based upon income and obligations.
- Applicant's willingness to pay which can be determined from the applicant's credit history.
- Applicant's potential profitability.

The costs associated with extending credit to lower-quality customers include:

- Increased costs of credit investigation
- Increased probability of customer default
- Increased collection costs

A business stand to lose the cost of the product or service sold to the customer if it cannot collect an account. If the cost is relatively high compared to the selling price, then a business needs to be particularly careful in assessing credit risks.

(a) **Consumer/Individual Credit:** Evaluation of any credit application depends upon a number of factors. In the case of an individual applicant, the firm considers the following:

- Employment history
- Employer's name and telephone numbers
- Current designation
- Current income
- Time on job
- Job security
- Monthly obligations (rent, loan payments, food, utilities, etc.)
- Bank balances
- Personal assets (house, cars, stocks, bonds, etc.)
- Credit standing
- Amount of credit desired
- Information Verification

Information on credit applications must be verified to ensure that it is correct, current, and complete. A good place to begin is the place of employment to verify that the applicant is employed and that income and time on the job have been reported accurately. Bank references should also be verified. While laws restrict the amount of information that banks can disclose, checking on this information can protect from obvious fraud and may give some indication of the applicant's ability to pay. Most banks will confirm the existence of an account and disclose a broad idea of the average balance. The bank may also indicate whether or not the account has been satisfactory.

Another important source of information for retail credit is the credit bureau. There is a nominal charge for each inquiry on a credit applicant.

In situations where the time or cost of a comprehensive credit check is not possible, a quick evaluation can be made based upon the applicant's stability. Stability is determined by the length of continuous employment and residence. This assumes that the person who has been employed for several years on the same job will most likely continue to be employed and therefore will be able to pay. Similarly, continuous residence indicates a desire to maintain standing in the community.

(b) Trade/Commercial Credit: In case of Trade or Commercial accounts, it is often difficult to verify information on income and expenses for businesses. It is also more difficult to make estimates of these factors for commercial accounts. Financial statement can be used before extending credit to the commercial accounts. But a manager must rely more heavily upon references such as banks and suppliers with whom the applicant does business, the applicant's reputation in the industry, identity of officers, and so on. The commercial applicant with a marginal credit rating will list only those suppliers with whom a satisfactory relationship has been maintained. However, a finance manager can use his own judgement and knowledge of industry to determine other suppliers with whom the applicant may have done business. If there is any doubt as to the credit worthiness of the applicant, it is advisable to contact these other sources to find out what their experience has been. In case of a trade account, the firm should consider the following factors:

- Company's name, address, telephone/fax numbers etc.
- Name of the principal owner or Chief Executive Officer
- Type of organisation: sole ownership, partnership, joint stock company or other
- Type of business — example: distributor, retailer, wholesaler
- Bank references: name, address, phone number, officer, type of account
- Trade references: name, address, phone number
- Year of business started
- Financial and operational information including facts and trends
- Agency rating
- Banking information
- Financial Statements
- Tax payment proofs.

Another source of information helpful in the evaluation of a customer can be company's own sales staff. Sales representatives are the company's first contact with a new customer and the most frequent contact with an established customer. Sales personnel can become an excellent source of credit information. Without even asking questions, sales representatives can obtain a great deal of information by observation only. They can judge the location and appearance of the place of business, its condition etc. They can observe the employees and management of the applicant firm. There is no better source of information about a business than the business itself. Personal contact with the staff provides the credit executive with financial details, bank and trade references, and other information of importance. How this information is requested and obtained will depend upon the time available for the investigation, the location of the customer, the relative importance of the credit exposure, and the degree of cooperation that can be obtained from the customer.

It must be noted that a delay in gathering and evaluating credit information may cause the loss of an order and possibly the customer. In addition to this, consideration must be given to the cost of gathering credit information, i.e., credit reports, calls for references, calls or visits to the prospective customer, mail handling, etc. in relation to the potential sale.

FIVE C'S OF CREDIT

Accurate credit granting decision requires an analysis of the asset relative to the five credit factors. The five credit factors, or the five C's of credit, which the credit manager evaluates in classifying loans are: capacity, capital, collateral, character, and conditions. The relative weight assigned to each credit factor varies with the circumstances of the individual situation.

The following provides a general description of each credit factor.

(i) **Capacity:** Capacity refers to the borrower's ability to repay. The determination of repayment capacity requires an analysis of cash flow, sources of repayment, and earnings history. Cash flow projections should be realistic in relation to past performance and should identify the source(s) of repayment. The source of repayment should be assessed to ensure repayments are expected from normal operations or from other recurring and reliable sources. Earnings history should evidence that future income is sufficient to meet all obligations, including normal living expenses, with some left for capital replacement and contingencies.

Following points should be considered during evaluation:

- Historic earnings performance;
- Repayment history;
- Stable and reliable income;
- Sources of repayment;
- Projected earnings; and
- Cash flow projections.

(ii) **Capital:** Capital relates to the ability to meet obligations, continue business operations, and protect against undue risk. The applicant's total assets, working capital and liquidity, amount of equity, contingent liabilities, financial progress, and history of earnings to date are significant measures of a borrower's capital position.

Following points should be considered during evaluation:

- Asset/liability structure;
- Working capital and liquidity;
- Owner equity position;
- Financial trends; and
- Earned net worth as a per cent of total net worth.

(iii) **Collateral:** Collateral is the security pledged on the loan. Where applicable, the collateral amount taken must comply with regulatory requirements—it should reasonably protect the lender, provide the necessary control of equity and repayment, and leave the borrower in a position to constructively manage the business. The type, quality, and location of collateral, as well as its ability to produce income, are relevant factors used to assess collateral adequacy. In addition, personal or entity liability in the form of guarantors or partial guarantors may provide added strength in extending credit. Sufficient analysis should be made of credit factors relevant to such guarantors or partial guarantors to ensure they can reasonably provide support for the loan.

Following points should be considered during evaluation:

- Reasonable lender protection;
- Current and accurate evaluation reports;
- Availability of additional collateral;
- Collateral risk (potential to decline in value); and
- Income producing and debt servicing ability of the collateral relative to its current market value.

(iv) Character: Character refers to the borrower's integrity and management ability. Character is an important aspect of the business credit decision; however, in most instances credit analysts do not actually appraise character—but rather the reflection of character as revealed by reputation and references. This factor is of such significance that it can affect the weight placed on the other credit factors, particularly if the evaluation of character is negative.

Analysis should include a careful evaluation of management of finance and operations.

Following points should be considered during evaluation:

- Realistic production and financial goals;
- Adequate financial records;
- Proven management experience;
- Borrower's marketing plan/approach; and
- Compliance with loan terms.

(v) Conditions: Conditions include the amount of loan, use of proceeds, and loan terms over which the lender has direct control. The conditions of a loan should be constructive in amount and purpose and practical as to repayment terms for both the borrower and lender. Conditions such as loan agreements, personal liability, additional collateral, and insurance should be required as each situation warrants.

Following points should be considered during evaluation:

- Prudent and productive loan purposes;
- Past experience in fulfilling conditions;
- Loan maturities coinciding with the purpose of the loan;
- Proper structure of loans financing specific major capital items; and
- Appropriate repayment plans/schedules established consistent with the source of repayment.

3. Collection Policy

'Collection' refers to obtaining payment of past due accounts. The establishment and execution of collection policies can minimize problems associated with accounts receivable. As with all policies, they must be re-evaluated from time to time in order to determine their effectiveness.

Collection may involve:

- Sending overdue delinquency notices
- Calling the customer
- Employing a collection agency
- Taking legal action against the customer

COLLECTION ANALYSIS TOOLS

Sound policies for credit and collection can eliminate many problems before they occur and minimize those that do occur. Many businesses are reluctant to enforce strict collection procedures. Some business people think that they might alienate a good customer and may lose an account. Some companies feel that rigorous enforcement of a collection policy can damage their reputation. It is not true. Whether or not a business chooses or use cash discounts or delinquency charges, a systematic follow-up procedure should be employed with all past-due accounts. Usually, this will take the form of a series of letters or telephone calls or both, as required.

Good business requires that collection of invoices be made promptly and without any damage resulting to the customer relationship. To retain the customers' goodwill makes the collection problem a difficult one and makes skill and tact essential in the handling of collections. Just how much pressure is to be brought to bear to obtain prompt collections and to what extent the relationship may be jeopardized in the effort are questions of collection policy. The collection problem should be analyzed and the collection policy defined in accordance with such objectives as:

- Sales department's policies and objectives
- General market conditions
- Customer relationship

Collection Process

It is the credit department's objective to maximize revenues through timely and systematic collection efforts and to apply cost-benefit principles to the collection of receivables. Effective collection efforts are essential to proper receivable management. Minimum collection efforts of receivables shall be:

(i) **Timely Billing:** Collection process starts with the customer invoice. Invoices should be prepared as soon as it is determined a receivable is due. Credit divisions should issue an invoice within the prescribed time of the provision of goods or services or determination of other debts. The invoice shall, at a minimum, include the amount due, the due date for payment, a brief description of why the amount is due, where to remit payment, and a contact for questions. The creditor should make sure that the billings go out promptly, preferably the same day as shipment, and that it has abided by the customer's request concerning correct billing addresses, duplicate invoices, etc.

Any decision not to bill valid obligations or any decision to cancel valid existing obligations must be justified and needs the approval of the head of the credit department. Each organisation should establish policies and procedures, the terms and/or conditions for payment at the time an account is created.

(ii) Prompt Collection: It is the responsibility of the credit department to monitor their accounts receivable to assure that timely and appropriate collection policies are in place. To increase the likelihood of collection, accounts should be collected immediately when they become due. Any account overdue should be given immediate attention and should be evaluated to determine if further credit should be granted or payments made to that recipient. Every effort should be made to collect receivables during the fiscal year of origin. This increases the likelihood of collection and maximizes the programme benefit.

Collection practices must be flexible. If the company is in the midst of a large promotion requiring customer cooperation, it may want to alter its normal timing until after the promotion is over. Conversely, if the company is facing a cash crunch, and needs cash more than new sales, it would tighten up.

The timing of collection should not be left up to individual collectors, but should be a part of a formal credit and collection policy. If the firm has different product lines with different type of customers, and different selling terms, the collection practices should be tailored to those differences. As a rule, the longer a customer ages past due, the more frequently a firm should contact them. The longer an account is past due, the less are the chances of collecting it.

Collection through in person is probably the best method of collecting dues, because it gives the chance of face-to-face communication with the customer. A problem with personal visits is that they are expensive. Telephoning is probably the most cost-effective collection method. It is fast, it gives the firm the opportunity to listen to what its customer has to say, and yet the manager is at its own desk with access to all the information he needs.

(iii) Standards for Collection Efforts: Receivable management is an important revenue producing activity. The business firm should ensure that receivable activities are well defined and that staff is adequately trained in collection efforts and properly supervised. The collection effort may be influenced by the amount due as indicated by levels of collection activity. The expenditure of time and money to collect a large amount is appropriate whereas the same effort expended to collect a small amount may not be. If one approach fails, another approach may result in a successful collection. For example, telephone contacts may be required if there has been no response to written communications.

Collection efforts should be regular and coordinated with at least one attempt to collect in each thirty-day period. Collection agencies are to be used when the organisation's efforts are not successful. Collection standards require thorough collection efforts for receivables which includes multiple strategies, including demand letters, telephone calls, instalment plans, a collection agency, tax intercept, liens, other legal action etc.

Credit department should promptly review the facts and circumstances of particular overdue receivables which may require additional collection efforts. In all cases, receivables are the responsibility of the organisation that incurred them. Approval of write-offs in accordance with the credit policy, assistance with collection and accounting efforts, and advice on further collection efforts should be available with the credit department of the firm.

The degree of collection efforts depends on a number of things— its selling terms, the practice in the industry, firm's competitive position and financial requirements. If the company is dominant in its industry, it enjoy a better chance of having customers adhere to its terms than if it is a small company, or new in the market, trying to expand its customer base. When an account becomes more than two weeks past due, the customer should be sent the first collection letter. Since the account cannot be considered seriously delinquent at this time, the tone of the letter should be moderate. Later letters should establish a firmer tone so that the customer is made aware of the seriousness of the situation. A second letter, a month later should be sent, if no response has been received from the customer. If again, this is unsuccessful, a stronger letter should be sent in two weeks time. In addition to this, an even more persuasive approach is through use of the telephone. The ground rules are basically the same. The telephone has the added advantage of flexibility since the caller can be more direct with better knowledge of the individual account. If the firm's own collection efforts fail, there are two courses of action that are left — the collection agencies and the courts.

In evaluating a delinquent customer, several factors should be taken into consideration such as amount owed by the customer, the time period the item has been unpaid, customer relationship past dealings with the customer etc. A company can afford to devote more time and effort to the collection of large balances than it can to smaller ones.

A firm with high debt delinquency rate should review its credit policy and recent information about its customer's paying habits with it as well as with the trade. Furthermore, it should review the customers' financial condition, and operations. All this information may give clues as to why the customer is not paying. Also, it will give the opportunity to ask more incisive questions and tailor payment request for better results.

(iv) External Help and Litigation: Collection agencies are businesses established to collect past due accounts receivable on behalf of creditors. The primary advantage that collection agencies offer is their superior knowledge of persuasive collection techniques. Additionally, creditors are usually anxious to clear invoices referred to collection agencies rather than further damage their credit ratings. The collection agency's fee is usually based upon a percentage of each account collected. The percentage ranges from 20% to 50% depending upon the size of the account or the total rupee volume of accounts referred to the agency for collection. This approach, while often effective, can be expensive. A business has to pay the agency's fee on any account referred for collection, whether payment is made to the agency or to the business firm. Although some creditors may resent making payment to a collection agency and prefer to pay the company directly, the company is still committed to pay the fee when the account is collected.

If the collection agency fails, the final recourse is through the courts. In litigation, a company is faced with a costly and time-consuming procedure. The best way of avoiding these time-consuming, costly procedures is to take prompt, strong action as early as possible.

In some instances the firm will better protect its interests by agreeing to a payout, rather than insisting on a full payment immediately. The firm should always confirm any payout plan in writing, and use actual dates and amounts of the payments.

Although it is not possible in every case, the firm should try to keep product or service flowing to the customer during the collection process. The ability to continue to support the customer and at what volume level, should be based on the gross margin return the company earns on the sale. This action may be defined in its credit and collection policy. In some cases the firm may wish to withhold shipments, but by doing this, it will cut off part of its relationship with the customer.

The time to terminate a collection effort is also crucial. The decision can make or lose money. Possibly outsourcing of collections based on rupees of exposure should be considered to control collection costs. Consideration of the age of the debt is also very important. The value of the receivable falls rapidly as a function of time, and the longer the debt has been owed, the less likely the firm will be paid. The firm should also note whether there have been partial payments or any effort to settle the debt. Has the customer made any sincere effort attempt to take care of the obligation? How long has the item been unpaid? How long the firm has been dealing with the customer? If the customer is new, the firm should have made its policy on collections clear from the start. Neglecting delinquency at this time is inviting problems forever with the account. If it is an old customer, how has the payment pattern been? How have any delinquencies been cleaned-up in the past? Is there a problem with the product or service? Answering these questions will throw some light on the choice of collection efforts and improvements in the credit policy.

When a firm should start legal action? This cannot be answered by any specific time frame. If the customer has not ordered from the firm, sent a payment, answered a letter, or returned a phone call for a long time, in spite of all the efforts, the firm should call some other suppliers and find out what they know. If there seems to be the same pattern, then it is the time to place the account with a collection agency or attorney.

Finally, if and when the customer files for protection under the bankruptcy laws, the firm must stop all collection activities against the debtor. The credit manager should contact its legal department for further information on this matter.

Principles of Collection

Following are the general guidelines and certain principles that are useful in the collection management.

(i) **Prompt Initiative:** The business firm should start collection efforts the day a payment is overdue. The primary job of the manager for collections is to collect the money as close to the terms of the obligation as possible. The credit manager should make sure that the terms have been clearly stated to the customer and the customer knew exactly *when* and *how much* was to pay, and *where* he was suppose to mail the cheque or the demand draft. The debtor has an obligation to pay within the terms of the agreement. It is the job of the collection person to make sure that this obligation is met. The tone may be indulgent at first, but should be intensified and accelerated as much as necessary to ensure payment by a debtor.

(ii) Feedback: The credit division should send the invoice as soon as the order ships and call as soon as the product or service is delivered to make sure the client is satisfied. Customers sometimes withhold payment because they are unhappy with the products or services delivered. The call gives the manager a chance to resolve the problem quickly. It is also an opportunity to ask if the customer needs additional products and services and to remind him of the payment terms.

(iii) Planning Collection Procedure: Managing the aged portion of accounts receivable portfolio requires planned action that reflects the mission and goals of the department. Written policy on important collection procedures will ensure consistent and effective receivable management that contributes to realizing those goals. The credit division should know:

- When to contact a customer?
- How to contact a customer?
- When to place an account on credit hold?
- How to resolve disputes, deductions, etc?
- When to turnover delinquent accounts to an outside collection agency?
- When to write an account off to bad debt?

After the initial contact with the delinquent customer, it is important to keep additional contacts on a strict schedule. If the customer, for example, says that a cheque will be mailed in a few days, it should be noted. If the cheque is not received at the promised time, a follow-up is essential; otherwise the collection effort will become ineffective.

Systematic follow-up of accounts, even those which cannot pay immediately, reinforces the serious nature of the outstanding debt and emphasizes the importance attached to it by the creditor.

(iv) Maintaining Goodwill: Even though the customer may be experiencing some difficulty in meeting payments, it does not preclude them from becoming a good customer in the future. Therefore, it is important to maintain goodwill while pressing for collection. This requires not only tact, but knowledge of the customer and industry. One of the advantages claimed by specialized collection personnel is that they can develop these techniques to their fullest. On the other hand, the team concept presents the opportunity for credit and customer service personnel to better understand the relationship of the customer to the industry and overall marketing objectives of the company.

The credit manager should never threaten a customer in writing or orally that their credit reputation will be ruined if they do not pay the dues. Also, he should not threaten legal action unless he is fully prepared to follow through, and has received the necessary approval from its management.

A write-off refers to the release of obligation of payment for debt and its removal from the receivables ledger. The forgiveness of debt may be total or partial. The process of approving and authorizing write-off should be a documented, objective process under strict controls of the upper management.

(v) Deciding Collection Strategies: In some cases, the firm may offer its customer the payout plan. A repayment or a payout plan is devised to help the customer and it is usually for a reasonable amount. The payout plan may be established provided it is in writing and signed by the debtor and a division/institution representative. If the payout plan includes taking any guarantees or security, credit manager should make sure that the legal department reviews and gives formal consent before they are finalized. During any payout arrangement where the firm continues to accept orders and deliver goods, it should be prepared to stop if:

- The firm is not receiving payments as agreed
- Other business firms have stopped accepting the orders or started legal action against the debtor
- A bank has called its loan

Many problems associated with credit can be avoided through the use of credit cards. In many businesses, particularly in the retail and consumer service fields, credit arrangements for customers are available through the use of these cards. Under these plans, there is little or no commitment of the business' own capital, and the costs and risks of administration and collection are almost entirely the responsibility of the credit card company or bank. Credit card services are particularly vital for businesses with a large number of relatively small accounts. They eliminate the need for credit approval, invoice preparation, record maintenance, and collections. They also minimize firm's commitment of capital and virtually eliminate the risk of bad debts. In some cases, the manager may ask the customer to send a series of post-dated cheques. While this does not guarantee they will all clear the bank. But, at least there remains some control on the mailing and deposit, and the firm need not have to rely on the customer to do it.

Use of letters is another effective method of collection. Letters are also useful for confirmation of telephone agreements. Letters should be addressed to a specific individual rather than to a designation or a title. They should be specific and to the point.

(vi) Reviewing Periodically: The credit manager should remember that credit policy will change over time as the business needs change, the economic conditions in the industry change, and the economic conditions in the country change. A credit and collection policy creates the structured environment that can safeguard a firm's most precious asset - accounts receivable. However, formulating such a policy is not a one-time effort. In order to maintain its relevance and continue to have a positive impact on cash flow and revenues, it must be routinely updated in response to the changing economy, market conditions, and competitive environment. The credit manager should re-evaluate policy periodically to determine if it is meeting the firm's needs.

FINANCING RECEIVABLES

Accounts receivable is usually the only major asset which is not safeguarded against future losses. With increasing pressure to do more with less, and the need to manage capital as accurately as possible, factoring has emerged as a very important and reliable source of financing receivable. The other source of financing is pledging of accounts receivable. It is the use of a firm's receivables to secure a short-term loan. This has been dealt with in the Chapter Working Capital Financing. Here, we will discuss in detail Factoring, its types and the issues involved.

FACTORING

Financing receivables with the help of factoring can help a company having liquidity without creating a net liability on its financial condition. Although in the western countries, factoring industry handles billions of dollars business every year, but business houses in India are still unsure about using it as a financial tool. At the instance of RBI, a committee headed by Shri C. S. Kalyanasundaram went in to the aspects of factoring services in India in 1988, which formed the basis for introduction of factoring services in India. In 1991, SBI (State Bank of India) established its subsidiary- SBI Factors Ltd. with an authorized capital of Rs. 25 crores to undertake factoring services.

Factoring grew specifically out of the need for working capital in some industries. Most of the new firms fail due to poor cash flow management. Cash flow needs are not restricted to start-up operations only — many established and even prosperous businesses occasionally face a cash crunch. One solution that is rapidly growing in popularity is Factoring. Factoring provides the means for businesses to convert receivables to cash before they are due without retaining liability for their payment. In its inception, factors acted as commission merchants handling goods on consignment. During the latter years of the 19th century and the early years of the present century, factors began to stop acting as sales agents for their clients. The general factor thus gradually evolved into the modern factor. The growth of factoring, the entry of a variety of financial institutions into this field, and the widespread uses of such financing in many different lines of business are all recent phenomena, developing since the beginning of the present century.

Whenever a company offers net terms on a sale to their customer, they are in fact lending that customer money until the invoice has been paid. What a factoring company does it purchase the obligation of the debtor/customer and makes immediate payment to the company. So, Factoring is the process of selling accounts receivables to a business firm known as 'Factor' rather than waiting to collect the money from the customer on due date. A receivable or an invoice, which has not been paid yet, has money value. It is a debt that customer has agreed to pay in the near future. Therefore, in a way, Factors are investors who will pay cash now for the right to receive the future payments on firm's invoices. The word 'Factor' comes from the Latin word *'factare'* meaning 'to make or to do'. Factoring is essentially the sale or assignment of a sale, trade, or receivable account for immediate cash. By definition, it provides, any business from start-up to mature companies of any size, access to immediate cash and improved cash flow for expansion or growth but without diluting equity or incurring debt.

The process of factoring accounts receivables can vary in many ways. The administration of funding invoices can differ with different finance companies. Also, the rate of funds in use can change based on variables of the deal like the rupee volume that will be financed and the length of time the company will be using the factor. The creditworthiness and number of customers also determines the price of a factor.

The factoring service can be: a) With Recourse b) Without Recourse

(a) With Recourse

The factor purchases accounts receivable with recourse to the client. A client may have made an independent decision to supply merchandise in excess of the limit the factor is responsible for. The factor will work the receivable until a specific date (usually a set number of days) then turn the receivable, which could not be collected, back to the client/ company for resolution. There can be many creative arrangements that can be made on the basic-rules for selling with recourse.

(b) Without Recourse

The factor purchases accounts receivable without recourse to the client, and bears the entire burden of collection and risk of bad-debt losses. This feature is especially attractive to a company which cannot afford extraordinary bad-debt losses.

Along with buying client's accounts receivable without recourse, factors offer a number of other services. Primarily among these is the lending of money against inventory. This method of secured borrowing is often used by customers to finance temporary needs for working funds. When the client sells the inventory, it turns over the resultant receivables to the factor and liquidates the loan.

COST OF FACTORING

A factor charges a commission or fee for performing the credit and collection function and for purchasing the client's receivables with or without recourse to the client for bad-debt losses. The factor's commission for service is usually based on the net face value of receivables bought over one year. Factors usually charge for their services in two ways: administration fees and finance charges. Service fees typically range from 1% to 3% of annual turnover. For the finance made available, factors levy a separate charge, similar to that of a bank overdraft. A number of conditions determine the costs for factoring service such as:

- The nature of the business, including considerations such as seasonable aspects, stability of products, whether the customer is a manufacturer or wholesaler.
- Annual sales volume of client firm. As volume increases, the percentage charged usually decline.
- Average size of order processed. Large orders are no more time consuming to process than small orders and produce more revenue for the factor. Therefore, the factor's commission rate may decline as the size of the individual orders rises.
- Average annual sales volume per customer. As this figure rises, there is less work and follow-up for the factor, since the client's business is becoming concentrated in few accounts. The commission rate tends to decline.
- Credit worthiness of the client's customers. If the risk is relatively small, the factor's commission may be lower.
- Client's selling terms. If the credit period is very lengthy, the factor must wait to collect its receivables, this requires a higher fee.

The essence of the credit sale transaction is the credit worthiness of the particular receivable account. Regardless of stage of development, immediate cash may be available. It should be noted that factoring is not a collection system for bad debts or even slow pay accounts. Use of factoring may, however, tend to speed up the payment from an otherwise slow-paying customer. As with any financial tool, there may be wide variations in applicable terms, conditions, and cost rates for its utilization. For example, advance rates (percentage of invoice paid in advance of collection) may vary due to account risk, industry, and factoring firm. The discount rate (fee charged by the factor for the financing) may also vary by actual risk in the account, industry, and/or factor firm. Transactions may either be with recourse or without-recourse. All of these variables are considered for a cost rate or fee for the factoring service. As with any type of financing, the greater is the perceived risk, the greater is the cost for the service.

Just like all financing options, the business firm must evaluate its own individual needs and requirements including a focused evaluation of all actual or potential advantages versus the costs in the transaction. In most circumstances, factoring, if properly utilized, can be a very valuable financial tool to achieve expanded sales and company growth.

BENEFITS OF FACTORING

Factoring is a flexible financial tool providing timely funds, efficient record keeping, and effective management of the collection process. Factoring offers a number of benefits to companies facing liquidity problems. Instead of having to wait for several weeks for payment on a product or service that has already been delivered, a business can factor its receivables for cash at a slight discount off the face value of the invoice. This instant cash can be used to meet payroll, fund marketing efforts, or provide working capital. This cash can provide the means for the manufacturing firm to replenish inventory and make more products to sell without having to wait for earlier sales to be paid. Factoring is not just a cash management tool for business firms. Factoring is especially appealing to new and rapidly growing companies. Since the process shortens their business cycle, these businesses can grow even faster. The inability to make more products to sell while waiting for invoices to be paid is largely eliminated. Such businesses usually net much more profit with factoring than without — even when the discount is considered. A typical business firm that extends credit usually has 10 to 20 per cent of its annual sales tied up in accounts receivable at any given time.

The reasons for using factoring are numerous and varied. Following are the chief benefits factoring provides:

- Factoring is the emerging financial tool that speeds client firm's cash flow and helps avoid the problems that slow-paying customers can create for growing companies. Factoring provides quick and convenient financing to a growing company that need capital to expand its business.
- Factoring is not a loan. There is no debt repayment, no compromise to balance sheet, no long-term agreements or delays associated with other methods of raising capital. Factoring allows the firm to use cash for the growth needs of today.

- Factoring provides the firm opportunity to take advantage of trade discounts or other early payment options with suppliers or vendors.
- A firm can increase its sales through credit granting and collection services provided by the factor. With this financing a firm gets the ability to re-invest immediately to acquire new sales opportunities.
- With the help of factoring, a firm can limit credit and collection expenses (including credit losses) to a definite percentage of credit sales. It can also reduce credit and collection expense ratio and can achieve more efficient performance of credit and collection function.
- Factoring helps smooth out the highly seasonal fluctuations, which boost credit, accounting activities, and collection efforts during peak season but leave the staff idle during the slack season.
- Since the factoring firm effectively assumes the credit evaluation risk of accounts receivable that may translate into decreased internal costs for accounts receivable administration, more efficient and effective customer accounts collection, and better information for management on the credit worthiness of the firm's clients.
- Factoring provides increased working capital turnover as well as a reliable means for turning receivables into *immediate cash.*
- Factoring service is quick and convenient to avail. Other financing options may not be timely available for firm's requirements. Moreover, there is no debt creation or no monthly or balloon payments are required.
- *It provides protection against bad debts.* A factor provides an experienced, professional approach to credit decisions and collection operations by examining each debtor's credit standing and determining credit worthiness from a credit manager's point of view. It provides comprehensive credit service support, credit screening and monitoring, early detection of customer service problems, detailed management reports, and professional collections etc.
- A factor gives no consideration of firm's credit rating. Hence, new firms can also get benefits of receivable financing.
- Factoring reduces overheads and it can replace in-house credit management. Moreover, it provides off balance sheet financing.
- The financing afforded by a Factor to its Client is based on sales volume, rather than on conventional credit considerations. Usually, the amount of credit obtainable is higher than the amount offered by a bank or other lender. This feature provides the business firm with additional financial leverage.
- *It improves management's productivity* by allowing the firm to concentrate on business. Management can focus on product development, sales, marketing, planning and business growth, rather than credit analysis and the administrative details of collections. Therefore, with the help of factoring, a firm can increase its profits by concentrating on core areas.

- Factoring has proven to be a useful financial tool for many businesses, particularly those with limited manpower for receivables processing and those which are unable to make satisfactory arrangements with a bank for revolving accounts receivable financing. Factoring can give a significant competitive edge in the marketplace. The business firm can sell products or services more aggressively, especially to new customers or those outside immediate geographical market.

PROCESS OF FACTORING

In factoring, the accounts receivable are purchased by the factor that assumes the credit risk normally without recourse to the seller. The seller's customers may be notified (in case of *notification arrangement)* to make payment directly to the factor or, may not be informed about the arrangement, and continue to pay to the seller (in case of non-*notification arrangement). In case of notified arrangement, a* factor notifies its customers that their invoices are being sold to the factor and each invoice is stamped to that effect. The client's customers pay directly to the factor who now owns the receivable. Therefore, client's customers are willing to deal and cooperate with the factor while submitting credit information and answering collection inquiries.

The business firm entering into a factoring agreement not only contracts to sell its receivables to the factor but also relieves itself of the credit and collection function, including the cost and risk of decision making regarding credit and collections. This role is assumed by the factor for a fee. Under no other method of short-term financing do business firms shift the credit and collection job to the financing institution. When a business is being factored with notification, it shows on its invoices a notice that payment for the goods is to be made to the factor.

After a decision is made by both parties to enter into a factoring arrangement, a Master Factoring Agreement is signed. This agreement sets forth the details of the factoring arrangement. As specific accounts receivable are purchased, this information is entered into the factor's file, invoices can be generated by the factor and the customer is notified to make payment directly to the factor. Following are the major phases in a factoring arrangement:

1. Credit Evaluation

A factor firm is staffed with credit analysts, collection specialists and skilled account executives. The experience of these employees in working with a broad range of businesses allows them to spot credit problems and other trends rapidly and to develop customized programs to meet specific business needs. When a factor checks credit, it takes over the credit and collection functions of its clients. The clients no longer need to conduct credit investigations and analysis, make credit decisions, keep records of accounts receivable, collect accounts receivable, and sustain bad-debt losses.

When an order is received from a customer, the client calls the factor for a recommendation. The factor usually has a credit file on the account or will set one up when the request is received. The file contains agency reports, memoranda of the factor's interviews with the principals and the accountant, trade reports, bank investigation, and other information normally contained in a credit file. In addition, there is a record of inquiries on the account, the factor's current exposure, and the recommendation. If the recommendation is favourable, the factor approves the client's order.

2. Purchase of Receivables

After the factor approves credit for the client firm. The client firm makes deliveries; it sends copies of the invoices and the documents to the factor. It may obtain immediate cash for the full net face value of the invoices from the factor, minus the commission for services rendered and a reserve to offset returned goods, merchandise claims etc. The remainder due the client is made available at the average due date of the invoices. Therefore, when the factor approves a client's order, there is a concurrent agreement that the receivables resulting from the order will be purchased by the factor. This distinguishes factoring from pledged borrowing. Factoring is the sale of an asset. A borrowing places a debt on firm's balance sheet, and it costs interest also. By contrast, factoring puts money in the bank without creating any obligation to pay. Moreover, loans are largely dependent on the borrower's financial soundness; with factoring, it is the soundness of the client firm's customer and not the client that matters. It is the major advantage to new businesses which are without an established track record. In factoring, title to the claim passes from the client to the factor. In case of borrowing, title remains with the client. In this way the client is assured of a stated amount of money each time the factor approves an order. There is no need for accounts receivable follow-up or for collection procedures. The likelihood of bad-debt losses is eliminated on *approved* accounts. Factoring is more expensive way of raising money than normal borrowing, but provides quick cash without collateral or charge on earnings.

In case the client firm delivers an order that has not been approved by the factor, the factor is not obligated to participate in the transaction. The order is made at *client firm's risk.* The factor reserves the right to turn down the receivable arising from that particular transaction or may advance money against it with recourse which makes the client contingently liable on the account.

3. Liquidation of Receivables

At any time after the receivable is created, the client firm turns it over to the factor. This function of the factor is called cashing receivables, or cashing sales, prior to maturity or at maturity. When accounts are purchased, the factor makes immediate cash payment of a substantial portion due on that account usually 90% or more to the client firm. The Factor's fee and any brokerage fees are deducted, and the balance of the account is designated as a reserve. The factor holds back the balance for such contingencies as returns and discount, disputed receivables and client's risk receivables. This provides the funds to the client before the due date of the invoice. The factor does not advance funds, but remits monthly on the average due date of the invoices bought in any given month. As payments are received from the debtors, the Factor is compensated for the cash advance originally made to the firm.

When the customers have paid the amount due to the factor, the reserve (less applicable fees) is remitted to the firm as per the terms of Master Factoring Agreement.

Reports on the ageing of receivables are generated on a regular basis and the factor follows up with the debtors if payment is not received in a timely fashion.

Because of the factor's experience in performing credit analysis and ability to keep records, produce reports and effectively process collections, many of the client firms simply purchase these services for a fee rather than selling their accounts receivable to the factor. Under these circumstances, the factor can even operate behind the scenes as the client's accounts receivable department without notifying the debtors of the assignment of accounts.

FACTORING PROBLEMS IN INDIA

Today, factoring industry in India is facing severe problems due to the absence of proper laws and legislations regarding factoring services. Government agencies and PSUs (Public Sector Units) neither promptly make payments nor they pay interest on delayed payments. Legislation is required to comprehensively support the establishment and operation of efficient and viable factoring services in India. This is required to empower factors to recover money from defaulting companies/institutions. The assignment of book debts attracts heavy stamp duty which makes factoring a costly affair and this should be waived off. Legislation is required to prevent restrictive stipulation being imposed by big corporate against use of factors. Legislation is also required to clarify that factor debts can be recovered; this requires amendment in the Order 37 of Civil Procedure Code. Proper legislation is required to exempt factoring firms from the provisions of money lending legislations.

- This section is based on the bulletins, Internet uploads and notifications issued by the RBI from time to time.
- An open account, or open-end credit, is credit extended by the selling company under a plan in which there is no formal documentation of the sale transactions, and the selling company sends a regular statement to notify its customers of their outstanding credit amounts.

Chapter 7

ADVANCES IN RECEIVABLE MANAGEMENT

(**Contents:** Introduction, Advances in Accounts Receivable Management: (1) Re-Engineer Receivable Process, Centralization, Alternative Payment Strategies, Customer Orientation (2) Evaluation of Risk (3) Use of Latest Technology: Electronic Commerce, Accounts Receivable Systems, (4) Receivable Collection Practices: Invoices, Open Account, Credit Terms, Periodic Statements, Use of Payment Incentives and Penalties, Record-keeping and Continuous Audit, Export Factoring, Business Process Outsourcing (BPO) (5) Use of Financial Indicators: Estimating Delinquent Accounts, Employee Performance Analysis, Sales Trend Analysis.)

"To go fast, row slowly."
— Norman Vincent Peale

INTRODUCTION

An integral part of the receivable management function is to develop a set of indicators which will measure progress over time. A firm may establish performance indicators to measure improvements which result from re-engineering the accounts receivable process. One simple approach can be the analysis of the data on time spent on each part of the process. The benefit of this approach is that it makes clear to managers the proportion of time that is spent on non-value adding activities in the accounts receivable cycle. This type of analysis is not an absolute indicator of cost effectiveness of processing, as it takes no account of costs. However, it does demonstrate the inter-relationship between the various steps in the process and opportunities to reduce non-value added activities.

The accounts receivable process commences with a receipt of a customer order and ends with the collection or writes off of a debt. Financial management functions such as accounts receivable have been traditionally viewed as transaction processing activities. The studies suggest that the elimination or reduction of non-value tasks can be effected through better work practices and automation of processes. This can be achieved by analysing current processes and redesigning them to remove as much manual intervention as possible, reducing re-keying and appraisal activities and minimising operator error. An important part of this analysis is a formal, structured risk assessment which identifies and measures exposures associated with the accounts receivable process.

Following are the major determinants for significant advances in accounts receivable management and process efficiency:

1. Re-engineer receivable process
2. Evaluation of risk
3. Use of latest technology
4. Receivable collection practices
5. Use of financial indicators

These measures of effectiveness in accounts receivable management are explained in detail as below:

1. RE-ENGINEER RECEIVABLE PROCESS

Some big organisations have achieved real cost reductions and performance improvements by re-engineering the accounts receivable process. Re-engineering is a fundamental rethink and re-design of business processes which incorporates modern business approaches. The nature of accounts receivable is such that decisions made elsewhere in the organisation are likely to affect the level of resources that are expended on the management of accounts receivable. An example of this point is the extra effort that must be put into debt collection where credit policy is poorly administered or too freely given. The strong linkages between different processes means that true improvements cannot be achieved without focusing on all aspects of the management of accounts receivable.

The following practices present opportunities to improve the accounts receivable function in a business firm.

(a) Centralisation

A better practice for the delivery of finance services is the adoption of centralised processing for finance functions such as accounts payable and accounts receivable. Centralised processing groups are typically high volume transaction processing centres servicing multiple operating groups. Their establishment achieves a number of benefits for the organisation. These include the achievement of a high degree of specialist expertise in the function supported, the establishment of centres of excellence that develop and enforce common practices and standards and the achievement of cost efficiencies through the co-locating of systems and staff. The establishment of these centres also frees up other staff for more value adding work.

(b) Alternative Payment Strategies

Research into better practice indicates that repayment rates are significantly enhanced by providing customers and debtors with alternative payment approaches. In addition to there being alternative payment methods there are also alternatives to issuing invoices in the traditional accounts receivable processing approach. These alternative payment strategies result in efficiencies in the management of accounts receivable.

An approach that is available to agencies which deliver services on a regular basis resulting in recurring invoicing and receipting cycles is to arrange for the provision by customers of standing payments. An annual or bi-annual settlement can be undertaken to reconcile payments to services provided. The process can be facilitated by providing customers with regular updates of fees charged.

The benefits of this approach to the service providers is the reduction of costs through the removal of the need for an invoicing and debt collection function and the more timely receipt of revenues. There is also benefit to the customer through the streamlining of payment processes. The approach is most effective if adopted in conjunction with payment by direct debit of customer bank accounts.

It has been observed that payment of accounts outstanding is likely to be quicker where a number of payment alternatives are made available to customers. Moreover, the availability of convenient payment methods is a marketing tool that is of benefit in attracting and retaining customers.

The following modern payment methods are available and provide the benefits of added customer service, reducing remittance processing costs and improving cash flow through faster debtor turnover:

(i) Direct Debit: Direct debit involves authorisation for the transfer of funds from the purchaser's bank account; this approach has the advantage of reduced processing costs.

(ii) Integrated Voice Response: Integrated Voice Response is a system which combines use of human operators and a computer based system to allow customers to make payments over the phone, generally by credit card; this

system has been proved highly successful in organisations which process a large number of payments regularly.

(iii) *Collection by Third Party:* Payments can also be collected by an external firm under a contractual arrangement. The payment method under this approach can be cash, cheque, credit card or Electronic Fund Transfer. This method increases flexibility and convenience to the customer which may lead to improvements in the rate of payment. A variant on this approach can be a system whereby banks act as outsourcing partners by collecting payments from suppliers' customers and directly crediting supplier accounts.

(iv) *Lock Box Processing:* Lock Box processing is an outsourced partner captures cheque and invoice data and transmits the file to the client firm for processing in that firm's systems. This approach transfers the cost of data collection to service/ provider.

Other payment methods such as payment via the Internet are likely to become readily available in the near future. Each of the above payment types have advantages and disadvantages which are likely to be peculiar to the environment that particular firm operate in. Firms need to balance the benefits in both the payment and receipt processes against the costs that some payment options may present to the firms. Most of the methods mentioned above are not appropriate for small firms and are not common in India.

(c) Customer Orientation

Where individual customers or a group of customers have some strategic importance to the firm a case management approach may be adopted to develop good customer relations. Under this approach all aspects of the relationship are drawn together including debt management. The increased knowledge of the customer that derives from the adoption of a case management approach can assist in the design of strategies for the prompt repayment of debt.

2. EVALUATION OF RISK

Risk assessment is a major component in the establishment of an effective control structure. Once risks have been properly identified, controls can be introduced to either reduce risks to an acceptable level or to eliminate them entirely. A proper risk assessment also creates opportunities for freeing processes from inefficient practices.

The risk analysis involves a re-think of processes and questioning the way that tasks are performed. A risk assessment opens the way for efficiency and effectiveness benefits in the management of accounts receivable. In particular, processes can be re-designed to achieve the following benefits:

1. Establishment of clear and concise policies for issuing credit and for recovery of debt
2. Removal of non-value adding tasks and procedures
3. Clarification of roles and responsibilities by streamlining delegations by:
   (i) The establishment of controls where exposures are experienced

(ii) Motivating staff to take more initiative and ingenuity to every day tasks

(iii) The identification of new and more effective ways of delivering services

The application of a credit policy will not be fully effective unless there has been a comprehensive risk analysis of the customer population performed. This can be achieved by having detailed information on the characteristics of customers (and potential customers) and through the establishment of criteria against which to assess the credit worthiness of individual customers.

It is a good practice to ask a potential customer for their last two financial year-end balance sheets and income statements. Generally, a customer that makes a complete financial disclosure is treated more favourably. Financial statements are a means of classifying customers into risk categories. If the prospective customer is approved, the initial financial statement can serve as a benchmark for future comparative analysis. The extent of the credit exposure and/or the importance of the product or service, may dictate the degree of financial information the firm requires and receives.

The criteria need to be laid out in the credit policy. Sufficient information on customers will need to be held on a comprehensive customer database.

Major components of an effective database are:

- Billing name and address
- Credit information
- Place of purchase
- Date of purchase
- Special service requirements
- Method of payment
- Payment history
- Customer type

This database will need to be regularly maintained and updated.

3. USE OF LATEST TECHNOLOGY

Advances in technology present an opportunity for improvement in accounts receivable processes. The principal innovations available are the integration of systems used in the management of accounts receivable, the automation of debt receivable systems and the use of electronic commerce.

(a) Electronic Commerce

Electronic commerce is a term applied to the use of computer and telecommunications technologies, particularly on an inter-organisational basis, to support trading in goods and services. It uses technologies such as electronic data interchange (EDI), electronic mail, electronic funds transfer (EFT) and electronic catalogue systems to allow the buyer and supplier to transact business by exchanging information between computer applications systems. This achieves cost savings by removing the need for direct negotiation between the parties. This potential is likely to increase in the future.

(b) Accounts Receivable Systems

Today, almost all the big companies develop and maintain automated receivable systems. Manual system of recording the transactions and manageingreceivables is not only cumbersome but ultimately costly also. In the past, automation of receivable systems was not easy task due to the unavailability of both hardware and software technology. In the mid-eighties almost all the companies that had used mainframe computer based system environments faced a lot of problems. Their systems had become more of a hindrance than an asset. These systems were very bulky in size and costly in investment. *Mainframe computers were* the largest and most powerful general-purpose systems, were designed to meet the computing needs of a large organisation by serving hundreds of computer terminals (dumb terminals, having no independent computing ability) at the same time. So there was a great need to replace these slow and heavy machines. The question was, what would they replace them with? Then came minicomputers and microcomputers. *Minicomputers,* though somewhat smaller, also are multi-user computers, intended to meet the needs of a small company by serving up to a hundred terminals. *Microcomputers,* computers powered by a microprocessor, are subdivided into personal computers and workstations (clients), the latter typically incorporating RISC processors (servers). Although microcomputers were originally single user computers, the distinction between them and minicomputers has blurred, as microprocessors have become more powerful. Linking multiple microcomputers together through a local area network or by joining multiple microprocessors together in a parallel-processing system has enabled smaller systems to perform tasks once reserved for mainframes.

As computers and their operating systems became more users friendly, smaller and less cumbersome, there arose the need for new software applications to perform likewise. In the late 80s came the appropriate technology i.e. client-server solutions. Today, many big companies are spending huge amounts of money on enterprise, knowledge-based systems such as SAP, Oracle, PeopleSoft etc. These integrated systems automatically update all the accounting records affected by a transaction. For example, if a transaction of credit sale to a customer is to be recorded; the system increases the amount the customer owes to the firm, reduces the inventory for the item purchased, and records the sale so that it appears in the Income Statement. This requires updating the databases for accounts receivable, inventory, and the ledger account. In a non-integrated system the operator would have to enter the transaction three times, once in each database—a lot of extra work, and a chance for error too.

The Accounts Receivable System of a company allows the application and tracking of receivables and collections. Using the automated Receivable System allows the company to store important information for an unlimited number of customers and transactions; and accommodate efficient processing of customer payments and adjustments.

The following list is the minimum that a credit and accounts receivable system should offer. The Computerized Receivable System should have these features and abilities:

- It should provide complete customer information, including alternate addresses, sales history, current balance, highest balance, open credits, deposits and last payment.

- It should be able to track customers' open credits and deposits.
- It should allow global (applicable to all) changes to more than one customer record at the same time.
- It should be able to create customer categories and classification of customers for reports and operations on selected customers.
- It should support on-line inquiry of customer status.
- It should provide separate cash records for cash sales.
- It should allow quick location of customers, standard items and Ledger accounts with a Search File feature.
- It should support multiple Accounts Receivable cash accounts.
- It should be able to maintain a number of provisions regarding sales tax, tracking taxable sales, sales tax, etc., by month, quarter and year.
- It should allow flexible payment terms including number of days, day of month, end of month and end of next month.
- It should indicate invoice discount dates and amounts, and due dates.
- It should track sales by customer, sales representative and sales account.
- It should support new customers entries.
- It should indicate when a customer exceeds credit limit.
- It should handle multiple descriptions for standard items.
- Recurring invoices can be posted on a monthly, bimonthly, quarterly, semiannual and annual basis
- It should provide warning of duplicate invoice numbers for each customer.
- It should be able to compute early payment discounts.
- It should offer the ability to print and later reprint credit memos and debit memos.
- Invoice description and terms should be easily modified at any time.
- Individual payments can be grouped into bank deposits.
- It should accept payments, deposit applications and open credit applications at time of invoicing.
- It should support user-defined ageingperiods and should be able to print the AgeingReport by invoice date or due date.
- It should generate Payment Analysis Report and Sales Analysis Report.
- It should support the sorting of records by customer ID, name or sales representative.
- It should provide cash flow projections based on customers' payment history.

A receivable system should, normally, generate the following reports:

- Customer Name List

- Customer Worksheet
- Customer History Report
- List of Recurring Invoices
- Detail Report
- Open Invoice Report
- AgeingReport
- Summary AgeingReport
- Cash Flow Report
- Sales Analysis Report by Customer
- Sales Analysis Report by Sales Account
- Sales Analysis Report by Sales Representative
- Delinquent Accounts Report
- Payment Analysis Report
- Open Credit Report
- Deposits Report
- Credit Limit Report
- Invoice Register
- Cash Receipts Register
- Adjustments Register
- Sales Tax Detail Report
- Sales Representative List
- Sales Account List
- Standard Items List
- Summary Report

4. RECEIVABLE COLLECTION PRACTICES

Debt collection processes should be undertaken with the objective of reducing outstanding accounts while keeping sight of the need to maintain customer goodwill, in an environment of cost restraint. The fundamental rule of sound receivables management is to minimize the time span between the sale and collection. Any delays that lengthen this span cause receivables to build to unnecessarily high levels and increase the risk of bad debts. This is just as true for delays caused by billing and collection procedures as it is for delays caused by the customer.

(i) Invoices

Proper collection procedures begin with invoice preparation. Invoices should be prepared promptly and accurately. Promptness eliminates one possible source of delay. Accuracy prevents those delays that occur when the customer disputes the invoice and returns it for correction, triggering a chain of events that is time-consuming and often costly. Invoices should clearly state payment terms.

(ii) Open Account

As stated earlier, an open account, or open-end credit, is credit extended by the selling company or a creditor under a plan in which there are no formal documentation and the creditor sends an regular statement to notify its customers of their current indebtedness. In other words, an open account is credit extended under a plan in which:

1. The creditor allows repeated transactions
2. The creditor may impose a finance charge from time to time on an outstanding unpaid balance, and
3. The amount of credit that may be extended to the customer during the term of the plan (up to any limit set by the creditor) is generally made available to the extent that any outstanding balance is repaid.

(iii) Credit Terms

Credit terms are the time limits a company set for its customers to pay for the merchandise or services purchased. Credit terms affect the timing of company's cash inflows. Offering trade discounts is one way to improve cash flow position.

(iv) Periodic Statements

Marketing and promotional activities can be used to promote timely payment. Firms should provide information on the nature of products or services available, the required payment cycle, payment options available and the consequences of non-payment. Customers should be aware of their liability at all times. A practical way of achieving this objective is the issue of monthly customer statements.

To keep customers advised of their account balances, monthly statements should be submitted to all open accounts. The statement should summarize the amount owed and any activity in the account within the month. The choice of payment terms will depend upon customary practices in the business. In order to stay competitive, it is necessary to offer payment terms that are equivalent to those offered by the rival business firms.

(v) Use of Payment Incentives and Penalties

The firms, which have problems with debtor turnover, can offer incentive for prompt payment to customers. Discounting can be used as an incentive for customers to pay upon receipt of services, thereby avoiding the use of credit terms. When selling to large accounts such as commercial, industrial, institutional, and governmental buyers, collection is often accelerated by the offer of a cash discount. The discount as an incentive is offered for payment within nominal time period. Most of the business firms take advantage of all such discounts. This way they can reduce commitment of capital to accounts receivable. Payment terms normally include discount terms and dating terms. Discount terms describe the discount available, if any, for prompt payment. Dating terms specify the time when payment is due.

The discount term is usually stated in the form: *x/y* net *z* indicating that the customer can deduct *x* percentage if the account is paid within *y* days; otherwise, the account must be paid within *z* days. Let us understand this with actual numbers.

For example the discount term is: 2/10 net 30.

As discussed earlier, 2% is the discount percentage and 10 is the number of days within which payment must be made in order to take advantage of the discount. In the above mentioned term, the customer can take a 2% discount for payment within 10 days. The '30' indicates that payment is due within 30 days. If no other date is specified, the 30-day period begins with the invoice date. For example, if the terms above appeared on an invoice dated June 2, the customer would be entitled to a 2% cash discount for payment by June 12. If the customer does not pay within this period, the net amount is due within 30 days, or by July 2.

If the customer (or the firm itself in case of considering payments to its suppliers) decides to forgo the discount and not pay until the final payment date, the annualized opportunity cost of passing up this *x*% discount and withholding payment until the zth day. The formula for the calculation of cost of not availing the discount is as follows:

$$\text{Annual opportunity cost of forgoing the discount} = \frac{x}{1-x} \times \frac{360}{z-y}$$

Given the trade credit terms of 2/10, net 30, the annual opportunity cost of passing up the 2 per cent discount and withholding payment until last day will be as follows:

$$36.73\% = \frac{0.02}{1-0.02} \times \frac{360}{30-10}$$

Now, this is a very high cost of credit, so a business firm must avail the discount offered to it for early payments.

Though discounting shortens the average collection period but it also reduces net revenue. Before offering discounts a firm must conduct proper analysis of the effect that the option of discounts will have on its net revenue. This estimate should be matched with the costs of holding receivables at their existing levels, which is effectively the market interest rate applied to the annual carrying cost of receivables. Another aspect for consideration is the alternative uses of the funds tied up in receivables which could have been used in the business.

In addition to incentives for early payment, a firm should also consider the imposition of penalties on late payment. A delinquency charge for late payment can be used to discourage chronic late payers. The delinquency charge may be 0.5% to 2% per month on all balances overdue. For example, if a customer's statement at the end of month indicates a total balance due of Rs. 990, of which Rs. 815 is more than 30 days overdue, the penal charge at the end of month will be as follows (assuming 1% delinquency charge):

Rs. 815 × .01 = Rs. 8.15

(vi) Record-Keeping and Continuous Audit

Debt collection requires adequate record keeping to demonstrate that thorough and concerted collection efforts were done, and to provide an audit trail for internal and external auditors. Most importantly, any legal action require complete documentation of all facts relating to the receivable, including documentation of the overpayment or invoice, any disputed amounts and their resolution and all collection activities. Record keeping for collection efforts includes dates and results of telephone calls, envelopes returned with address unknown and certified letter stubs. Electronic records or a hard copy should be preserved as the relevant audit trail. The loss of any of these materials could jeopardize further collection activities.

Better practice in debt collection includes the following:

- Assessment of debts against a financial threshold before proceeding with recovery action;
- Review of the accuracy of invoices following failure by debtors to respond to a letter of demand;
- Categorise debtors in accordance with their ability and willingness to pay. Tailor debt collection processes in accordance with results of this analysis;
- Priorities debt on the basis of risk indicators. The indicators could include the payment history of the customer, debt level, demographics, etc;
- Communicate directly with debtors most probably by phone and obtain personal commitment as to repayment schedule;
- Staff have the authority to negotiate payment options within guidelines, without further approval from management;
- Large accounts often specify certain requirements for invoice preparation. They may require reference to a purchase order, proof of delivery, or a certain number of copies. These conditions are met when the invoice is first prepared and submitted in order to avoid delays and duplication of effort.
- Treat debt collection as a specialist function. Recruit specialists as required and provide appropriate training; and
- Consider outsourcing all or part of the debt collection process to a private collection firm.

Of vital importance in the design of debt collection procedures is the need to be proactive about the recovery process. The best time to initiate pursuit of outstanding balances is immediately. As an account gets further behind, the balance often increases, while the chances of collection decrease. Present time is the best time to start enforcing a rigid collection policy, making whatever arrangements are necessary to be sure that the firm receives the money due in a reasonable period of time. Credit industry advice is that the more a debt ages, the greater is the risk of non-recovery. Estimates are that allowing a debt to age more than 90 days increases the risk of non-recovery by at least 20 per cent.

(vii) Export Factoring

In case of companies exporting internationally, a factor can help offer competitive terms of sale while controlling the risks involved. Factors provide comprehensive credit management, protection against losses, collection services, and working capital to assist international business. In addition to relieving exporters of the time-consuming administrative burden of approving international credit and collecting sales, export factoring lets exporters safely offer their foreign customers competitive open account payment terms. Most importantly, factors help convert export receivables into cash by advancing funds to the company prior to collection.

Export factoring eases much of the credit and collection burden created by international sales. By outsourcing this credit function, the firm can convert the high fixed cost of operating an international credit department into a variable expense. Commissions are based on sales volume so the costs fluctuate with actual sales, resulting in lower costs for the firm when the sales are down.

Export factoring provides credit protection for 100% of the value of the invoices billed. Additionally, the factor collects the proceeds from sales and can assign them to a bank. The factor manages the whole process; from invoicing through collecting to full financial reporting.

Many companies use export financing as a method to increase their borrowing ability from their lender since many lenders refuse to lend money against foreign receivables. By having the export receivables factored, the factor purchases the accounts receivable and assigns the proceeds to the bank. The bank is then able to lend against those receivables.

(viii) Business Process Outsourcing (BPO)

Management of the credit function varies widely from company to company. There is no universal method for the selection of a specific tool to be used by a credit manager. The utility of a particular tool involves both knowledge and judgement on the part of a credit manager.

BPO can be viewed as a strategic business tool whereby an outside vendor assumes the entire responsibility for manageinga business process. The commitment is long term in nature. The outside vendor has the responsibility to fully manage a non-core business activity. There is a widely embraced goal of enhancing shareholder wealth that is pushing managers in all functional areas of business toward the use of outsourcing. For credit managers, the placement of selected accounts for collection with a collection agency has been a common practice for many years. The introduction of a third party, coupled to freeing up time for the credit manager, can often lead to successful results.

The placement of selected accounts is called transactional outsourcing. BPO differs from transactional outsourcing because an entire process is outsourced, not just selected transactions. By having customers send cheques directly to a bank lockbox operation an entire process is being outsourced; this is an example of BPO. Reasons that a company may move toward BPO are driven by long-term efficiency improvements and lower costs. Specific reasons often cited for outsourcing entire processes include:

1. To improve the corporate focus and increase shareholder value
2. To cut costs and thereby improve competitiveness
3. To gain access to new technology
4. To free up funds invested into assets
5. To provide managers with more time to focus upon core problems
6. To improve the management of a process where management skills are scarce.

The quantitative analysis of a BPO decision is similar to the analysis of a make or buy decision used in accounting by a manufacturer. The alternative costs associated with buying from an outside supplier are compared to the alternative costs of making the product internally. The incremental cost difference pinpoints the quantitative aspect of the make or buy decision; the lower the costs the more highly preferred the alternative.

The qualitative aspects of a make or buy decision can drive the final decision. For example: Is the outside supplier reliable? Will the outside supplier deliver quality merchandise? These qualitative aspects of the analysis are where BPO analysis can become complex. Credit managers need to be trained to ask questions that pertain to both the quantitative and the qualitative aspects during BPO analysis.

BPO may have certain pitfalls. Through BPO analysis a business will give up some control over the process that is outsourced. The quality of the work may suffer. How can a credit manager quantify a need for customer intimacy when considering outsourcing? Sometimes BPO has a negative connotation with existing employees. There is often a threat of layoffs in an attempt to reduce costs while implementing BPO. BPO can actually lead to an increase in costs. The changes that are planned often use estimates of future costs; these may or may not come to fruition.

There are a number of credit management and accounts receivable related activities that lend themselves to BPO. Each of the activities requires the use of judgement in terms of whether or not they are appropriate at a particular company. For example, there is a need to differentiate as to whether the collection process being considered for BPO can be handled better because the credit department has a strategic advantage, or is the collection process a commodity type process. If there are many small balance accounts with little technical collection knowledge then perhaps collections could be outsourced. Economies of scale could provide BPO cost savings. On the other hand, if the credit manager has large balance accounts that require close personal contact and a high level of product knowledge then collections should probably be handled internally.

Decisions that pertain to BPO are too often made at the top of an organisation chart and then flow down to credit managers. Credit managers could benefit from, and contribute to, the direct involvement in BPO decision-making. In order for credit managers to contribute to informed BPO decision-making, costs of servicing and performing tasks should be clarified. Making cost comparisons to the value added has become the key driver for outsourcing decisions. For the most part credit managers perform tasks that are a part of the core competencies that establish value for their employer; the non-core practices are the likely candidates for BPO.

5. USE OF FINANCIAL INDICATORS

Credit, collections, and accounts receivable personnel have the myriad measures available for performance measurement and analysis. It is evident that choosing a single or group of measures is a personal, company, or industry preference. Credit executives plan and direct the credit, collection, and accounts receivable functions to increase sales and profits. While pursuing these goals, they use their decision-making capabilities to foster growth, optimize cash inflows, and improve the quality of work performed by the staff. Meaningful measures supports the organisation's mission and help reach organisational goals.

Using valid measures of performance is critical in this process. The need is to understand the performance measures and use them appropriately. The prudent credit professional will have a clear understanding of the importance of spending the necessary time and effort to understand the measures of performance and implement the appropriate measures to meet the needs of their organisation. The measure used must have a standard. The standard can be a set value or a range. A measure must be compared to some standard otherwise it has no meaning. Standards may be set according to past organisational or industry values or trends. Organisations should communicate all measures and standards to those individuals who are responsible for executing the action plan that will help the organisation reach its goals. Measures of performance should be graphed or charted as a part of the reporting process. The right measure is the one that meets organisational needs and supports the plans of the company, division, or department.

Following are some of the important performance indicators for a receivable function.

(a) Estimating Delinquent Accounts

When it is highly probable that some accounts will prove delinquent and the rupee amount can be reasonably estimated, estimates of bad debt expense should be made and recorded in the period in which the sale takes place. Two methods of accounting for bad accounts are used in practice — the allowance method and the direct write-off method.

When the seller can make a reasonable estimate of the rupee amount to be written off, the allowance method should be used. The allowance method provides an expense for delinquent receivables in advance of their write-off. The use of the allowance method serves two purposes. First, it reduces the value of the receivables to the amount of cash to realize in the future. Second, it matches the delinquent expense of the current period with the related revenues of the period.

The allowance for delinquent accounts is reported on the balance sheet as a deduction from accounts receivable and is called a contra asset account. Because the receivables are reported net of the allowance, the net receivables balance is the amount of cash that is expected to be collected in the near future and thus satisfies the financial reporting objective of providing information about future cash inflows to the company.

The estimate of delinquents at the end of a fiscal period should be based on past experience and forecasts of future business activity. When the general economic environment is favourable, the amount of the expense should normally be less than when the trend is in the opposite direction.

Following are the three generally accepted procedures that are used in applying the allowance method:

(i) Percentage of Sales: This estimate of delinquent accounts is based on a historically determined percentage of each period's credit sales. For example, if your company's experience indicates that ultimate delinquent accounts average about two per cent of credit sales, an adjusting entry would be made at year-end that expensed two per cent of the receivables with an offsetting credit to the reserve for bad-debt.

(ii) Percentage of Receivable: Under this method the percentage of the ending balance of accounts receivable not expected to be collected is determined. The allowance account is then adjusted to equal this percentage. The method emphasizes valuation of the receivables at net realizable value on the balance sheet.

(iii) Ageing of Receivable: The accounts receivable Ageing Schedule is a listing of the customers making up the total accounts receivable outstanding balance. Most businesses prepare an accounts receivable ageing schedule at the end of each month. Analyzing the accounts receivable ageing schedule periodically helps identify potential cash flow problems.

The following is a sample accounts receivable ageing schedule from ABC Ltd.:

Books of ABC Ltd.
Accounts Receivable Ageing Schedule
as on August 31, 2004

Customer Name	*Total Amount*	*Current*	*1-30 Days Past Due*	*31-40 Days Past Due*	*41-50 Days Past Due*
Shubi World	Rs. 12400	Rs. 3200	Rs. 6000	Rs. 1000	Rs. 2200
Monney Farma	4800	1200	2000	1600	—
Prayri & Co.	2000	1800	200	—	—
Dharam Inc.	4050	—	1,050	3000	—
Chetna Ltd.	9000	1000	7000	1000	—
Sharma Bros.	1800	600	1200	—	—
Total	Rs. 32 050	Rs. 7800	Rs. 17 650	Rs. 6600	Rs. 2200

As discussed earlier, analysis of average collection period helps identify and measure receivables problems in total. However, immediate corrective action requires identification of individual problem accounts. Problems in individual accounts can be detected through analysis of receivables by ageing. Ageing considers that the longer a receivable is outstanding, the less likely it is to be collected. Analysing ageing schedule allows management to spot problems in accounts receivable early enough to protect the firm from major revenue problems. It also assists in highlighting individual delinquent accounts. A separate estimate of the percentage of delinquents is applied to each age classification group instead of applying an overall percentage. A receivable ageing schedule divides each customer's account into amounts that are currently due, 1-30 days old, 31-60 days old, 61-90 days old, and so on. The longer an account is overdue, the more serious is the problem. Ageing can identify these quickly, and corrective action can be initiated promptly. As per example of ABC Ltd., a total outstanding of Rs. 12400 is due from Shubhi World; of this amount, Rs. 6000 is 1-30 days old, Rs. 1000 is 31-60 days old, Rs. 2200 is 61-90 days old. The recovery of Rs. 2200 which is more than 61 days old requires some prompt action. Totals are entered for each age group. It is often useful to calculate the percentage of total receivables in each age group to indicate whenever overdue receivables become excessive.

The allowance method emphasizes reporting delinquent accounts expense in the period in which the sales occur. This emphasis on matching expenses with related revenue is the preferred method of accounting for delinquent receivables.

In situations in which it is impossible to estimate, with reasonable accuracy, the delinquents at the end of the period, the direct write-off method should be used. Under the direct write-off method, no entries are made until a customer actually defaults on payment, at which time the delinquent account receivable is written off; therefore, no allowance account is required.

Setting a reserve for delinquents is a valuation reserve, since it writes-down accounts receivable to a probable liquidation value. Whether the reserve is adequate, is a matter of judgment. Often, conservative management prefers to establish an allowance for delinquents on the high side, so that any portion of the allowance not needed at the end of the accounting period can be released into the profit column after a reasonable balance has been retained for the new accounting period. This approach has distinct advantages if a serious number of insolvency's are encountered. On the other hand, it is sometimes criticized by auditors for being unrealistic and leading to understated profits in the course of the business year as the large allowance is accumulated.

(b) Employee Performance Analysis

(i) **Active Debtor Accounts per Employee:** This figure represents the total number of active debtor accounts per employee of the credit department. Generally, the higher the number of accounts per employee, the more efficient the use of technology and people. This measures the department's efficiency. The formula for this is as follows:

$$\text{Active Debtor Accounts per Employee} = \frac{\text{Number of Active Debtor Accounts}}{\text{Number of Total Department Employees}}$$

In the same way, Active Debtor Accounts per Credit Executive can be calculated which is an individual performance measure. *This figure represents the total number of active* accounts for an individual credit representative or collector. Generally the higher the number of accounts per employee, the more efficient is the executive.

$$\text{Active Debtor Accounts per Credit Executive} = \frac{\text{Number of Active Debtor Accounts}}{\text{Number of Total Credit Executives}}$$

(ii) **Operating Cost per Employee:** This figure represents the total rupee spent per employee. The lower the cost, the more effective is the functioning of the department. The following is the formula for calculation:

$$\text{Operating Cost per Employee} = \frac{\text{Departmental Operating Costs}}{\text{Number of Department Employees}}$$

(iii) Transaction Turnover per Employee: This turnover indicates the number of transactions processed per individual employee. All employees involved in accounts receivable are included because their combined duties are directed in some fashion to processing transactions of all types. This includes secretaries, administrators, supervisors, and managers. A transaction includes all invoices, credits, deductions, and payments. A higher turnover rate implies that a more efficient system is employed. This measure could include automated remittance processing. Once the parameters are set, they should not change in like comparisons.

$$\text{Transaction Turnover per Employee} = \frac{\text{Number of Transactions Processed}}{\text{Number of Employees}}$$

(c) Average Collection Period

An important indicator of the effectiveness of credit and collection policy is average collection period. The average collection period is a ratio that expresses the total amount of receivables outstanding in terms of an equivalent number of average daily credit sales.

The average collection period is calculated as follows:

$$\text{Average Collection Period} = \frac{\text{Accounts Receivable}}{\text{Average Daily Credit Sales}}$$

For example, if a business had average monthly credit sales of Rs. 6,000 and outstanding accounts receivable of Rs. 9,000, the collection period would be calculated as follows:

$$\text{Average Daily Credit Sales} = \frac{\text{Average Monthly Credit Sales}}{\text{30 (days in month)}}$$

So in this example, Rs. 6,000/30 would equal 200.

So in this example Rs. 9,000 /Rs. 200 would equal 45 days. Or, viewed another way, the total amount owed by customers is equivalent to 45 days' credit sales, on the average.

This indicates that, on the average, customers are taking 45 days to pay their accounts. Some formulas for calculating the average collection period consider only net credit sales. This is determined by subtracting an estimated allowance for bad debts from total annual credit sales.

The average collection period can be compared with some predefined base. For example, if the payment terms of sale specify payment within thirty days and average collection period is greater than this, it indicates that customers are not complying with the terms and a problem exists. Or past performance can be used as a basis for comparison. Performance in previous periods indicates whether or not collections are improving or declining. The other popular base can be the use of Industry averages.

Comparison with the experience of other companies in the same industry will determine whether or not credit and collection policies are as effective as those of the competitors.

The extent of the receivables' excess can be measured by comparing the actual receivables with a target level. For example, assume that the terms of sale specify payment within 30 days, and the industry average collection period is approximately 30 days. A suitable target for receivables would then be 30 days' average credit sales.

If average daily credit sales are Rs. 200, then a target for receivables will be calculated as follows:

Average daily Sales × Collection Period = Receivables

Rs. 200 × 30 = Rs. 6,000

If actual receivables were Rs. 9,000, then it is an average of Rs. 3,000 (Rs.9,000 – Rs.6,000) in receivables that require attention.

A relatively high average collection period indicates that a problem exists and corrective action must be taken. Prompt attention should reduce the collection period, speed conversion of receivables to cash, minimize capital tied up in accounts receivable and, at the same time, reduce the risk of bad debts.

(d) Sales Trend Analysis

(i) Analysis of Past Sales Trend: If the company's sales fell compared to the previous year, the level of corresponding receivable accounts will drop too. If the receivable account did not decrease from the prior year, even though sales did, this may indicate that the company is keeping receivables too long or not collecting fast enough. To check, the manager should do an analytical comparing the company's percentage change from current year to prior year to that of other firms.

(ii) Cost per Sales (in rupees): This calculation relates rupees spent in the credit and collection effort to credit sales generated, or how much it cost the company to process each rupee in credit sales. A higher percentage signifies that a more effective operation is employed. This ratio is calculated as follows:

$$\text{Cost per Sales (in rupees)} = \frac{\text{Departmental Operating Costs}}{\text{Credit Sales}}$$

Is cost per credit sales rupee justified? This question is relative. It could be answered by benchmarking with other organisations or measuring itself against its own past performance.

(iii) Accounts Receivable to Sales Ratio: This ratio can be used to highlight trends in the level of investment in accounts receivable. Where accounts receivable as a proportion of monthly revenue exceeds an established bench-mark, thereby indicating the possibility of interest foregone, the matter can be highlighted for management attention. Following is the formula for calculation.

$$\text{Accounts Receivable to Sales Ratio} = \frac{\text{Total Monthly Accounts Receivable}}{\text{Monthly Sales}}$$

In addition to measuring the effectiveness of the accounts receivable process as a whole specific debt collection techniques and their effectiveness should be monitored. This information can be used when assessing alternative debt collection strategies. It is of assistance when conducting assessments of this type to be cognisant of the costs of the relative collection strategies.

An important consideration in this process is the cost of measuring and analysing performance data. It is also critical that reports be timely, present information in a readily digestible fashion and that they are directed to the appropriate levels of management. Reports presented to higher levels of management are more effective when they are presented in summary form, often with table or chart form presentations. Reports containing too much data are unlikely to be effective. Better practice should be to obtain management input into the design of reports to ensure that the reports are used as intended.

Chapter 8

INVENTORY MANAGEMENT

(**Contents:** Introduction, The Nature of Inventory, Types of Inventory - Raw Materials, Work in Progress, Finished Product, Consumables, Spares. Benefits of Inventory, The Cost of Inventory — (1) Holding/Carrying Costs (2) Ordering Costs, (3) Stockout/Shortage Costs (4) Set-up Costs. Inventory Valuation — (1) First-In First-Out (FIFO), (2) Last-In First-Out (LIFO), 3. Average Cost (AVECO). Inventory Control, Just-In-Time Control System, The Efficiency of Inventory – (1) Inventory Turnover Ratio (2) Average number of days of inventory (Days sales in inventory) (3) Re-Order Time (4) Inventory Adjustments. Profit Analysis — (1) Gross Margin Return On Inventory Investment (2) Break-Even Analysis (3) Analysis of COGS (cost of goods sold), Inventory Pricing, Level of Inventory, Economic Order Quantity (EOQ) Model, Sporadic Usage Inventory, Budgeted Inventory Investment.)

"Success is not to be measured by how much material wealth is possessed, but whether you are able to create at will what you need".

— Sri Sri Paramahansa Yogananda

INTRODUCTION

For many business firms, Inventory is one of the most visible and tangible aspects of doing business. Raw materials, work in process and finished goods all represent various forms of inventory. Each form represents money tied up until the inventory leaves the company as purchased products. Likewise, merchandise stocks in a retail store contribute to profits only when their sale puts money into the cash register. In simple words, inventory refers to stocks of goods necessary to do business. These stocks represent a large portion of the business investment, therefore, must be well managed in order to maximize profits.

In fact, for a business firm, inventory is both an asset and a liability. Too much inventory consumes physical space, causes a financial burden, and increases the possibility of damage, spoilage and loss. Also, too much inventory frequently compensates for poor and inefficient management, wrong forecasting, haphazard scheduling, and inadequate attention to process and procedures. On the other hand, too little inventory disrupts manufacturing operations, engenders chaos on the shop floor, and increases the likelihood of poor customer service. In many cases good customers are lost if the desired product is not immediately available. Many businesses cannot absorb the types of losses arising from poor inventory management. Unless inventories are controlled, they are unreliable, inefficient and costly. This thin line between keeping too much inventory and too little is not the only problem faced by a business. Others include:

- Maintaining a wide assortment of stock
- Increasing inventory turnover but not sacrificing the service level;
- Keeping stock low but not sacrificing service or performance.
- Obtaining lower prices by making volume purchases
- Having an adequate inventory on hand

Therefore, successful inventory management involves balancing the costs of inventory with the benefits of inventory. Many business firms fail to appreciate fully the true costs of carrying inventory, which include not only direct costs of storage, insurance and taxes, but also the cost of money tied up in inventory.

THE NATURE OF INVENTORY

The Inventory, which is shown in the balance sheet of a firm, can take a number of forms. Inventory consists not just of finished goods waiting to be sold but also of semi-finished products (work in progress) and raw materials waiting to be used in the production process. Thus, for an automobile company, a pile of doors for the body of a motorcar is an item of Inventory even though the doors themselves are not for direct sale. Similarly, the paint that is used in the paint shop of the car manufacturer is also to be entered as Inventory in the balance sheet.

Two types of Inventory — finished products and work-in-progress, tend to play different roles in the production and selling process. Finished products are needed in order to sell to the customers without the inconvenience of waiting for the product to be manufactured. This is also true of firms producing items needed by other firms. For example, a firm producing tyres for a vehicle manufacturing firm may lose its contract to supply if it upset the production processes of its customer by asking it to wait. Such Inventories also have another role. In batch processes, where quantities of similar items are produced in one production run, it is often more efficient to build up Inventories.

TYPES OF INVENTORY

The objective of inventory management is to provide right goods, in sufficient quantities, in right place at the right time. In a business firm Inventory is required mainly for two reasons:- to enable items to be produced or to be sold; to act as a buffer against an unpredictable high usage. The most common amount of inventories is as piece parts in stores, from which material is taken for production, or as a store for final products that are to be dispatched to customers. So, inventory may be finished goods, spares, consumables, work-in-progress, or raw materials. There are three phases to the flow of goods:

- Raw materials flow into the manufacturing company from a physical supply system.
- Raw materials are converted into finished goods after certain manufacturing processes.
- Finished goods are distributed to the customers through a distribution system.

RAW MATERIAL

Raw materials are purchased material or goods required for production. Manufacturing process transforms raw materials into a finished product. Raw material stocks are held because:

- Future supply may be uncertain.
- Production comes to a halt without raw materials supply.
- Already purchased and stocked material offers convenience and cost benefit.
- Quality control tests may be needed on raw materials.

WORK-IN-PROGRESS

It takes time to convert raw material into finished product. Work-in-Progress (WIP) is tied up stock and needs to be kept to a minimum. WIP occurs from:

- Delays in doing work, long movement times between operations and queque bottlenecks.
- Workshop stations may hold bins or pallet of issued raw materials and WIP/sub-assemblies to buffer flows or enable rapid response to demand/factory call-off.

FINISHED PRODUCT

Finished product is stocked to be ready for customer sales. It also buffers manufacturing from unpredictable market demand. The firm can then supply from a well-managed capacity plan. Making a large batch may be cost effective even when demand is low.

CONSUMABLES

Computer and photocopying paper, brochures, envelopes, cleaning materials, lubricants, etc are used in many operations and are usually treated as raw materials.

SPARES

Spares are held as a after-sales service for products supplied to customers. It is important to differentiate their management from that of finished goods stock so that they may not be used for production. Spares for maintenance of the firm's equipment may be held in a site stores or be held on-call by the supplier.

BENEFITS OF INVENTORY

Inventory is a major part of a business's current assets that are intended for sale or are in process of being produced for sale, or are to be used in producing goods. It includes all goods and materials that are used in the production and distribution process. Raw materials, component parts, subassemblies, and finished goods are all part of inventory. Every business firm requires some Inventory in order to facilitate its operations. On the other hand, financial institutions and other service industries hold less Inventory and, for them, investment in Inventories is not of the same importance.

Inventory is held in order to have goods available for sale or raw materials for production. Holding inventory is especially important if sales or production are not stable, continuous and predictable. In a well-planned and standardized production, inventory can be reduced to nil with just-in-time deliveries of supplies. Inventory is non-existent in utilities, transportation and services. It is only important in manufacturing, wholesale and retail. Especially in retail business, it can represent two thirds of the assets of the company; the examples of such businesses are automobile companies and dealers, jewellers, clothing, shoe, sporting goods stores etc. In manufacturing, inventory management must deal with scheduling production, as well as holding inventory for sale. But raw materials inventory usually represents a small amount of funds, and work-in-progress inventory is dictated by the need for finished goods. Thus, the most important role of inventory is to make immediate sales possible even if the timing of demand is not known. Some of the major benefits of inventory are as below:

- Inventory forms the basis for doing business. This may be the product line inventory in the retail store.
- Inventory provides a favourable return on investment. Sometimes inventory have value and can be traded for that value.
- Inventory allows the buyer to take advantage of quantity discounts. It may be cost effective to buy in quantities larger than the cycle stock and store the excess because the discount for buying in large lots is substantial.
- Inventory protects against fluctuations in demand, delayed supply, and inflation.
- Inventory provides a buffer time from the customer. For example, a manufacturer may wish to make a long production run for economies of scale in production. The production run may result in more items than current demand. The excess is placed in inventory until the next demand period.

THE COST OF INVENTORY

Inventory whether produced or purchased resides all the time in the firm. It is not immediately sold and moreover sale proceeds comes after some time. The cost of Inventory is the purchase price of the raw materials, on which some trade credit is extended, and the costs incurred in transforming the raw materials into semi-finished and finished products. Some of this cost is the wages and other production expenses. There is always a time lag between buying the Inventory and selling it. The gap between paying for the Inventory and receiving the money for it – the cash cycle – is period during which the firm incurs a cost of carrying the Inventory. All this requires financing, so money will have to be borrowed to fund the time between paying for the production and receiving payment. Usually this gap is bridged by means of a bank overdraft, which will mean that interest payments have to be made.

One of the major reasons for Inventory management is that it requires storage. This requires the use of space in the form of warehousing, extra shelf space, larger floor areas for production facilities and so on. Therefore, the level of fixed assets of the firm will have to increase and this will require a corresponding increase in the level of liabilities. If these liabilities are in the form of long-term debt it means that interest payments will have to be incurred. If it is in the form of equity it follows that higher profits will have to be generated in order to give the return required by shareholders.

In either case high Inventory levels will impinge on fixed assets and so, not only will the Inventory turnover ratio be reduced, so too will the fixed asset turnover ratio, the return on equity and the return on assets.

1. Holding/Carrying Costs

Holding or carrying costs are associated with keeping stock over time. Holding or carrying costs includes interest, insurance, taxes, depreciation, obsolescence, deterioration, spoilage, pilferage, breakage, warehousing, opportunity costs etc. Most of the inventory holding cost is linked to the capital cost tied up in inventory. Storage costs includes cost of space, heating and lighting, cost of supervision and the cost of maintaining records. Insurance costs are also important for the valuable stock. In some cases, raw materials have deterioration costs where First In, First Out (FIFO) system is used. This means that the raw material that arrives first to the store is used first for production. Another can be the cost of any spoilage or shrinkage. The chances of theft and proliferation cannot be overruled.

2. Ordering Costs

Ordering costs includes determining how much to order, cost of invoices, clerical/labour costs of processing orders, temporary storage, inspection and return of poor quality products, transport costs, handling costs etc. Order costs are related to the clerical and managerial time required for placing and processing an order, shipping and billing costs, cost of receiving and placing the raw materials in inventory. It also includes the cost of using the computers to update the stock records. In some cases the order costs include the set-up cost of machines and the scheduling costs.

3. Stockout/Shortage Costs

A stockout occurs when we have insufficient stock to supply customers. Usually stockouts occur in the order lead-time, the time between placing an order and the arrival of that order. Stockout or Shortage costs are incurred when demand exceeds the supply of inventory on hand including not making sale, delayed delivery, loss of firm's goodwill etc. Stock out costs are difficult to calculate as they depend on the type of business involved. They include lost profits, cost of buying raw materials at premium, loss of goodwill and customers, loss of market share, and line stop cost, poor staff relationships and a halt in the production process, delivery penalties, overtime charges, cost of a line shutdown, line changeover due to parts unavailability etc. In other words, stockout cost can be expressed as the cost of not having inventory. In theory, we can see that these cost elements are relevant it can often be difficult to arrive at an appropriate figure e.g. if the stock is stored in a building used for many other purposes, it is not possible to decide an appropriate allocation of heating/lighting/security costs etc.

4. Set-up Costs

Set-up costs results when changing over from one fixture type to another, involved with product changes, cost of labour and fixture. Analytical techniques are used to determine inventory size and minimise overall costs of the company. Complex techniques are applied to control raw materials that account for a major share of the inventory costs. Implementing various techniques can thus reduce inventory costs.

INVENTORY VALUATION

The accounting method that a company decides to use to determine the costs of inventory can directly impact the balance sheet, income statement, and statement of cash flow. There are three inventory-costing methods that are widely used by both public and private companies:

1. First-In-First-Out (FIFO)

This method assumes that the first unit making its way into inventory is the first sold. FIFO gives us a better indication of the value of ending inventory (on the balance sheet), but it also increases net income because inventory that is several months/years old is used to value cost of goods sold. Increasing net income is good, but at the same time it also has the potential to increase the amount of taxes that a company must pay.

2. Last-In-First-Out (LIFO)

This method assumes that the last unit making its way into inventory is sold first. The outdated inventory is therefore left over at the end of the accounting period. LIFO is not a good indicator of ending inventory value because the left over inventory might be extremely old and perhaps obsolete. This results in a valuation that is much lower than today's prices. LIFO results in lower net income because cost of goods sold is higher.

3. Average Cost (AVECO)

This method is quite straight forward, it takes the weighted average of all units available for sale during the accounting period and then uses that average cost to determine the value of cost of goods sold and ending inventory. Average cost produces results are somewhere in the middle between FIFO and LIFO. In the absence of inflation, all of the three inventory valuation methods will produce the exact same results.

INVENTORY CONTROL

Inventory Control is the collection of activities, techniques, and methods of maintaining an accurate stock of items at a desired level. To maintain an in-stock position of wanted items and to dispose of unwanted items, it is necessary to establish adequate controls over inventory on order and inventory in stock.

One of the most important aspects of inventory control is to have the items in stock at the moment they are needed. This includes going into the market to buy the goods early enough to ensure delivery at the proper time. Thus, buying requires advance planning to determine inventory needs for each time period and then making the commitments without delays.

The purchasing plan must include accounting for the depletion of the inventory. Before a decision can be made as to the level of inventory to order, you must determine how long the inventory you have in stock will last. For instance, a retail firm must formulate a plan to ensure the sale of the greatest number of units. Likewise, a manufacturing business must formulate a plan to ensure enough inventory is on hand for production of a finished product. In nutshell, the purchasing plan must answer the questions: When the orders should be placed? When the first delivery should be received? When the inventory should be peaked? When reorders should no longer be placed; and when the item should no longer be in stock. Well-planned purchases affect the price, delivery and availability of products for sale.

The inventory management is concerned with answering the two major questions, they are: what should be the size of inventory and how often should it be replenished? Demand for the product and the lead-time for the supply of raw materials are the factors that determine the size of inventory. Assumptions about inventory are to be made depending on the past experiences.

Inventory management involves making decisions concerning how much inventory to order and when. The basic criterion in making these decisions is to minimize total inventory costs, such as the cost to carry inventory, the cost to order inventory, and the item cost, subject to meeting demand for the items. Inventory control involves process, procedures, and infrastructure to maintain the inventory at the desired level. The main objective is to reduce the overall cost of the inventory system.

JUST-IN-TIME CONTROL SYSTEM

The Just-In-Time (JIT) inventory control system was originally developed in Japan by Taiichi Okno, the vice-president of Toyota. Originally, the system was called the 'kanban' system, named after the cards that were placed in the parts bins that were used to call for a new supply. JIT is also known as stockless production or lean production system. The idea behind the system is that the firm should keep a minimum level of inventory on hand, relying on suppliers to furnish inventory 'just in time' when required. This is contrary to the traditional inventory philosophy, which is sometimes referred to as a 'Just-In-Case' system, which keeps high levels of safety stocks to ensure that production will not be interrupted.

The Just-In-Time (JIT) inventory control system is more than just an inventory control system; it is a production and management system. Not only inventory is cut down to a minimum, but the time and physical distance between the various production operations are also reduced. Just-In-Time (JIT) is a process for achieving excellence in a manufacturing company based on the continuing elimination of waste. Waste is considered as those things which do not add value to the product. JIT accomplishes this by moving material to the necessary place at the necessary time. Each operation is closely synchronized with the other subsequent operations to make just-in-time delivery possible. JIT involves employee participation, involving workers so as to gain from their knowledge and experience. Such participation is meant to ensure that workers feel involved with the system and make suggestions for improvements, cooperate in changes, etc. In a JIT system, quality is the responsibility of every worker, not of quality control inspectors only. In addition, management develops close relationships with suppliers and promotes speedy replenishment of inventory in return for the ability to hold less safety stock.

JIT system is based on the elimination of waste. Inventory is also regarded as an unnecessary waste. In his system waste is eliminated by:

- **Just-in-Time** – Inventory is only moved through the production system as and when needed.
- **Automation** – Automation of the production system so as to include inspection - human attention is only needed when a defect is automatically detected whereupon the system stops and does not proceed until the problem has been solved.

Okno regarded waste as a general term including time and resources as well as materials. He identified a number of sources of waste that he felt should be eliminated:

- Overproduction — waste from producing more than is needed
- Time spent waiting — waste such as that associated with a worker being idle whilst waiting for another worker to pass him an item he needs (e.g. such as may occur in a sequential line production process)
- Transportation/movement — waste such as that associated with transporting/ moving items around a factory
- Processing time — waste such as that associated with spending more time than is necessary processing an item on a machine
- Inventory — waste associated with keeping stocks
- Defects — waste associated with defective items

Therefore, in JIT instead of holding stock the firm receives the items it needs 'just in time'. So that, for example, a car manufacturer needs not keep a large stockpile of tyres. Rather the tyres would arrive in very small batches just when they are needed. It is sometimes argued that the reason for such systems is to reduce the cost of holding stock but the original idea was that by having no stock, the overall production process would become more efficient. Other major benefits of JIT are — better quality products, less amount of scrap and rework, reduced cycle times, lower setup times, smoother production flow, less inventory, cost savings, higher productivity, higher worker participation, reduced space requirements and improved relationships with suppliers.

In Japan, where this system is used by most of the large companies, JIT companies have established very close ties with their suppliers. As the suppliers have to deliver the required items 'just in time' it implies that very close links are required to ensure that the system works smoothly. One of the benefits of this is the co-operation of the companies in question in the design process. For example, if the suppliers of car mirrors are included in the design process for a new model, JIT system can reduce the overall costs of producing the new model of car. Thus, suppliers are crucial to JIT success. Supplier gets — long-term and guaranteed contract, good price for their supplies, steady demand, and minimal paperwork e.g. use electronic means to order - such as email or Web or Electronic Data Interchange etc. In return, the supplier agrees to — quality components e.g. zero defects material, guaranteed delivery times, a partnership with its customer, contingency plans to cope with disruptions like bad weather, strike etc.

JIT is a suitable production system when a firm:

- has steady production of clearly defined standard products
- makes a reasonable number of units
- has a high value product
- has flexible working practices and a disciplined workforce
- has short setup times on machines
- values quality, e.g. zero defects products/material

With respect to the western production philosophy, JIT only began to impact on manufacturing in the late 1970s. Books by Japanese authors about JIT in Japan were not published in the west until the late 1980s. Although the just-in-time inventory system is conceptually very appealing, it has not proved easy to implement. It should be absolutely clear to the management that implementing a JIT system is a task that cannot be undertaken lightly. It is expensive in terms of management time and effort, in terms of the initial set up costs and in terms of the continuing effort required to run the system.

Long distances from suppliers and plants constructed with too much space for storage and not enough access (doors and loading docks) to receive inventory have limited successful implementation. Firms rely on suppliers to deliver high-quality parts and materials immediately, so they must have a close, long-term relationship with them. All this is very difficult, if not impossible. However, many firms have been successful in changing the relationships with their suppliers. Despite the difficulties of implementation, many firms have moved to cut inventory through the use of a just-in-time inventory system. General Motors, Dell Computer, Toyota are just some of the many firms that are successfully using just-in-time system.

THE EFFICIENCY OF INVENTORY

For almost all the manufacturing or retail business firms inventory is the single largest asset on the balance sheet. To determine inventory productivity Inventory Turnover is the common measure.

1. Inventory Turnover Ratio

Liquidity of inventory is best assessed with the inventory turnover ratio. Inventory turnover is the number of times a company sell its average investment in inventory each year. This is a common measure of the efficiency with which a firm manages its Inventory, it is calculated as follows:

$$\frac{\text{Cost of Goods Sold from Stock Sales during year}}{\text{Average Inventory Investment during year}}$$

For example, if a company has total annual sales (at cost) of Rs.12,000,000 and its average inventory value is Rs.3,000,000, its inventory turnover is four turns per year (12,000,000 ÷ Rs.3,000,000). If the results of the inventory turnover equation are to accurately reflect the performance of a firm's investment in stock inventory, we must take great care in determining the values for both cost of goods sold and the average inventory value. Let us look at these two components.

Cost of Goods Sold: The value appearing in the numerator of the equation should reflect the cost of goods sold from stock over the previous 12 months. For example, if we are calculating turnover at the end of April, 2004, turnover should be based on the total cost of goods sold from May 2003 through April 2004. Direct deliveries (sales of material sent directly from a vendor to a customer) are not included because the material never passes through the warehouse, and as a result is not reflected in the average inventory value appearing in the denominator of the equation. That means, the firm did not make an investment in inventory in order to generate these sales.

Special order items (i.e. products ordered for a specific customer order that are not normal inventory items) are also not included in turnover calculations because they do not remain in inventory for a significant period of time. They normally are shipped to customers within several days of their receipt from the supplier. Including the cost of special order items in the cost of goods sold used in the equation tends to exaggerate turnover.

In order to calculate the turnover for the company, the manager should only include the cost of goods sold of items delivered to customers. This includes amounts sold to customers as well as quantities used for repairs and in assemblies. A company, while continually transferring material from one location to another without ever selling it to a customer, should not include such transfers in turnover. Otherwise, the company will have incredibly high inventory turnover, but no sales. However, in case of a central warehouse, one should include transfers in the calculation of inventory turnover. Central warehouses are facilities that serve as the normal source of supply for other company locations. These branches are customers of the central warehouse. If we do not consider transfers in the inventory turnover of a central warehouse, the resulted turnover will be less than the actual turnover for that facility.

Most companies use average cost in the calculation of the cost of goods sold. The manager can use other cost basis (e.g. last cost, FIFO, LIFO, etc.) as long as he is consistent from month to month. Also, it must be noted that the cost basis used for the cost of goods sold in the numerator is the same cost basis used for the average inventory value in the denominator of the equation.

Average Inventory: This is the average value of stock inventory over the previous 12 months. It should include all material in the warehouse, even the dead stock. Average Inventory is usually the average between Closing and Opening inventory, but more appropriate average is the average of monthly inventory throughout the year.

The amount recorded as inventory is significantly affected by the choice of standard cost versus full-absorption cost method, whether revaluation of inventory for lower of either cost or market was performed, and inventory accounting used: LIFO, FIFO or Average.

The firms that use standard costs for their inventory allocate a portion of overhead to each item produced. These standard costs also do not change from year to year, whereas in the full-absorption cost method, only direct costs are assigned to produced items, and consequently, unit costs change from year to year. The revaluation of inventory at market price can be based on replacement cost or on salvage value less cost of disposal. A note to financial statements should indicate which method is used. LIFO increases cost of goods sold and reduces inventory amounts on the balance sheet in periods of inflation. Thus, the turnover ratio can be significantly inflated. When comparing inventory turnover, one must keep in mind that a switch from FIFO to LIFO will automatically increase the ratio, and therefore, when comparing over time, a recalculation is desirable.

For manufacturing companies, inventory turnover should be calculated for components (i.e. raw materials, work-in-progress and finished goods) of inventory rather than for the inventory as a whole. For each of the three types of inventory, the turnover ratio is

$$\text{Raw Materials Turnover} = \frac{\text{Raw Materials Used in Production}}{\text{Average Inventory of Raw Material}}$$

$$\text{Work-in-Progress Turnover} = \frac{\text{Annual Volume of Finished Goods}}{\text{Average Inventory of Work-in-Progress}}$$

$$\text{Finished Goods Turnover} = \frac{\text{Cost of Goods Sold}}{\text{Average Inventory of Finished Goods}}$$

It is also desirable to know which portion of inventory is slow moving. Comparing with companies in the industry may be difficult because, while the breakdown of inventory into its elements is common, data on volume of production is managerial information that even company's accounts may not provide.

Companies that manufacture and assemble products may also have to consider factors other than the cost of raw materials (or components) in turnover calculations. If the cost of goods sold amount in the numerator includes any labour or other charges necessary for producing or assembling finished goods inventory, the average inventory value should include the same non-inventory charges for both the current work in progress (WIP) inventory as well as the finished goods inventory. If the cost of goods does not include any labour or non-material charges, the average inventory value should only include the actual cost of the components or raw material.

Interpretation of Turnover Ratios: Inventory beyond the need for the current operating period should be classified as non-current and included in the fixed asset portion of the balance sheet. The determination of what constitutes the portion of inventory needed for the current operating period is essentially a management decision. Nevertheless, analysts within the firm and even outside analysts can gauge the presence of idle inventory stocks on the basis of sales volume over several years. Such break out can be helpful in industries such as metals, construction, precious stones, where turnover can be understated if inventory reserve stocks are considered as current inventory.

Another adjustment that is normally performed after inventory taking at the end of year, is recording losses due to spoilage, obsolescence or theft (also known as shrinkage and/or shortage). There is always a possibility that inventory is overstated because unsealable inventory may not be written off if the firm wants to improve its profits.

Certain industries have their own methods of inventory accounting. At inventory taking, the end-of-year inventory is arrived by dividing inventory by the average mark-up (i.e. profit margin). Comparing that amount to purchases plus beginning inventory, minus sales net of mark up gives the amount of shortage due to theft for the year.

From a working capital point of view, a company with a high turnover requires a smaller investment in inventory than one producing the same sales with a low turnover. This ratio indicates management's efficiency in turning over the company's inventory, which can be compared with other companies in the same field. It also suggests how adequate a company's inventory is for its business volume.

There is no standard yardstick for this ratio since inventory turnover rates vary from industry to industry. Companies in the food industry, for example, will turn over their inventory faster than heavy manufacturing companies, where a longer period of time is required to process, manufacture and sell the finished product.

If a company has an inventory turnover rate that is above average for its industry, it will generally mean that a better balance is being maintained between inventory and sales volume. So, there will be less risk of (i) heavy inventory balance in the event of a decline in the price of raw materials, or in the market demand for products, and (ii) wastage through materials and products standing unused for longer periods than anticipated with consequent possible deterioration in quality and/or marketability. On the other hand, if inventory turnover is too high compared to industry norms, problems may arise from shortages in inventory, resulting in lost sales. Since much of a company's working capital is usually tied up in inventory, how the inventory is managed has an important and direct effect on earnings. Some examples of high turnover industries are hotels, cosmetics, dairy products, food chains, industries dealing in perishable goods and low cost item industries. Some examples of low turnover industries are aircraft manufacturers, distillers, heavy machinery manufacturers, steel, and wineries etc.

A ratio that is high and a ratio that is low can be either better or worse. An accurate interpretation of turnover ratios requires further analysis because a high ratio may indicate efficient management due to: Low cost of inventory, Just in time purchasing and production, Inventory maintained fresh, up-to-date and in demand, or a high ratio may indicate total mismanagement and other problems such as: Delays in shipping and excessive shipping costs, Overtrading, Sales lost because of inadequate assortment on hand, Sales vulnerability (i.e. seasonal or cyclical demand not met), Inability of the firm to maintain purchasing and/or production in line with growing demand.

In the same manner, a low turnover ratio may indicate either efficient management because of: No sales are lost, Preparedness for expanding sales, Avoidance of raw materials shortages, Potential appreciation of value of precious items on hand, Low risk for lenders or total mismanagement from: Inefficiency in working capital management (e.g. excessive cost), Presence of unsealable goods, Ineffective marketing strategy, Poor sales staff, Unforeseen decreasing demand.

The only way of finding out if inventory is too large is to look at the merchandise in the warehouse, and physically observe if it is old. And the only way of knowing if inventory is too small is to ask sales staff if they lost sales because of stock outs. As stated earlier, inventory turnover measures the number of times a firm sells average investment in inventory each year. To put it another way, it is the number of opportunities a firm must have to earn a profit on the money it has invested in inventory. It is a crucial measurement that must be calculated accurately.

2. Average Number of Days of Inventory (Days Sales in Inventory

Average number of days of inventory is calculated as

$$\frac{\text{Average Inventory}}{\text{Cost of Goods Sold}/360}$$

Or to calculate days inventory, we can divide the number of days in a year (360) by the inventory turnover ratio.

$$\text{DSI} = \frac{360}{\text{Inventory Turnover}}$$

Combined with the average collection period, it gives the cash or operating cycle of the firm. An ageing schedule of inventory, a statement similar to accounts receivables ageing schedule, reveals obsolescence of stock on hand and it is more informative, but it is usually not obtainable by outsiders.

Average number of days of inventory (days sales in inventory) measures the number of days it takes, on average, to sell the finished inventory. This ratio is simply the inverse of the inventory turnover ratio. Since only finished goods are used in calculating inventory turnover, days inventory also reflects only finished goods. The fewer the number of days that finished goods are kept in stores the better it is for the firm, hence, a lower figure is preferable.

3. Re-Order Time

The second factor that impacts inventory is termed as 'Re-order Time' or simply what is the time required to be re-supplied the stock. The longer the time the greater is the amount of inventory a firm has to carry. The re-order time begins at the moment a firm determines that it needs more inventory.

Safety stock is additional inventory that a firm carries just in case something goes wrong. The supplier may have a problem in shipping or picking up the item and it may be delayed by a few days or a customer may buy more than expected or the item gets more popular for a short time. Any or all of these factors may cause a firm to have adequate safety stock. However, it should be very careful about increasing the safety stock level as it not only increases inventory levels but it decreases stock turnover at the same time. Any decision to build in a safety stock should only be made after careful consideration and an understanding of the impact on store performance.

4. Inventory Adjustments

From time to time inventory adjustments should be done. Why? Because most inventory adjustments are the result of problems encountered in the normal handling of material. Here are some common reasons for inventory adjustments:

- Material is missing from inventory.
- More material for a product is in inventory than is recorded in the books.
- Some material/product in inventory is damaged and cannot be sold.
- Some material/product in inventory is outdated or cannot be sold because it has been in inventory for a long period of time.
- The material/product is obsolete.
- The remaining inventory in stock is less than the quantity a customer normally purchase.

Along with the quantity and item, the company should accurately record the reason for each adjustment. Every month, a summary of adjustments (by item and reason) should be reviewed to see if changes to policies and procedures are required to prevent future discrepancies.

PROFIT ANALYSIS

Nature of the stock (product or service) also affects inventory productivity. Customers purchase some products every day; some products weekly and some are purchased even occasionally. For example, a customer may buy five or six bathing soaps a month, or six or seven shirts a year, or nine or ten tubes of toothpaste per year. Conversely, he/she will buy only one television set every eight to ten years. Products that have a high purchase frequency always have a lower replacement price. For example, if toothpaste costs as much as a TV set, purchase frequency will be less. On the other hand, merchandise with a low purchase frequency has often a higher price. So, the customer often has to take some time to consider and analyse his buying decision. This is very common in case of furniture, jewellery, electronics appliances and many other comfort and luxury items. Even in consumable items there may be certain sizes or types of merchandise that is more specialized and takes longer to sell. Which leads us to the measure of inventory analysis for judging profitability i.e. Gross Margin Return On Inventory Investment.

1. Gross Margin Return on Inventory Investment

Gross margin return on inventory investment is a financial measure that tells us what return we are making on our inventory investment. It is the only financial ratio formula that returns a rupee answer not a percentage. It computes the return for every rupee invested in inventory. The formula for this is as below:

$$\frac{\text{Gross Margin (The Profit / Return on investment in selling an item)}}{\text{Average Inventory}}$$

Gross margin return on inventory investment is the measure that helps in balancing the turnover of an item and its sale price. If a firm has an item that turns only twice a year, it requires a much higher profit on that item as it is only making the profit two times and yet paying to keep the item entire year. The investment in the slow turning items is longer and therefore more costly.

2. Break-Even Analysis

Break-even analysis is widely used by the production and inventory management. It is used to determine the impact of price and cost strategies on a firm's ability to remain solvent without excessive risk. The analytical procedure for break-even analysis is short run, i.e. a time framework within which a firm does not change its methods of production. This popular method calculates the volume of sales after which profits occur or in other words, break-even point is the sales level where the rupee amount of contribution margin is just equal to total fixed costs.

The actual or projected sales volume is compared with the break-even volume. If the actual volume is smaller or very close to the break-even volume, it indicates that either the pricing strategy should be revised or the product should be discontinued because it is not sufficiently profitable. If the actual volume is only slightly above the break-even volume, the profitability may be adequate or not dependent on the sales stability. If sales are unstable, the actual sales must be significantly above the break-even volume; otherwise, the revenues may fall and that will put the company in financial difficulty.

A business's goal is to make a profit not just break even, but by knowing where that number is, a firm can accomplish its objective. Managers often want to know the production level where profits earned from a product cover the cost of resources used to create it. Break-even analysis is how we determine this level. The point at which total sales revenues covers the costs of committed resources is called the break-even point. In addition to knowing the break-even point, managers may also want to know the point at which sales volume reaches a pre-set target-profit level.

To calculate the break-even point of a firm, the costs are divided into: Variable Costs and Fixed Costs. Total variable and fixed costs are compared with sales revenue in order to determine the level of sales volume, sales value or production at which the business makes neither a profit nor a loss i.e. break-even point.

Variable Costs: Variable costs (VC) are those costs which vary directly with the volume of production, such as raw materials and direct labour and production costs included in costs of goods sold, as well as selling expenses, freight, and other costs that increase as volume increases.

Variable cost can also be divided between Direct variable costs and Indirect variable costs. Direct variable costs are those costs which can be directly attributable to the production of a particular product or service and allocated to a particular cost centre. Raw materials and the wages those working on the production line are good examples.

Indirect variable costs cannot be directly attributable to production but they do vary with output. These include depreciation (where it is calculated related to output e.g. machine hours), maintenance and certain labour costs.

Fixed Costs: Fixed costs are those business costs that are not directly related to the level of production or output. In other words, even if the business has a zero output or high output, the level of fixed costs will remain the same. Fixed costs (FC) are normally unavoidable, such as rent, staff salary, insurance, depreciation, research and development expenses, general and administrative expenses etc. In the long term, fixed costs can be altered as a result of investment in production capacity e.g. adding a new factory unit or through the growth in overheads required to support a larger, more complex business.

Semi-Variable Costs: Practically, there are some costs which are fixed in nature but which increase when output reaches certain levels. These are largely related to the overall scale and complexity of the business. These costs have both, a fixed and a variable portion, such as overheads, cost of utilities, advertising expenses etc. They are separated in their constituent parts and are termed as Semi-Variable Costs.

Calculation of Break-even Point

The break-even point is that quantity Q for which, Q = FC / (P - VC)

Where Q = break-even sales volume

FC = fixed costs

SP = unit price

VC = unit variable cost

(P-VC) = contribution margin

The formula is obtained by equating Total Revenue with Total Cost i.e. where profits are zero.

$Q \times SP = Q \times VC + FC$

The break-even revenue in rupees can be calculated as follows:

Break-Even Sales (Rs.) = (Break-Even units) × (Selling Price)

Let us understand this with the help of an illustration. For Example, a firm manufactures a particular type of toy. Each unit retails at Rs.5. It costs the firm

Rs. 2 to make each piece, and the fixed costs for the period are Rs.750. What will be the break-even point in units and in sales revenue?

SP = Rs. 5.00

VC = Rs. 2.00

FC = Rs. 750.00

Break-even units, Q = FC/(SP - VC)

= Rs. 750/(Rs. 5 - Rs. 2)

= Rs. 750/Rs. 3

= 250 units

Break Even Sales Revenue = Break-Even units × SP

= 250 x Rs. 5

= Rs. 1,250

In other words, the firm will have to manufacture 250 units to break-even, which results in a revenue of Rs.1,250.

The break-even point for a business is when the total revenue equals total costs. Break-even graph can be used to show total costs and total revenue; the point where the two lines cross is the break-even point. The total sales revenues rises with each additional unit sold at the rate of price SP (i.e. Rs. 5), the total cost starts at FC and is rising at the rate of unit variable cost VC (i.e. Rs. 2). Profit is zero where Total Cost intersects Revenue (i.e. that is where units sold equal 250).

Break-even analysis shows the level of sales that are needed to break-even. It can also be used to investigate the impact of a price change or be presented to the bank with application for a loan. Break-even point can also be used to know the margin of safety. That is the amount by which demand can drop before the company makes losses.

There are three ways to lower break-even volume, only two of them involve cost controls which should always be one of the major goals for inventory department.

1. A firm should try to lower direct costs, which will raise the gross margin. A firm should be diligent about purchasing material, controlling inventory, or increasing the productivity of labour by more cost effective scheduling or adding more efficient technology.

2. A firm should exercise cost controls on fixed expenses, and should try to lower the necessary total fund requirements.

3. Another way can be to raise prices of the product/material. In today's highly competitive market, most of the business firms hesitate to follow this strategy.

Break-even Chart: In its simplest form, the break-even chart is a graphical representation of costs at various levels of activity shown on the same chart as the variation of income (or sales, revenue) with the same variation in activity. The point at which neither profit nor loss is made is known as the break-even point and is represented on the chart below by the intersection of the two lines:

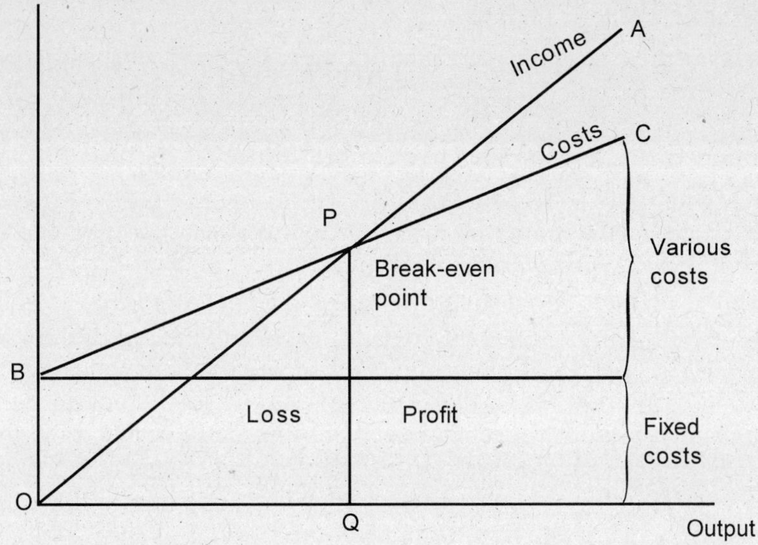

Fig. 8.1

In the diagram above, the line OA represents the variation of income at varying levels of production activity (output). OB represents the total fixed costs in the business. As output increases, variable costs are incurred, meaning that total costs (fixed + variable) also increase. At low levels of output, Costs are greater than Income. At the point of intersection, P, costs are exactly equal to income, and hence neither profit nor loss is made.

3. Analysis of COGS (Cost of Goods Sold)

In both, cash and the accrual accounting methods, the cost of goods sold matches costs to revenues. The cost of the goods that are sold is naturally that portion of inventory sold during the year. However, only where a continuous inventory method (i.e. maintaining records for each individual items on hand) is the process of matching cost and revenue one to one. And only in industries where very expensive items are handled such as works of art, automobiles or precious stones, can companies afford the expense of maintaining continuous or perpetual inventory records. For most other industries, firms calculate cost of goods sold from the inventory on hand at the beginning of the year, plus purchases or production during the year, minus inventory at the end of the year:

COGS is calculated for any given period as follows:

	Opening Inventory
+	Purchases
=	Goods available for sale
-	Closing inventory
=	**COGS**

Opening inventory is the amount of inventory at the end of the previous period. Closing inventory is the amount of inventory at the end of the current reporting period. Both items are taken from the balance sheet. Purchases are inventories bought over the period anchored by beginning and ending inventory. Therefore,

Cost of Goods Sold (COGS)= Inventory at beginning of year + purchases and/or production – inventory at end of year

A manager is not able to verify the calculation of cost of goods sold because numbers on purchases and production are practically never given in annual reports. Moreover, inventories are significantly affected by accounting methods used. It is necessary to rely on auditor's opinion that the company uses appropriate GAAP accounting policies in a consistent manner.

Cost of goods sold is very much affected by the unit pricing method a company uses for its inventory. Full-absorption costing combines direct costs only, while standard cost includes an allocated portion of overhead. Because overhead is large in some industries, when firms that need to be compared, use different inventory pricing methods, the comparison may be difficult, if not meaningless. But the difficulty may be more apparent than real because it is common for all firms in a given industry to use accounting methods that are most appropriate and, therefore, very similar. This is also true for revaluation of inventory at lower of cost or market. On the contrary, the use of LIFO or FIFO is not universal and it is dictated by two considerations. The first one is the rate of inflation. The second one is the need of the firm to manipulate its net earnings in a very effective and legal manner, for LIFO was specifically invented to deflate earnings. Both of these reasons are not related to any particular industry, and consequently comparison of firms using different methods is inappropriate. It may seem possible to make corrections to the cost of goods sold of firms that offer footnote details on current costs for those firms that use LIFO. But the conversion is not free from errors and it is not possible from FIFO to LIFO. In recent years, the slowing of inflation has prompted most firms to switch back to FIFO. Only occasionally, a firm under study will be an added challenge because it still uses LIFO.

The cost of goods sold differs considerably depending on the volume of production and the experience a firm has in producing an item. It is generally known fact that as a person becomes more skilled in producing or making an item he/she requires less time and effort for it. For instance, a carpenter may take two days or more to create a particular type of furniture. To make two or three copies of the same furniture would require less time. When producing dozens of similar furniture, each of the parts of the furniture can be cut in series or batches, thus saving even more production time, and assembling of furniture may be speeded up by division of labour resulting into additional savings in time and unit cost. It implies that increases in sales volume and reduction in cost are goals in themselves. The manager must be convinced that the goals are achievable and that the savings from a larger volume will bring about reductions in unit costs. Therefore, volume and unit cost strategies will have a positive impact on the profitability of the concern.

INVENTORY PRICING

As discussed above, profit margin is the end result of unit cost and volume strategies, as well as pricing strategy.

The gross profit is the difference between the sales revenue and cost of goods sold. Gross profit margin is stated as a percentage, dividing gross profit by revenue from sales.

$$\text{Gross Profit Margin} = \frac{\text{Sales Revenue - Cost of Goods Sold}}{\text{Sales Revenue}}$$

How prices are determined varies from industry to industry and from company to company. One very common form of pricing is the Cost-Plus method in which the cost is incremented by some percentage (known as mark-up) or rupee amount. In this method, the price is the by-product of a profit margin strategy which is guided by the need to cover overheads, taxes and returns to the shareholders. There are many variations of the cost-plus method of pricing. In many practical circumstances, managers entering a particular market for the first time find it most reasonable to use the profit margin of competitors as an appropriate return for the firm. Other firms use pricing strategies that align their own prices proportionately under that of the market leader.

When cost-plus method of pricing is used, there are dangers which the manager must assess. First, cost-plus pricing does not encourage efficiency of production since the costs are simply passed on to consumers. Second, pricing of products can be sub-optimal from a market point of view. When a firm prices its products according to market demand, price should correlate with quality. The reason is quite simple - the ultimate consumer will judge a product by intrinsic benefits so the better quality product will be in much greater demand than the lower quality product at the same price. It also implies that the consumer will pay a higher price when product shortages occur. But when the cost-plus method is used, differences in production costs determine prices, not quality as perceived by the market.

In theory, pricing should be based on consumer preferences. Market research exists for the purpose of helping managers to choose optimum marketing and pricing strategies. Historical data on consumer reaction to price changes is most useful. But, it can only provide answers on existing sales. When a new product is introduced, it is important to adjust price as experience tells when the product is over or under priced. Marketing research provides comparable test markets to gather empirical information.

Economic theory tells us that total revenue is maximized at the point where the demand price elasticity is one. The rationale behind it is that if a price is either increased or reduced, the consequent change in quantity reduces total revenue. But firms do not necessarily set total revenue as their goal. Rather, it is profit that they seek to maximize at the point where marginal revenue is equal to margin cost. The result is that prices and costs are dependent on volume. Therefore, a monopolist will try to price its products at a much higher price than a firm in perfect competition. In addition, the monopolist will also try to segment its markets and price discriminate among different groups of customers, so that the profit is maximized from each individual sale rather than from total profit. A firm in a monopoly position is clearly more profitable than a firm with many competitors. However, firms that take undue advantage of their customers, such as in the case of Microsoft, finds that this leads to customer unhappiness and government intervention.

The manager must ensure that the firm has given all necessary attention to customer preferences and the product is not over or under priced. It is customers' attitudes and preferences that should determine price.

LEVEL OF INVENTORY

Inventory consists of a stock of items, the size of which is called the inventory level. In a manufacturing concern, Inventory constitutes around half of the level of current assets and about one tenth of total business assets. So, Inventory represents an important investment for firms and it is important that it is properly managed. From the concept of operating cycle we know that Inventory is paid for before the revenues from its sales are received. In other words, inventory is an asset so it must be financed by liabilities of some sort. The Inventory can be financed by trade credit, bank overdrafts or other liabilities that require some sort of payment, for example, interest on short-term debt. If Inventory is too high the payments on these liabilities will be very high and the firm will not be able to maximise its profits. On the other hand, Inventory provides some benefits to firms. If Inventory is too low, profits will be sacrificed. Too much Inventory suggests that storage costs are too high and that no sales will be lost. For a manufacturing firm it means that there will be no stoppage in the production process. Thus, costs are higher than necessary and profits get lowered. On the other hand, low levels of Inventories may increase costs by disrupting production process and require frequent re-ordering. Lost sales due to no/low Inventory decreases revenues and profits.

Thus, there exits an optimum Inventory level. The best Inventory level will be that where the marginal cost of holding one extra unit of Inventory is equal to the marginal benefit. Conceptually, this is true but such observations are not very useful in a practical context. Managers want to know, in routine, what is the best actual Inventory level. Without a quantitative evaluation of the various costs and benefits, it is not possible to decide what level of Inventory is 'too high' and what is 'too low'. Practically, many firms decide their Inventory level on a judgemental basis. Management knows, with experience, that there is always some Inventory left over and so the Inventory level must have been too high or on the other hand, Inventory ran out before new Inventory arrived and so Inventories must have been too low. Further, the optimum Inventory level will be that which maximises profits and this will depend on the relative costs and benefits of Inventory. If costs are high and benefits low, a relatively low Inventory level is indicated and vice versa. This way, on the basis of past experience, observation and knowledge some idea of the optimum Inventory level can be arrived at. However, there exists Economic Order Quantity (EOQ) model that attempts to identify this optimum Inventory level given certain assumptions. It is one of the best-known mathematical management models and is the basis of many computerised Inventory control systems. The principal goal of inventory control is to determine the minimum possible annual cost of ordering and stocking each item. Two major control values are used: (1) the order quantity, that is, the size and frequency of orders; and (2) the reorder point, that is, the minimum stock level at which additional quantities are ordered. The Economic Order Quantity (EOQ) formula is most widely used method of computing the minimum annual cost for ordering and stocking each item. The EOQ computation takes into account the cost of placing an order, the annual sales rate, the unit cost, and the cost of carrying inventory. Let us discuss the EOQ model in detail.

ECONOMIC ORDER QUANTITY (EOQ) MODEL

The optimum level of inventory is determined by minimizing the combined cost of holding inventory and being out of stock. The cost of holding inventory is known as the carrying cost, and consists of warehousing, insurance, funds required, spoilage and obsolescence. The cost of being out of stock divides into reordering cost and cost of lost sales. Ignoring lost sales first, inventory control theory offers a precise derivation of economic order quantity (EOQ) by minimizing Total Cost (TC).

TC = Annual ordering cost + Annual carrying cost

TC = (No. of orders × cost per order) + (average inventory × unit carrying cost)

TC = ((D/Q) × S) + ((Q/2) × C)

where D = number of units sold, consumed or depleted per year

S = cost per order

C = unit carrying cost

Q = quantity ordered each time

D/Q = number of orders per year

Q/2 = average inventory (i.e. maximum inventory = Q, minimum = 0)

The economic order quantity is obtained by taking the first derivative of TC with respect to Q, and is equal to

EOQ = Square Root ((2 S × D)/C)

The value of the average stockholding = (Q/2 × item cost/value) where Q is the order quantity. The holding cost/unit (C) is derived from the average inventory value multiplied by the cost of carrying the item over the period expressed as a % of the item cost/value.

Order cost is derived from the number of orders placed (D/Q divided by order quantity) multiplied by the cost of placing an order.

The order/acquisition cost (or set-up cost for a make-to-stock situation).

Therefore Total cost = TC = ((D/Q) × S) + ((Q/2) × C)

These relationships can be shown graphically as below:

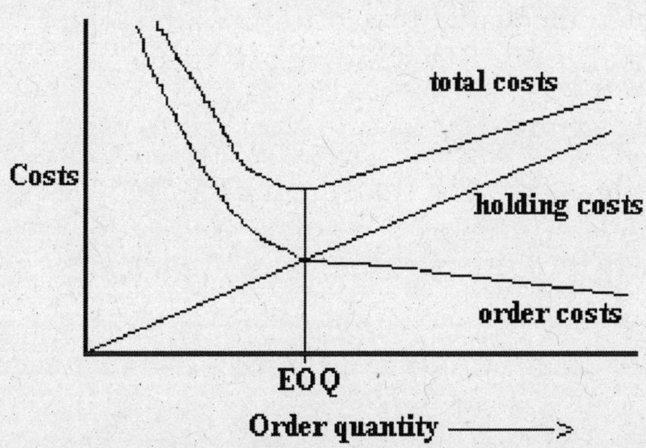

Fig. 8.2

The EOQ is found at the lowest point on the total cost curve. Here the order size optimises the cost of stockholding with the cost of acquisition. The equation is:

EOQ = Square Root ((2 S × D)/C)

For example, in a company where order cost is estimated at Rs. 10 and with a holding cost of 25% of item value if annual demand is 1000 units at a supply price of Rs. 36, if we substitute these figures in the EOQ formula then the EOQ is (47.1) 48 units.

EOQ ASSUMPTIONS

- Demand (units of supply) is known and steady so average inventory can be estimated.
- Quantity discounts do not apply - the effect of buying discount/price breaks needs to be calculated additionally.
- Orders arrive in one batch with a known lead time arriving just as stock is exhausted
- Some order placement/receiving costs are independent of order quantity, others are dependent.
- Economies or diseconomies of scale do not apply to holding stock.

So, as per assumptions, orders must be placed at a reordering point before the inventory is completely depleted, with sufficient time for the ordered quantity to be shipped and delivered by the supplier (i.e. the time it takes to receive the order is called lead time).

The inventory level must be reviewed on a continuous basis. This is generally the case when we are considering relatively expensive items. When the items are relatively inexpensive, the inventory manager may often review the inventory level every fixed time period, like once a month, and then place an order based on that level.

To avoid lost sales due to stock outs, a company must maintain a safety stock so that it is never completely out of inventory. This implies ordering ahead of the reordering point. For seasonal sales, in addition to safety stock it is advisable to adjust EOQ upwards for both anticipated higher demand and longer lead-time at season's peak demands. Such inventory planning is strictly a concern of middle level management. Though this managerial task cannot be even delegated to accountants, but the task can be eased by software that computes automatically EOQ and safety stocks.

SPORADIC USAGE INVENTORY

In many large organisations, roughly half of the stocked products have sporadic usage – that is, they are not sold or used on a regular, predictable basis. In other words, a firm has no idea when they will be sold or used. We can divide the total inventory into three categories:

(a) ***Dead Inventory:*** Inventory with no sales or recurring transfers during the last year.

(b) ***Slow-Moving Inventory:*** Inventory with a very low turnover is termed as slow moving inventory for example, inventory having less than one and a half turns a year.

(c) ***Other Items:*** This is normal or good inventory whose turnover is more than one and a half times per year.

Dead and slow moving inventory constitutes the sporadic usage inventory. Sporadic usage items are not used or sold on a predictable basis, so it is very difficult to calculate an average investment for these items. Therefore, a firm has to consider an estimated value of sporadic inventory items to be equal to the target stock level quantity times the average cost. It is true that a firm may occasionally use some of the stock of sporadic items, so the value of the target inventory will overstate the average value of some items. But this is the most accurate method known so far of determining the value of sporadic inventory items.

BUDGETED INVENTORY INVESTMENT

Most business firms spend a lot of time developing sales projections and budgets for expenses. Each month these forecasts are compared to actual sales and expenses. If sales are lower, or expenses higher than the projections, management takes corrective action to ensure that the company remains profitable.

Budgets are good management tools. Unfortunately, a few business firms maintain budgets and projections for inventory. It is critical to the success of an inventory management system, to develop a budget for the value of stocked inventory maintained in each warehouse. This provides the budgeted inventory investment. To calculate budgeted inventory investment, we use a variation of the formula used to calculate inventory turnover:

Budgeted Inventory Investment

$$= \frac{\text{Projected Annual Cost of Goods sold from Stock Sales}}{\text{Budgeted Inventory Turnover}}$$

Let us look at an example which illustrates how increased stock turnover leads to lower inventory investment:

Budgeted Annual Sales	*Budgeted Inventory Turnover*	*Budgeted Inventory Investment*	*Saving in Inventory Investment*
Rs. 20000000	5.0	Rs. 4000000	Current Inventory
Rs. 20000000	5.1	Rs. 3921569	Rs. 78431
Rs. 20000000	5.2	Rs. 3846154	Rs. 153846
Rs. 20000000	6.0	Rs. 3333333	Rs. 666667

It is quite clear from the figures in the above table that the increase in inventory turnover results in a continuous decrease in inventory investment. As the target inventory turnover of six is obtained, target inventory investment comes down to Rs. 3333333 (Rs. 20000000/6 turns).

To reduce the overall inventory investment to meet turnover goals, a firm should reduce dead stock and slow-moving items. The manager must realize that if an item is not selling, it does not contribute to generating the profits and is an expense for the business. However, there are some valid reasons to maintain an inventory of items that do not currently sell on a regular basis. This may include the item that might be a repair part or other item that a business must have on hand to handle customer emergencies or it may be an item in which the firm has invested in today, to receive profits in the future. Whatever the case may be, a firm must control the amount of dead stock and slow-moving inventory in order to enhance profitability.

Chapter 9

FINANCIAL ANALYSIS

(**Contents:** Introduction, 1. Ratio Analysis – a) Liquidity Ratios: Current Ratio, Working Capital, Acid Test or Quick Ratio, Cash Ratio, b) Solvency Ratios: Leverage, Debt to Assets Ratio, Loan Capital Ratio, Total Debt to Equity Ratio, Interest Coverage Ratio, Debt Service Coverage Ratio (DSCR), Long-term Debt to Net Working Capital Ratio, c) Profitability Ratios: Net Profit Ratio, Gross Profit Ratio, Return on Assets (ROA), Return on Equity (ROE), Return on Investment (ROI), d) Efficiency Ratios: Net Working Capital Turnover Ratio, Total Asset Turnover Ratio, Inventory Turnover Ratio, Accounts Payable Ratios, Accounts Receivable Ratios, 2. Common Size Analysis, 3. Operating Cycle and Net operating cycle, 4. SWOT Analysis: Internal Analysis, External Analysis, 5. Trends in Earning Per Share (EPS) and Price to Earnings (P/E), 6. Economic Value Added (EVA).)

"If we can really understand the problem, the answer will come out of it, because the answer is not separate from the problem".

— J. Krishnamurti

INTRODUCTION

Financial analysis is a key to business success. It provides a means of assessing a firm's strengths and weaknesses. The major goal of any financial analysis is the identification of major changes in the trends, investigation of the reasons underlying those changes, and the inter-relationships in the relevant variables. The judgement process can be improved by experience and the use of analytical tools. Among the most widely used financial analysis technique is the ratio analysis. Using data from the balance sheet and income statement, various ratios can be calculated, which can be compared directly to those of competing firms of varying sizes. Comparing the firm's operating results with those of specific competitors or the industry as a whole helps identify relative strengths and weaknesses. In addition, comparing changes in a firm's ratios over time can highlight improvements in performance or problem areas needing attention.

This chapter focuses on the major traditional and modern financial analysis tools as follows:

1. Ratio Analysis
2. Common Size Analysis
3. Operating Cycle and Net operating cycle
4. SWOT Analysis
5. Trends in Earning per Share (EPS) and Price to Earnings (P/E)
6. Economic Value Added (EVA)

Following is the detailed description of each financial analysis tool.

1. RATIO ANALYSIS

Financial ratio analysis is the calculation and comparison of ratios which are derived from the information in a company's financial statements. A financial ratio is a mathematical comparison between two or more items from a firm's Income Statement/ Profit and Loss Account or Balance Sheet. In other words, ratio analysis is a way of reviewing inter-relationships between different items or accounts. The level and historical trends of these ratios can be used to make inferences about a company's financial condition, its operations and attractiveness as an investment. Although a single ratio is not likely to be useful, it becomes meaningful when compared to prior periods, or averages for comparable firms in context with other ratios.

Financial ratios are usually expressed in percentage or times. The financial ratios are calculated for the purpose of evaluating aspects of a company's operations, progress of the business, uncover trends, and point to potential problem areas. Bankers and investors often analyze these numbers to decide if they want to lend money or invest in the company.

Financial ratios can be categorized as following:

(a) Liquidity Ratios

(b) Solvency/Leverage Ratios

(c) Profitability Ratios

(d) Efficiency or Turnover Ratios

Liquidity ratios measure a firm's ability to meet its *short-term* obligations. Solvency *ratios* measure the degree of protection of suppliers of long-term funds, the degree of leverage, and can also aid in judging a firm's ability to raise additional debt and its capacity to pay its liabilities on time. *Profitability ratios* measure management's ability to earn a return on the resources committed to the business. *Efficiency or turnover ratios* provide information about management's ability to control expenses and to earn a return on the resources committed to the business. These Liquidity, Solvency, Profitability, and Efficiency Ratios allow the analyst to identify trends in a business and to compare its progress with the performance of others through data published by various sources. The analyst may thus determine the business's relative strengths and weaknesses.

Given the large quantity of variables included in financial statements, a very long list of meaningful ratios can be derived. A standard list of ratios or standard computation of them does not exist. The following ratio presentation includes ratios that are most often used in evaluating the financial strength of a business firm.

(a) Liquidity Ratios

In order to stay in business, a firm should be able to pay its obligations as they become due even when profits are low and cash flows are tight. To do this a firm has to maintain some reserves that can be used to cover cash flow deficits in the short-run. These reserves can either be cash or they can be a line of credit. The availability of credit hinges in part on whether a firm has the ability to come up with some cash within a year. This ability to come up with cash quickly is known as liquidity. A firm is said to be 'liquid' if it has the ability to raise the cash that is needed to pay all financial obligations coming due.

(i) Current Ratio: The Current Ratio is one of the most popular measures of financial strength. This ratio provides an indication of the liquidity of the business by comparing the amount of current assets to current liabilities. A business's current assets generally consist of cash, marketable securities, accounts receivable, and inventories. Current liabilities include accounts payable, current maturities of long-term debt, accrued income taxes, and other accrued expenses that are due within one year. This measure of liquidity reflects how many current assets are available per rupee of current liability. In general, businesses prefer to have at least one rupee of current assets for every rupee of current liabilities. At a minimum one wants this ratio to be equal to 1. A value of 1.25 or greater is desirable for this ratio. However, the normal current ratio fluctuates from industry to industry. A current ratio significantly higher than the industry average could indicate the existence of redundant assets. Conversely, a current ratio significantly lower than the industry average could indicate a lack of liquidity. A current ratio of 2:1 or higher is looked upon well. This ratio indicates that the firm is able to meet all debts and if the business gets in trouble, they can liquidate the firm's assets and get their money back. It is calculated as below:

$$\text{Current Ratio} = \frac{\text{Total Current Assets}}{\text{Total Current Liabilities}}$$

A generally acceptable current ratio is 2 to 1. But whether or not a specific ratio is satisfactory depends on the nature of the business and the characteristics of its current assets and liabilities.

(ii) Working Capital: As stated time and again, Working Capital is simply the amount that current assets exceed current liabilities. Working capital is computed as follows:

Working Capital = Current Assets – Current Liabilities

This formula is very similar to the current ratio. The only difference is that it gives us a rupee amount rather than a ratio. It, too, is calculated to determine a firm's ability to pay its short-term obligations. Working capital compares current assets to current liabilities, and serves as the liquid reserve available to satisfy contingencies and uncertainties. A high working capital balance is maintained if the business firm is unable to borrow on short notice. The ratio indicates the short-term solvency of a business and in determining if a firm can pay its current liabilities when due.

Working Capital can be viewed as somewhat of a security blanket. This financial measure indicates the amount of money needed to cover all of the debts and liabilities due within a year. The greater the amount of working capital, the more security an investor can have that the company will be able to meet its financial obligations. Therefore, the more investment a business has in working capital, the greater is its ability to make current payments. Thus it is desirable to have positive balance of working capital.

(iii) Acid Test or Quick Ratio: Quick Ratio measures how well a company can pay its debts without selling inventory. It is same as the current ratio except it takes inventories out of the analysis. A quick ratio above 1.0 generally indicates the company can meet its obligations. The purpose of this ratio is to test the firm's ability to meet its current obligations. Like current ratio, it is a measurement of the liquidity position of the business. The quick ratio compares the cash plus cash equivalents and accounts receivable to the current liabilities. The primary difference between the current ratio and the quick ratio is the quick ratio does not include inventory and prepaid expenses in the calculation. Consequently, a business's quick ratio will be lower than its current ratio. It is a stringent test of liquidity.

$$\text{Quick Ratio} = \frac{\text{Quick Assets}}{\text{Current Liabilities}}$$

$$\text{or } \frac{\text{Cash} + \text{Marketable Securities} + \text{Accounts Receivable}}{\text{Current Liabilities}}$$

Quick assets are total current assets minus inventory and pre-paid expenses. The quick ratio (or acid-test ratio) is found by dividing quick assets by current liabilities. This test does not include inventory to make it a stiffer test of the company's liquidity. It tells if the business can meet its current obligations with quickly convertible assets should sales revenue suddenly cease.

(iv) Cash Ratio: Cash ratio is a better indicator of liquidity than the Acid test ratio. If there is a considerable delay in the collection of accounts receivable, then the acid test ratio will not be useful. Ultimately, cash is required to discharge the current obligations. That is why; cash ratio is also termed as Absolute liquidity ratio. It indicates a conservative view of liquidity such as when a company has pledged its receivables and its inventory, or the analyst suspects severe liquidity problems with inventory and receivables.

$$\text{Cash Ratio} = \frac{\text{Cash Equivalents}}{\text{Cash Liabilities}}$$

Where, cash equivalents consist of short-term, highly liquid investments such as treasury bills, commercial papers, and money market instruments. The ideal cash ratio is 1:2.

(b) Solvency Ratios

Solvency relates to the ability of a business firm to pay-off all of its financial obligations. By definition a business is solvent when it has enough money from the sale of assets to pay all its debts and liabilities. The survival and continuity of a business depends whether it is able to stay solvent. As a business increases its assets relative to debt it becomes more solvent and more likely to survive over time. Conversely a business' existence becomes increasingly less certain as the business becomes less certain.

The availability of credit for a firm depends on how much cash flow the business can generate and how much of the cash flow is available for servicing debt. As more cash is available for servicing debt, more credit is available. Conversely credit resources diminish as cash flows become tight. The company should monitor its credit activities and have an idea of how much credit it can afford to borrow. A company can do this by monitoring its repayment capacity and coverage margin.

(i) Leverage: Leverage is a ratio that measures a company's capital structure. In other words, it measures how a company finances its assets. This ratio measures who has the major stake in the business — shareholders or debenture holders. Do the firm is strictly on equity? Or, it is using a combination of equity and debt? The answers to these questions are of great importance to investors. The formula for leverage is as follows:

$$\text{Leverage} = \frac{\text{Long-term Debt}}{\text{Total Equity}}$$

A firm that finances its assets with a high percentage of debt takes the risk of bankruptcy in case it is unable to make its debt payments. A firm with a lower percentage of debt has a bigger safety cushion because of less fixed charge. Another drawback of being highly leveraged is the unwillingness of lenders to provide more debt financing. In this case, a firm that finds itself in a financial crisis may have to issue stock on unfavourable terms. So, a company being highly leveraged is generally viewed as being disadvantageous due to the increased risk of bankruptcy, higher borrowing costs, and decreased financial flexibility. On the other hand, using debt financing has advantages. Stockholder's potential return on their investment is greater when a firm borrows more. Borrowing also has some tax advantages also.

From an investor's viewpoint, the optimal capital structure for a company depends on the type of investor. A bondholder would prefer a company with very little debt financing because of the lower risk inherent in this type of capital structure. A stockholder would probably opt for a higher percentage of debt than the bondholder in a firm's capital structure. Yet, a company that is highly leveraged is also very risky for a stockholder.

When a firm becomes over leveraged, bankruptcy[1] can result.

(ii) Debt to Assets Ratio: The Debt to Assets Ratio is probably the easiest to understand. It is calculated by dividing total debt by total assets, as shown in the Balance Sheet. The higher the debt, higher will be the ratio. A good ratio is 1:2 or 50%. Anything over 2.0 and is not desirable and indicates less asset base in comparison to debt liability. This ratio provides information about the company's ability to absorb asset reductions arising from losses without jeopardizing the interest of creditors. This ratio is a commonly used measure of solvency that reflects how much debt (liability) a business has per rupee of asset. A high value for this ratio is an indication a business is an aggressive user of debt and approaching insolvency.

It is computed as follows:

$$\text{Debt to Assets Ratio} = \frac{\text{Total Debt}}{\text{Total Assets}}$$

Lenders look at this ratio when they are evaluating the credit worthiness of the borrower. Whenever the debt to asset ratio rises above 0.75, lenders tend to be hesitant to approve additional credit to a borrower. Thus, a business firm should attempt to keep this ratio from rising much above 0.75.

(iii) Loan Capital Ratio: Loan Capital Ratio is also known as capitalization ratio. This ratio indicates long-term debt usage or the ratio of long-term loans to total capitalization. A high Loan Capital Ratio indicates too much dependence of the company on outside borrowings. It is calculated as follows:

$$\text{Loan Capital Ratio} = \frac{\text{Long Term Loans}}{\text{Long-term Loans} + \text{Owners Equity}}$$

(iv) Total Debt to Equity Ratio: The total debt to equity ratio measures how much debt a company is using to finance its operations. If this number is too high it may signify future liquidity problems. If this number is too low it can signify inefficient use of the financing alternatives available to a company. This ratio is calculated by taking the total debt of a company and dividing it by the shareholders' equity. The analyst should make sure to include the company's lease and other fixed interest obligations when calculating long-term debt.

It is calculated as follows:

$$\text{Total Debt to Equity ratio} = \frac{\text{Total Debt}}{\text{Total Equity}}$$

1. Business Policy, Text and Cases, Edmund P. Learned, C. Roland Christansen, Kenneth Andrews and William D. Guth, Havewood, IL: Irwing 1969.

A ratio of more than 2:1 is not generally favoured by the stakeholders. Debt includes not only debentures issued by the company but it also include all fixed interest bearing securities issued by the company. It is very important that a company should maintain a proper balance between its equity and debt. The capital structure of a company should not be highly geared with debt. It indicates how well creditors are protected in case of the company's insolvency.

Start up companies which have access to the debt markets, often have higher ratios than more established companies. In addition, the amount of debt a company can safely issue varies by industry. For example, companies with large manufacturing facilities often have more long-term debt than companies that provide services or software. Therefore, it is useful to look at the ratios of numerous companies in the same industry before drawing any conclusions.

(v) Interest Coverage Ratio: This ratio measures a company's capacity to meet interest obligations. In this ratio attempts to find out as to what extent the net profits earned will cover fixed charges or interest payments. This ratio is also known as Fixed Charge Coverage Ratio. Net profits for the calculation of this ratio means Earnings Before Interest and Taxes (EBIT). The satisfactory interest coverage ratio is 6 to 7 times. Following is the formula for the calculation of this ratio:

$$\text{Interest Coverage Ratio} = \frac{\text{EBIT}}{\text{Interest / Fixed Charges}}$$

(vi) Debt Service Coverage Ratio (DSCR): This ratio is on the lines of interest coverage ratio. This ratio measures the company's ability to meet not only the interest obligations but also the periodical payments of the principal amount of the debt. To calculate the debt service coverage ratio, divide the net operating income (NOI) by the debt payments as follows:

$$\text{DSCR} = \frac{\text{Net Operating Income (NOI)}}{\text{Total Debt Service}}$$

Total Debt Service includes the principal and interest payments of all loans. It should be noted that taxes and insurance are not to be included in the debt service, as they have already been accounted for when we arrived at net operating income (NOI). Obviously the higher the DSCR, the more net operating income is available to service the debt. From a lender's viewpoint it should be clear that they want as high a DSCR as possible.

The borrower, on the other hand, wants as large a loan as possible. The larger the loan, the higher the debt service. If the net operating income remains the same, and the loan size and therefore the debt service increases, then the DSCR will fall, which is not a good sign.

A DSCR of 1.0 is called a break-even cash flow. That is because the net operating income (NOI) is just enough to cover the debt payments. A DSCR of less than 1.0 would be a situation where there would actually be a negative cash flow. A DSCR of say .95 would mean that there is only enough net operating income (NOI) to cover 95% of the debt payment. This would mean that the borrower company would have to come up with cash out of other sources/projects every month to keep the project afloat.

(vii) Long-Term Debt to Net Working Capital Ratio: Long-term Debt is employed in the business to improve profitability (as debt is a low cost source of finance) and to have overall financial soundness. This ratio computes the proportion of working capital in relation to long-term debt. In other words, this ratio provides insight into the ability to pay long-term debt from current assets after paying current liabilities. The formula for the calculation of this ratio is as below:

$$\text{Long-term Debt to Net Working Capital Ratio: } \frac{\text{Long-term Debt}}{\text{Current Assets - Current Liabilities}}$$

(c) Profitability Ratios

A central objective of a business is to generate profits using the limited capital resources available at a given point in time. Businesses are continually assessing their profitability and trying to determine if they are doing as well as they could be in terms of generating profits. Profitability ratios show the effectiveness of the company by the returns from investments and sales. Profit margin measures how much a company earns relative to its sales. A company with a higher profit margin than its competitor can be termed as more efficient.

Following are the ratios that reflect the profitability of a business.

(i) Net Profit Ratio: This ratio is a measure of how much of a return to assets a business is able to generate per rupee of total income. The higher the value of this ratio the greater the likelihood that there will be profits. This is a measure of overall profitability of a business firm. This measure of net income rupees generated by each rupee of sales can be calculated as below.

$$\text{Net Profit Ratio} = \frac{\text{Net Income from operations}}{\text{Net Sales}}$$

Low net profit margins can result when there is a little difference between the selling price and per unit cost of production. Thus low net profit margins can be a sign that the cost of production is too high and/or the selling price for output is too low.

(ii) Gross Profit Ratio: This is one of the most widely used ratios for the measurement of profitability. For better analysis this ratio should be compared with industry data. Otherwise, it may indicate excessive purchasing or high labour costs.

$$\text{Gross Profit Ratio} = \frac{\text{Gross Profit}}{\text{Net Sales}}$$

This ratio establishes the relationship between net sales revenue and the cost of goods sold. Net sales means the sum of cash and credit sales out of which sales returns are deducted. The cost of goods sold includes opening stock of goods with the firm plus the price of further purchases (less purchase returns) including direct expenses incurred for the procurement of raw material less closing stock at the end of the year. The figure of cost of goods sold is deducted from the sales to arrive at the figure of gross profit.

(iii) Return on Assets (ROA): This ratio reflects the earnings that are generated per each rupee of asset or in other words this ratio measures the company's ability to utilize its assets to create profits.

$$\text{ROA} = \frac{\text{Net Income from operations}}{\text{Average Total Assets}}$$

$$\text{Where, Average Total Assets} = \frac{(\text{Beginning} + \text{Closing Total Assts})}{2}$$

A high ROA is preferred to a low one because the profitability of a business typically increases as ROA rises. Thus a high ROA is generally a sign of good management while a low ROA is a possible indication of inefficiency in the system. At a minimum, the ROA needs to be higher than the interest rate paid on debt if a business is to be able to use credit profitably. If a business interest rate on debt is greater than the ROA, the business might want to consider its use of credit.

(iv) Return on Equity (ROE): This ratio is a measure of the profit that a business earns per each rupee of equity (net worth) that is invested in the business or in other words, it measures the income earned on the shareholder's investment in the business.

$$\text{ROE} = \frac{\text{Net Income from operations}}{\text{Equity Capital}}$$

High values for ROE are an indication of profitability and good management. Alternatively low values for this ratio are generally signs of poor management. At a minimum one would expect the ROE to be greater than zero. A ROE equal to the rate of inflation is desirable because this is a sign that a business is at least keeping up with inflation. In the best cases a business will have an ROE that equals or exceeds the ROA.

(v) Return on Investment (ROI): On the lines of ROE and ROA, ROI can be calculated. This ratio measures the income earned on the invested capital. The ROI is the most important ratio of all. It is the percentage of return on funds invested in the business by its owners. In short, this ratio tells the owner whether or not all the effort put into the business has been productive. If the ROI is less than the rate of return on an alternative, risk-free investment such as a bank savings account, the investors may put the money in such savings instruments. The ROI is calculated as follows:

$$\text{ROI} = \frac{\text{Net Income from operations}}{\text{Long-term Liabilities} + \text{Equity Capital}}$$

(d) Efficiency Ratios

A business firm's profitability is very much determined by its financial efficiency. Firms that are able to achieve high levels of efficiency tend to be the most profitable while inefficient firms typically suffer losses and go out of business over time. A firm is said to be efficient when it is able to produce maximum income per rupee of expenditure or expense. There are generally two ways a farm business achieves efficiency. One is to adopt operating procedures that result in minimum costs per unit of output. The other is to maximize production or output per rupee invested in assets. These ratios are very useful in determining a business' overall financial efficiency.

(i) Net Working Capital Turnover Ratio: This ratio measures the number of times the working capital is turned over during the year. In a way this ratio also throws light on the duration of operating cycle (conversion of current assets into cash) of the company. A low ratio indicates slow moving operating cycle and it is a sign of inefficiency. Whereas a high level implies that the company's current assets are being utilized efficiently.

$$\text{Net Working Capital Turnover Ratio} = \frac{\text{Net Sales}}{\text{Average Working Capital}}$$

(ii) Total Asset Turnover Ratio: Measures the activity of the assets and the ability of the business to generate sales through the use of the assets. In other words, this ratio measures how productively the firm is managing all of its assets to generate Sales. When comparing Total Assets Turnover Ratios of different firms it is important to note that the values for Fixed Assets reported on the firms' Balance Sheets are book values which can be very different from market values. This ratio is calculated by dividing sales by average total assets as follows:

$$\text{Total Asset Turnover Ratio} = \frac{\text{Net Sales}}{\text{Average Total Assets}}$$

(iii) Inventory Turnover Ratio: Inventory turnover ratio measures the liquidity of the inventory in a manufacturing firm by establishing the relationship between the cost of goods sold and the average inventory. This ratio finds out the number of times inventory is turned over on an average in a year. The inventory may include raw material, work in progress and finished products. The objective of calculating this ratio is to find out to what extent the inventory has been utilized efficiently and what proportion of working capital has been locked up in inventory. Average inventory is computed by dividing the sum of opening and closing inventory by 2. The formula for this is as follows:

$$\text{Inventory Turnover Ratio} = \frac{\text{Cost of Goods Sold}}{\text{Average Inventory}}$$

Inventory Turnover in Days: This ratio is another version, with small variation, of inventory turnover ratio. This indicates the liquidity of the inventory in days. This ratio is also known as Inventory Conversion Period.

$$\text{Inventory Turnover Ratio} = \frac{\text{Average Inventory}}{\text{Cost of Goods Sold}/360}$$

Here, 360 refer to the number of days in a year.

Accounts Payable Ratios

(iv) Accounts Payable Turnover Ratio: This ratio measures the number of times creditors are discharged during the year. Or in other words, it indicates the liquidity of the firm's payables. A high payable turnover ratio indicates that the creditors' bills are discharged in a shorter period. The higher the turnover, the shorter is the time between purchase and payment. A low turnover may indicate that there is a shortage of cash to pay bills or some other reason for a delay in payment. The formula for this ratio is as follows:

$$\text{Payable Turnover Ratio} = \frac{\text{Purchases}}{\text{Average Accounts Payable}}$$

Accounts Payable Turnover in Days

This ratio indicates the liquidity of the firm's accounts payables in days.

$$\text{Payables Turnover Ratio (in days)} = \frac{\text{Average Accounts Payable}}{\text{Purchases}/360}$$

(v) **Accounts Payable to Sales Ratio:** This ratio is obtained by dividing the Accounts Payables of a company by its Annual Net Sales. This ratio gives an indication as to how much of the suppliers' money does the company use in order to fund its Sales. Higher the ratio means that the company is using its suppliers as a source of cheap financing. The working capital of such companies is funded by its suppliers.

$$\text{Accounts Payable to Sales Ratio} = \frac{\text{Accounts Payables}}{\text{Net Sales}}$$

Accounts Receivable Ratios

(vi) **Accounts Receivable Turnover Ratio:** Accounts Receivable Turnover ratio measures the number of times per year a company completely clears all of its outstanding debt. This ratio indicates the average period for which sales revenue will be held in accounts receivable. This measures the efficiency and effectiveness of receivables collection. The higher the number the better it is. This number indicates the liquidity of the company's receivables by measuring how many times a firm's receivables are turned into cash during the year. This ratio is obtained by dividing the net sales on credit by the average receivable for the year.

$$\text{Accounts Receivable Turnover Ratio} = \frac{\text{Net Sales}}{\text{Average Gross Receivables}}$$

This number of time figure (turnover ratio) can be divided into 360 (number of days in a year) to determine the average number of days being taken to collect a receivable. This measure is known as Average collection period.

$$\text{So, Average Collection Period} = \frac{360}{\text{Accounts Receivable Turnover}}$$

(vii) **Days' Sales in Receivable (DSO):** This ratio, also known as *Receivable Turnover in Days,* determines how many days' worth of sales are still uncollected. This ratio indicates the average time in days that receivables are outstanding (DSO). It helps determine if a change in receivables is due to a change in sales, or to another factor such as a change in selling terms. An analyst may compare the days' sales in receivables with the company's credit terms as an indication of how efficiently the company manages its receivables. It is derived by dividing the accounts receivable balance by the average sales per day (which is sales divided by 360). A DSO of 25 to 30 is usually a good benchmark. Following is the formula for this:

$$DSO = \frac{\text{Gross Receivables}}{\text{Annual Net Sales}/360}$$

(viii) Bad Debt to Accounts Receivable Ratio: Bad debt to Accounts Receivable ratio measures expected uncollectibility on credit sales. An increase in bad debts is a negative sign, since it indicates greater realization risk in accounts receivable and possible future write-offs.

$$\text{Bad debt to Accounts Receivable Ratio} = \frac{\text{Bad Debts}}{\text{Accounts Receivable}}$$

(ix) Bad-Debt to Sales Ratio: This expresses the percentage of credit sales that were written off to bad debt. An increase in bad debts is a negative sign, since it indicates greater realization risk in accounts receivable and possible write-offs. *A lower percentage signifies that effective credit policies and procedures are employed.*

$$\text{Bad-Debt to Sales Ratio} = \frac{\text{Bad Debts}}{\text{Credit Sales}}$$

Helping in this analysis is the figure of Previous Month's Overdue Collected. *This percentage expresses the amount that has been collected in the current month of the prior month's past due amount. This is calculated as follows:*

$$1 - \frac{\text{Current Month's Past Due Age Categories}}{\text{Beginning Receivables of Prior Month}}$$

The performance measures related to Accounts Receivable are discussed in detail in the Chapter: Advances in Receivable Management.

2. COMMON SIZE ANALYSIS

In vertical analysis of financial statements, an item is used as a base value and all other accounts in the financial statement are compared to this base value.

On the balance sheet, total assets equal 100% and each asset is stated as a percentage of total assets. Similarly, total liabilities and stockholder's equity are assigned 100%, with a given liability or equity account stated as a percentage of total liabilities and stockholder's equity.

On the Income Statement/Profit and Loss Account, 100% is assigned to net sales, with all revenue and expense accounts then related to it.

3. OPERATING CYCLE AND NET OPERATING CYCLE

Investment in working capital is influenced by the major events in the production and sales cycle. These events are — Purchase of raw materials, Payment for purchase, sale of finished goods on credit, and collection of cash for the sales made. The period between purchase of raw materials and production of finished goods is known as the inventory period. The period between sale of finished goods and the collection of receivables is known as the accounts receivable period. The time duration of operating cycle indicates the time between the acquisition of inventory and the realization of cash from sales of inventory. Usually the operating cycle is less than one year, but in some industries it can be longer. It is calculated as follows:

Operating Cycle in Days =

Receivable Turnover in Days + Inventory Turnover in Days - Payables Turnover in Days

Regular measurement of the operating cycle, which determines the short-term financing requirements of the business, enables the company to monitor its working capital performance against targets and identify areas for improvement.

Net Operating Cycle

Net operating cycle, also known as Cash conversion cycle, indicates how cash is moving throughout a company in terms of duration. The time lag between the purchase of raw materials and the collection of cash for sales is referred to as the operating cycle for the company. The time lag between the payment for raw materials purchases and the collection of cash from sales is referred to as the net operating cycle or cash conversion cycle.

This ratio is vital because the cycle represents the number of days a firm's cash remains tied up within the operations of the business. It is calculated as follows:

Net Operating Cycle or Cash Conversion Cycle = Average Inventory Collection Period + Average Receivable Collection Period - Average Payable Period

The cash conversion cycle, or net operating cycle, simply indicates the duration of time it takes the firm to convert its activities requiring cash into cash returns. This ratio is vital since it represents the number of days a firm's cash is occupied with its operations. In finding the cash conversion cycle, the analyst should pay attention to the trend of its three general components i.e. Inventory Collection Period, Receivables Collection Period and Payables Period, with special emphasis on the payables processing period. Sometimes shorter processing periods for inventory and/or receivables can be largely offset by increases in the processing period for accounts payables. The processing period for accounts payables will increase if the firm is paying its creditors and suppliers at a slower rate. However, an understanding of each of the three components can help pinpoint the trend not only in the cash conversion cycle but also in the individual processing periods themselves. Naturally, a firm wants its cash conversion cycle to be as short as possible. Therefore, a downward trend in this cycle is a positive signal while an upward trend is a negative signal.

If the firm reduces the average age of its inventories, it might shorten the cash conversion cycle. With the smaller average inventories which might result, the possibility of stockouts and subsequent lost sales could increase. There is a somewhat inverse relationship between average inventory age and level of sales, i.e., as inventory age decreases, possibility of lost sales increases, and vice versa. When the cash conversion cycle shortens, cash becomes free for other uses such as investing in new capital, spending on equipment and infrastructure, as well as preparing for possible share buy-backs etc. On the other hand, when the cash conversion cycle lengthens, cash remains tied up in the firm's core operations, leaving little freedom for other uses of this cash flow.

4. SWOT ANALYSIS

Using the SWOT[1] approach requires an internal survey of strengths and weaknesses of the firm and an external market survey of threats and opportunities. The external environment has a profound impact on a business firm. Recent shifts from an industrial to information based society and from a manufacturing to a service-oriented economy have significantly influenced the business conditions and environment. Existing products and services, and those planned for the future irrespective of the type of industry, should be based on a careful consideration of future trends in society.

SWOT (Strengths, Weaknesses, Opportunities, and Threats) is a simple, easy to understand technique. It can be used in formulating strategies and policies for the business manager. However, it is by no means an end in itself. SWOT analysis can be simply understood as the examination of an organisation's internal strengths and weaknesses, and its environments, opportunities, and threats. It is a tool useful in the preliminary stages of decision-making and as a pre-requisite to strategic planning. If properly applied, a firm gets an overall picture of its present situation in relation to its competitors, and the industries its customers may enter. Understanding of the external factors for threats and opportunities, along with an internal examination of strengths and weaknesses assists in forming a vision of the future.

SWOT analysis is a simple framework for generating strategic alternatives from a situation analysis. It is applicable to either the corporate level or the business unit level and frequently appears in marketing plans. SWOT analysis is useful when a very limited amount of time is available to address a complex strategic situation.

The internal and external situation analysis can produce a large amount of information. Although, much of that information may not be highly relevant. The SWOT analysis can serve as an interpretative filter to reduce the information to a manageable quantity of key issues. The SWOT analysis classifies the internal aspects of the company as strengths or weaknesses and the external situational factors as opportunities or threats. Strengths can serve as a foundation for building a competitive advantage, and weaknesses may hinder it. By understanding these four aspects of its situation, a firm can better utilize its strengths, overcome its weaknesses, capitalize on opportunities, and face threats.

Internal Analysis

The internal analysis is a comprehensive evaluation of the internal environment's potential strengths and weaknesses. Factors should be evaluated across the organisation in areas such as:

- Company culture
- Company image

- Organisational structure
- Key staff
- Access to natural resources
- Position on the experience curve
- Operational efficiency
- Operational capacity
- Brand awareness
- Market share
- Financial resources
- Exclusive contracts
- Patents and trade secrets

The SWOT analysis summarizes the internal factors of the firm as a list of strengths and weaknesses.

External Analysis

An opportunity is the chance to introduce a new product or service that can generate superior returns. Opportunities can arise when changes occur in the external environment. Many of these changes can be perceived as threats to the market position of existing products and may necessitate a change in product specifications or the development of new products in order for the firm to remain competitive. Changes in the external environment may be related to:

- Customers
- Competitors
- Market trends
- Suppliers
- Partners
- Social changes
- New technology
- Economic environment
- Political and regulatory environment

The SWOT analysis summarizes the external environmental factors as a list of opportunities and threats. When the analysis has been completed, a SWOT profile can be generated and used as the basis of goal setting, strategy formulation, and implementation.

While useful for reducing a large quantity of situational factors into a more manageable profile, the SWOT framework has a tendency to oversimplify the situation by classifying the firm's environmental factors into categories in which they may not always fit. The classification of some factors as strengths or weaknesses, or as opportunities or threats is somewhat arbitrary. For example, a particular company culture can be either a strength or a weakness. A technological change can be either a threat or an opportunity. What is more important than the conceptual classification of these factors is the firm's awareness of them and its development of a strategic plan to use them to its advantage. In order to be most effectively used, a SWOT analysis needs to be flexible. Situations change with the passage of time and an updated analysis should be made frequently. SWOT is neither cumbersome nor time-consuming and is effective because of its simplicity. Used creatively, SWOT can form a foundation upon which to construct numerous strategic plans for the business firms.

5. TRENDS IN EARNING PER SHARE (EPS) AND PRICE TO EARNINGS (P/E)

Earning per share is simply the earning available for common stockholder/number of shares of common stock outstanding. Since earnings increase equity, and increased equity increases investors' value in the form of a higher market price, EPS is a very popular indicator for measuring financial growth of a share. EPS is computed by taking profit after tax and dividing it by number of shares issued as paid-up capital.

EPS is defined as below:

$$\text{EPS} = \frac{\text{Net Income}}{\text{Number of common shares outstanding}}$$

EPS can be directly computed out of the official figures published by the company. Investors and analysts consider earning per share (EPS) as an important measure of financial performance. EPS is applied in computing price-earnings (P/E) ratio, also termed as earnings multiple. The analysis of EPS is carried out along with other financial information. The prevailing practice is that no financial analysis is considered as complete without computation of book value per share, return on shareholders' equity, sales per share and net profit margin, but these bench-marks are studied independently and in isolation, not as a framework that accurately accounts for change in EPS. No ideal EPS ratio is suggested as this ratio will fluctuate, depending upon the volume of profits available for equity shareholders. The higher the ratio, the better it is for the equity shareholders.

EPS needs to be seen as a product of book value per share and return on shareholders' equity ratio, as these reflect changes in financial position. On the other hand, EPS reflects changes in financial performance when viewed as a product of sales per share and net profit margin. Combined, the two elements of EPS offer new insight into the financials of a company.

EPS can also be expressed as follows:

Earning per share = Book value per share x Return on Shareholders' equity

Book value per share (Rs.) = Net assets / Number of shares

The Book value (or net asset value) per share shows the amount of shareholders' equity attributable to each share. Shareholders' equity comprises paid-up capital and reserves. Alternatively, shareholders' equity can also be seen as surplus of assets over liabilities (equity equals assets minus liabilities). In terms of net assets, book value per share reflects the amount of assets attributable to each share.

The return on shareholders' equity is computed herewith reference to shareholders' equity as on balance sheet date (dividends paid during the year or payable are ignored). The essence of this relationship lies in its capability for deriving any unknown variable provided the other two are known. The target return on shareholders' equity can be found by taking estimated EPS and dividing by book value per share. This knowledge can be useful in performing other analysis based on estimates of any two financial indicators.

The EPS, in its second form, can be expressed as follows-

Earning per share = Sales per share x Net profit margin

The sales per share show the amount of sales attributable to each share. This ratio reflects the impact of increase in number of shares in a given year, which would otherwise remain concealed in terms of absolute numbers.

The Net profit margin relates the profit after tax to sales. EPS and profit per share refer to the same concept but note that the standard term is 'earning per share' and not 'profit per share'. The term earnings is a broader concept than profits.

In other words, one angle of looking at EPS is as a return on book value (net assets) of a company per share; the other is to look at it as a return on sales per share.

Examining EPS figure, in pairs, as a product of book value per share and return on shareholders' equity, and as a product of sales per share and net profit margin, reveals clearly the reason for its change.

Price to Earnings (P/E)

A high Price/Earnings (PE) greater than the industry average indicates that the market expects the company to be profitable in the future. The price to earnings ratio, or P/E, is calculated by dividing the stock price by the company's earnings per share (EPS). This ratio compares the earning per share with the market price to forecast investment possibilities.

The P/E is calculated as follows:

P/E = Market Stock Price/Earning per share

For example, if a company's Earning Per Share is Rs. 1.78 and the Market Price of a share is Rs. 15.00 then the PE Ratio will be 8.43 (Rs. 15 ÷ Rs. 1.78). Therefore, the Price of the share is 8.43 times of its earning potential. Generally, if the price of the share is several times higher than the earning potential of that share, we can conclude that there is high demand for the shares. The reason for this high demand is generally attributed to the thinking of the public that the company is growing.

The P/E is a performance bench-mark that can be used as a comparison against other companies or within the stock's own historical performance. For instance, if a stock has historically run at a P/E of 40 and the current P/E is 18, the potential investor will want to explore the reasons for the drastic change. If he believes that the ratio is too low, he may want to buy the stock in anticipation of high P/E in the future. Companies with high P/E are considered as recognized by the market for their future profitable growth and a low P/E indicates the opposite.

6. ECONOMIC VALUE ADDED (EVA)

EVA, in simple words, is the gain or loss that remains after assessing a charge for the cost of all types of capital employed. What an accountant calls profits in an income statement includes a charge for the debt capital employed which is commonly referred to as interest expense. However, an income statement does not include a charge for the equity capital that was employed during the accounting period. Therefore, EVA goes beyond conventional accounting standards by including a provision for the cost of equity capital. The cost of equity needs to be factored into business investment decisions in order to enhance shareholder value.

EVA can be used as a performance measure to evaluate an overall company, a division within a company, a location within a division, or an individual manager. By setting goals, EVA can become a motivational tool at various levels of management. EVA can also be used in downsizing decisions.

EVA can help to facilitate communication thereby enhancing coordination within a company. Managers need to train to recognize the opportunity to strive for an increase in economic value added. Once properly trained, managers can then pinpoint key financial focal concerns germane to decisions. The formula to calculate EVA is as follows:

EVA = Net operating profit after taxes less the after tax cost of capital employed

The operating profit includes deductions from sales revenues for the cost of goods sold and for the operating expenses. The interest expense is then subtracted to cover the cost of the debt capital used, income taxes are then subtracted, and finally, a cost for the equity capital is subtracted from the net income after tax to obtain the EVA.

The cost of equity capital can be derived by using any one of several approaches. The simplest approach is to use the interest rate that a company can borrow at and then add a risk premium. The risk premium is added because investors require a higher return to invest in stock than they require on bonds. A typical equity risk premium is for example, about 6%, so if a company can borrow at 12% then its cost of equity capital would be 18%. There are other approaches that can be used to calculate the cost of equity capital. Two such approaches that are commonly used are the Capital Asset Pricing Model Approach and the Dividend Yield Plus Growth Rate Approach.

EVA can become a management focus at all levels. Individual unit managers may find ways to cut costs or increase revenue. Corporate managers can focus upon allocating capital to divisions, units, or profit centers that can generate higher EVAs. Managers can be rewarded or replaced based upon EVA. Perhaps a manager will take more time to consider using less capital which would create efficiency gains for a business.

However, there are potential pitfalls also. EVA can be used subjectively which could lead to faulty decisions. Finally, EVA can be subject to manipulation by individual managers seeking rewards. The purpose of EVA is to create value for the owners of a firm. If used properly it can be an effective tool in the hands of a manager.

Chapter 10

GLOSSARY OF FINANCIAL TERMS

"Understanding can overcome any situation, however mysterious or insurmountable it may appear to be".

— Norman Vincent Peale

A

ABC Approach	Inventory is subdivided into three or more groups and the groups are analyzed to determine the relationship between inventory value and quantity represented in each group.
Accounting	Process of recording and summarizing the business transactions of a firm during a period of time to find the income or loss for the period.
Accounting Policies	The concepts, conventions, rules and procedures adopted by management in preparing and presenting financial statements.
Accounts Payable	Money owed to creditors or suppliers.
Accounts Receivable	Money owed by debtors or customers.
Accounts Receivable Turnover	Gauges the number of times a business recycles each dollar invested in its accounts receivable during the year.
Accruals	Continually recurring short-term liabilities. Examples are accrued wages, accrued taxes and accrued interest.
Accrued Interest	The amount of interest owing but not paid.
After-tax Cash Flow	Total cash generated by an investment annually, defined as income after tax plus depreciation.
Agency Problem	The agency problem occurs when management places personal goals (wealth, job security, etc.) ahead of corporate goals (share price maximization). In this situation, managers may avoid risk to maintain their personal goals.
Ageing Schedule	A break-down of receivables accounts by age.
Amortization	Liquidation of an asset or a loan on an instalment basis.
Annual Report	A report, issued annually by companies to their shareholders, that contains basic financial statements as well as management's opinion of the past year's operations and future prospects.
Annuity	A series of payments of a fixed amount for a specified number of years.
Asset	Asset is a resource that a business owns to produce goods and provide services.

Asset Backed Securities	Bond or securities secured by the assets of a company.
Asset Coverage	Extent to which a company's net assets cover a particular debt obligation.
Asset Turnover	A measure of asset efficiency.
Average Collection Period	The average length of time a firm must wait after making a sale before receiving cash.
Account	In the context of book-keeping, refers to the ledger pages upon which various assets, liabilities, income, and expenses are represented.
Account Executive	An employee who handles accounting work.
Accounting Earnings	Earnings of a firm as reported on its income statement.
Accounting Exposure	The change in the value of a firm's foreign currency-denominated accounts due to a change in exchange rates.
Accounting Insolvency	Total liabilities exceed total assets. A firm with a negative net worth is insolvent on the books.
Accounting Liquidity	The quickness with which assets can be converted to cash.
Accounts Receivable Financing	A short-term financing method in which accounts receivable are collateral for cash advances.
Accounts Receivable Turnover	The ratio of net credit sales to average accounts receivable, which is a measure of how quickly customers pay their bills.
Accrual Accounting Convention	An accounting system that tries to match the recognition of revenues earned with the expenses incurred in generating those revenues.
Accrual Basis	In accounting, expenses and incomes are accounted for as they are earned or incurred, whether or not they have been received or paid.
Acquisition	When a firm buys or acquires another firm.
Ageing Schedule	A table of accounts receivable broken down into age categories (such as 0-30 days, 30-60 days, and 60-90 days), which is used to determine if customer payments are keeping close to schedule.
Automated Clearinghouse (ACH)	A computer-based clearing and settlement system, operated by a Bank, established for the

exchange of electronic transactions among participating depository institutions.

Automated Teller Machine (ATM) Automated terminals through which customers may withdraw or perform other transactions as they would through a bank teller.

B

Balance Sheet Financial statements providing the status of a company's assets, liabilities and shareholders equity on a specific date.

Banker's Acceptance A short-term credit investment created by a non-financial firm and guaranteed by a bank as to payment. Acceptances are traded at discounts to face value in the secondary market.

Bank Float Time required for processing and clearing a cheque through the banking system.

Bank Rate Bank rate is the minimum rate at which the central bank provides loans to the commercial banks. It is also called the discount rate.

Bankruptcy Inability to pay debts. A legal procedure for formally liquidating a business firm under the jurisdiction of courts of law.

Balloon Payment A large extra payment that may be charged at the end of a loan or lease.

Bear Market Any market in which prices exhibit a declining trend.

Below Par Less than the nominal or face value of a security.

Bill of Exchange A term used for a document demanding payment.

Bill of Lading A contract between an exporter and a transportation company in which the latter agrees to transport the goods under specified conditions that limit its liability. It is the exporter's receipt for the goods as well as proof that goods have been or will be received.

Black-Scholes's Model A model developed by Fischer Black and Myron Scholes in 1973 for pricing call options based on arbitrage arguments. Model uses the stock price, the exercise price, the risk-free interest rate, the time to expiration, and the expected standard deviation of the stock return.

Bond	A fixed-interest security under which the issuer contracts to pay the lender a fixed principal amount at a stated date in the future and a series of periodic interest payments.
Bootstrap	Term used to describe the start-up of a company with very little capital.
Book Value	The accounting value of an asset.
Book-keeping	The process of collecting, classifying, recording and summarizing a business's financial transactions in what are known as journals and ledgers.
Break-Even Point	Break-Even Point is the point at which sales equal costs. A firm's break-even point is the level of sales at which all fixed and variable operating costs are covered. An increase in fixed operating costs and variable operating costs will increase the operating break-even point and vice versa. An increase in the selling price per unit will decrease the operating break-even point and vice versa.
Bridge Loan	A short-term loan to cover immediate cash requirements until permanent financing is received.
Budget	A quantitative expression of a contemplated plan of action. It is useful to formulate plans, allocate resources and evaluate organisational and managerial performance.
Break-Even Point: Business Plan	Document prepared by management that summarizes the operational and financial objectives of a business and the detailed plans and budgets showing how the objectives are to be realized.
Business Risk	Business risk is the risk that the firm will be unable to cover its operating costs. Business risk along with financial risk results into the total corporate risk.
Budget Deficit	The amount by which government spending exceeds government revenues.
Bullish	Word used to describe an investor's attitude. Bullish refers to an optimistic outlook, while bearish means a pessimistic outlook.
Buyback	When a firm repurchases some of the shares trading in the market.

Buydown	A lump sum payment made to the creditor by the borrower or by a third party to reduce the amount of some or all of the consumer's periodic payments to repay the indebtedness.

C

Call	An option that gives the holder the right to buy the underlying futures contract.
Callability	Feature of a security that allows the issuer to redeem the security prior to maturity by calling it in, or forcing the holder to sell it back.
Capital	Money invested in a firm.
Capital Account	Net result of public and private international investment and lending activities.
Capital Asset	A long-term asset, such as land or a building, acquired for carrying on the business of a company with a life exceeding one year.
Capital Budget	A firm's planned capital expenditures.
Capital Budgeting	The process of selecting long-term assets for revenue generation.
Capital Gain	When an asset is sold for a profit. It is the difference between the net sales price and net cost.
Capital Investment	It refers to money invested in a business to purchase permanent assets rather than to cover day-to-day operating expenses.
Capital Market	The market for trading long-term (more than one year) instruments.
Capital Rationing	Capital rationing is a situation where a firm has only a limited amount of funds available for capital investments. In most cases, implementation of the acceptable projects would require more capital than is available. Capital rationing is common for a firm, since most firms do not have sufficient capital available to invest in all acceptable projects. In theory, capital rationing should not exist because firms should accept all projects with positive NPVs or IRRs greater than the cost of capital.
Capital Structure	The mix of the various types of debt and equity capital used by a firm.

Capitalization	Total debt and equity mix that a firm uses for funding its assets.
Capital Turnover	Annual sales divided by average stockholder equity.
Cash Asset Ratio	Cash and marketable securities divided by current liabilities.
Cash and Equivalents	The value of assets that can be converted into cash immediately, as reported by a company. This includes marketable securities and bank accounts.
Cash Budget	A forecast of a firm's expected cash inflows and cash outflows.
Cash Conversion Cycle	The cash conversion cycle (CCC) is the number of days in the firm's operating cycle (OC) minus the payable payment period for inputs to production. The CCC takes into account the time at which payment is made for material; this spontaneous form of financing partially or fully offsets the need for external financing while resources are tied up in the operating cycle.
Cash Discount	Offered by sellers to induce early payment by the purchasers. Not taking the discount involves a cost of credit for the purchaser.
Cash Equivalents	Instruments or investments of such high liquidity that they are near to cash.
Cash Management	Concerned with holding sufficient cash to meet demand and investing cash balance to maximize return.
Cash Ratio	Ratio of cash and cash equivalents to liabilities.
Cash Reserve Ratio (CRR)	All commercial banks are required to keep a certain amount of its deposits in cash with RBI. This percentage is called the cash reserve ratio.
Cash Turnover	The number of cash cycles completed in one year.
Certificate of Deposit (CD)	A certificate issued by a bank that indicates a specified sum of money has been deposited. A CD has a maturity date and a specified interest rate.
Clearinghouse	An institution where mutual claims are settled between accounts of member depository institutions.

Clearinghouse Interbank Payments System (CIPS)	An automated clearing system used primarily for international payments.
Collateral	Security that is offered to secure a loan or other credit and that becomes subject to seizure on default.
Collection Effort	The sequence of steps taken in collecting overdue accounts.
Collection Float	The period between the time a cheque is deposited in an account and the time funds are made available.
Collection Policy	Collection policy describes the procedures a firm follows in attempting to collect its accounts receivables. Collection policy has to do with only overdue accounts; it consists of letters, phone calls, personal visits, and legal actions.
Collection Ratio	The ratio of a company's accounts receivable to its average daily sales, which gives the average number of days it takes the company to convert receivables into cash.
Commercial Paper (CP)	A short-term, unsecured promissory note can be issued only by high rated, creditworthy companies in order to raise short-term funds.
Common Shares	Shares representing ownership and voting rights in a company.
Concentration Account	A centralized account into which funds collected lockboxes are transferred.
Concentration Banking	Concentration banking utilizes regionally dispersed collection centers to collect money; then receipts are deposited into nearby concentration banks from which wire transfers of funds to a central disbursing bank can be made.
Contribution Margin	Contribution of each unit sold that goes toward paying fixed costs.
Cost of Capital	The required return for a capital budgeting investment.
Credit	The promise to pay in the future.
Credit Analysis	Estimating probability of default for individual customers to determine who receives credit and at what terms.
Credit Card	A card that is repeatedly used to borrow money or buy goods and services on credit.

Credit History — A record of how an individual or company has borrowed and repaid debts.

Credit Period — Amount of time allowed for payment.

Credit Policy — It consists of credit standards, credit terms, and collection policy.

Credit Risk — Risk that a borrower may default on obligations; risk that the borrower will not settle an obligation for full value.

Credit Scoring System — A statistical system used to determine whether or not to grant credit by assigning numerical scores to various characteristics related to creditworthiness.

Credit Standards — Credit standards are used to determine whether the credit application and the amount of credit will be accepted.

Credit Terms — Credit terms are composed of the size of the cash discount, the amount of the cash discount, the credit period, and maturity date.

Creditworthiness — A creditor's measure of an individual or company's past and future ability and willingness to repay debts.

Current Assets — Assets are expected to be turned into cash within one year's time. These include cash, accounts receivable, inventory and marketable securities.

Current Liabilities — Financial obligations that will have to be paid within one year. These include accounts payable, bank loans and short-term notes.

Current Ratio — Indicator of short-term debt-paying ability. It is calculated by dividing current assets by current liabilities.

D

Day's Sales to Inventory — The amount of inventory a business needs to satisfy its average daily sales requirements.

Debit Balance — The amount that is owed to a broker by a margin customer for loans the customer uses to buy securities.

Debit Card — A card that resembles a credit card but which debits a transaction account with the transfers

	occurring contemporaneously with the customer's purchases.
Debt Capacity	An assessment of ability and willingness to repay a loan from anticipated future cash flow or other sources.
Debt to Equity Ratio	A comparison of debt to equity in a company's capital structure.
Debt Ratio	Total debt divided by total assets.
Debt to Total Assets Ratio	Measures the proportion of all debts provided by lenders to finance all assets.
Debt Service	Interest payment plus repayments of principal to creditors.
Debt Service Coverage	The ratio of cash flow available to the borrower to the annual interest and principal payments on a loan or other debt.
Debtor	Borrower of money.
Debtor Management	Concerned with the trade off between extending credit to increase sales and profits the interest and administrative cost of carrying debtors and the cost of bad debts
Debenture	A written acknowledgment of debt, usually secured by a lien on assets.
Default	Failure to meet the terms of a credit agreement.
Demand Loan	A loan that must be repaid in full on demand.
Depreciation	An accounting term reflecting reduction in value of an asset used by a business.
Derivative	A financial contract whose value is based on or derived from a security such as a stock, bond, commodity or a market index.
Disbursement Float	Disbursement float is the lapse between the time when a firm deducts a payment from its books of accounts and the time when the funds are actually withdrawn from its account. The objective of the financial manager is to minimize collection float and maximize disbursement float.
Discount	A discount is an incentive offered to a customer to pay the account before the due date.
Discount Rate	The rate of return used to convert a future investment into present value.

Discounted Cash Flow (DCF)	A technique for establishing the relative worth of a future investment by discounting the expected net cash flow from the project.
Discounting	The process of finding the present value of a series of future cash flows.
Divestiture	Sale of part of a company. It is the opposite of merger.
Dividend	A cash or in kind such as share, warrant payment to shareholders.
Dividend Coverage	Number of times a company's dividend is covered by earnings available to pay it.

E

Earnings	Refers to a company's total sales minus the cost of sales and operating expenses, including interest and income tax.
EBIT	Earnings before interest and taxes.
EBITDA	Earnings before interest, income taxes, depreciation and amortization
Economic Value Added (EVA)	A method of performance evaluation that adjusts accounting performance for investors' required return on investment. In other words, it is the after-tax operating profits a firm earns from an investment minus the cost of funds used to finance the investment. If the resulting value is positive (negative) shareholders wealth is increased (decreased) by the investment. EVA is used for determining if an investment will result in an increase in shareholder wealth and should be continued in order to fulfil the financial management function of maximizing shareholder wealth.
Economies of Scale	Achievement of lower average cost per unit through increased production.
Efficient Frontier	Efficient Frontier, developed by Harry Markowitz, is the combinations of securities portfolios that maximize expected return for any level of expected risk, or that minimizes expected risk for any level of expected return.
Efficient Market	Market in which prices correctly reflect all relevant information.

Electronic Fund Transfer (EFT)	A system for transferring funds electronically rather than by cheque.
Entrepreneur	A person who starts a business and who takes all the associated risks.
Equity	Ownership interest in a firm.
Equityholders	Equityholders are the shareholders who hold shares of the company.
Equity Buyback	The equityholders' ownership of a company that can be reacquired by the company.
Exchange Risk	The risk associated with an asset or liability denominated in a foreign currency.
Expected Return	The return (amount of money) an investor anticipates to receive from an investment.
External Funds	Funds acquired through borrowing.

F

Face Value	The nominal value that appears on the face of a document.
Factoring	Factoring is an arrangement in which a company sells its receivables to another company at a discount. The purchasing company obtains title to the accounts receivable.
Field Warehouse	Warehouse rented by a company on another firm's premises.
Finance	A discipline concerned with making financial decisions. The finance function allocates resources, acquires resources, finance resources, and manages resources. It is the art and science of managing money. Finance affects all individuals, businesses, and governments in the process of the transfer of money through institutions, markets, and instruments.
Finance Charge	The total amount paid to get credit.
Financing Instruments	The term refers to different forms of financing a firm may use. For example, shares debentures, bonds, loans etc.
Financial Analyst	A professional who analyzes financial statements and research market trends in order to purchase, sell or hold various stocks.
Financial Assets	Claims on real assets.

Financial Leverage	Financial leverage refers to the sensitivity of earnings available to common shareholders to changes in earnings before interest and taxes.
Financial Control	The management of a firm's costs and expenses in relation to budgeted amounts.
Financial Innovation	Design of new financial instruments such as Deep Discount Bonds, Swaps etc.
Financial Institution	An enterprise such as a bank whose primary business and function is to collect money from the public and invest it in financial assets such as stocks and bonds.
Financial Planning	Financial planning is concerned with the evaluation of investment and financial options available to a firm.
Financial Policy	Financial policy is concerned with a company's choice regarding its debt-equity mix, method of financing investment projects, and hedging decisions with an objective of maximizing the value of the firm.
Financial Position	The financial status of a firm's or an individual's assets and liabilities as reflected by its financial statement.
Financial Risk	Financial risk is the risk that the firm will be unable to meet required financial obligations. It increases as the firm increases its dependence on such financing as debts, preferred stock, and leases. The more fixed-cost components in a firm's capital structure, the greater is its financial leverage and financial risk.
Financial Service	Financial service is the area of finance concerned with the design and delivery of advice and financial products to individuals, businesses, and government.
Financial Structure	The way in which a company's assets are financed, such as short-term borrowings, long-term debt, and owners' equity. Financial structure is different from capital structure in the sense that capital structure accounts for long-term debt and equity only.
First In First Out (FIFO)	An accounting method for valuing the cost of goods sold that uses the cost of the oldest item in inventory first.

FIS	FIS (Financial Information System) is a subsystem of computer based information system that provides information to persons and groups both inside and outside the firm concerning the firm's financial matters. Information is provided in form of periodic reports, special reports, results of mathematical simulations, electronic communications, and the advice of expert systems.
Fiscal Policy	Government spending and taxing for the specific purpose of stabilizing the economy.
Five Cs of Credit	Five Cs of credit are: Character, Capacity, Capital, Collateral, and Conditions. These characteristics are used to make judgement about a debtor's creditworthiness.
Fixed Assets	Fixed assets are the assets which are acquired not for the purpose of resale but for the purpose of revenue generation in the long run. Fixed assets include real estate, plant, and equipment, patents, trademarks etc.
Fixed Expenses	The expenditure which does not change with the volume of business. Examples are rent, insurance premium, light etc.
Fixed Asset Turnover Ratio	The ratio of sales to fixed assets.
Fixed Annuities	Contracts in which an issuing financial institution such as an insurance company pays a fixed rupee amount of money per period.
Fixed Charge Coverage Ratio	A measure of a firm's ability to meet its fixed-charge obligations: the ratio of (net earnings before taxes plus interest charges paid plus long-term lease payments) to (interest charges paid plus long-term lease payments).
Fixed Cost	A cost that is fixed in total for a given period of time and for given production levels.
Fixed Rate	An approach to determining the finance charge payable on an extension of credit. A predetermined and certain rate of interest applied to the principal of a loan or credit agreement.
Float	Float refers to funds that have been dispatched by a payer but are not in a form that can be spent by the payee. The three components of float are mail float, processing float, and clearing float.

Forfaiting	A form of factoring that involves selling large, medium to long-term receivables to buyers (forfaiters) who are willing and able to bear the costs and risks of credit and collections.
Foreign Exchange	Foreign exchange refers to the number of units of one currency required to buy another.
Forfeiture	The loss of rights to an asset outlined in a legal contract if a party fails to fulfil obligations of the contract.
Front-end Loading	Charges or fees that are greater at the start of a loan or investment contract than in its later stages.
Funding Costs	The price of obtaining capital either borrowed or equity to carry on business.
Futures Contract	A contract calling for delivery of a particular commodity or financial instrument at a fixed date in the future.

G

Gain	The gain is the difference between the cost and the sale.
Gearing	Financial leverage.
Generally Accepted Accounting Principles (GAAP)	The overall conventions, rules, and procedures that define accepted accounting practices.
Going Public	When a private company first offers shares to the public market and investors.
Gross Interest	Interest earned before taxes are deducted.
Gross Profit	Sales minus the cost of goods sold.
Going Concern Value	The amount received when a firm is sold as an operating business.
Gross Margin on Sales	The interrelationship between a firm's sales structure and its purchase and production costs.

H

Hedge	A transaction that reduces the risk of an investment.
Horizontal Merger	A merger involving two or more firms in the same industry that are both at the same stage in the production cycle; that is, two or more competitors.

Hurdle Rate	A predefined bench-mark rate of return.
Hypothecation	The pledge of property and assets to secure a loan.

I

Illiquid	It denotes absence of cash flow needed to fulfil financial debts and meet obligations.
Impaired credit	Result of a borrower's reduced credit rating.
Indenture	Agreement between lender and borrower that details specific terms of the bond issuance.
Indirect costs of financial distress	Costs such as lost business as a result of bankruptcy or liquidation.
Industry	The category describing a company's primary business activity. This category is usually determined by the largest portion of revenue.
Inflation	Inflation refers to a persistent rise in prices of goods and services. It is a situation of too much money and too few goods. Thus, due to scarcity of goods and the presence of many buyers, the prices are pushed up.
Insolvent	A firm that is unable to pay debts (its liabilities exceed its assets).
Interest	The price paid for borrowing money.
Interest Coverage Ratio	The ratio of earnings before interest and taxes to annual interest expense. This ratio measures a firm's ability to pay interest.
Income Statement	A financial statement that displays a break-down of total sales and total expenses.
Insolvency	A financial condition of a firm in which the value of its debts is greater than the realizable value of assets.
Interest	A charge for the use of money supplied by a lender.
Internal Financing	Funds made available from retained earnings and depreciation reserve for capital budgeting and working capital expansion through the normal operations of the firm.
Internal Rate of Return (IRR)	Internal rate of return is the rate that will make present value of net cash flows equal to investment.

Inventory Costs	There are two basic types of costs associated with current assets in general and inventory in particular - carrying costs and shortage costs.
Inventory Turnover	Ratio used to evaluate the effectiveness of inventory management.
Investment Banker	One who underwrites and distributes new investment securities.

J

Joint Stock Company	A form of business organisation that falls between a company and a partnership. The company sells stock, and its shareholders are free to sell their stock, but shareholders are liable for all debts of the company.
Just-in-time inventory systems	Systems that schedule materials to arrive exactly when they are needed in the production process.

K

Key Industry	An industry that plays a critical role in a nation's economy.
Kiting	Used in banking to refer to the practice of depositing and drawing checks at two or more banks and taking advantage of the time it takes for the second bank to collect funds from the first bank.

L

Last-In-First-Out (LIFO)	A method that fixes the cost of inventory to the most recent purchases. So in case of inflation when the prices are generally rising, LIFO method will lead to lower profitability.
Late Charge	A penalty fee charged for a late payment.
Lead Time	Lead time is delivery time.
Lender	A firm or a person that provides loans to others.
Lender of Last Resort	The Central Bank which is Reserve Bank of India (RBI) in case of India, which assists, banks and stabilizes the banking system.

Letter of Credit	A guarantee of payment by an issuing authority usually a bank to a lender/seller on behalf of a borrower/buyer for a specific amount of money.
Leverage	Leverage is the use of fixed cost assets or funds to magnify the returns to owners. Leverage is closely related to the risk of being unable to meet operating and financial obligations when due.
Leverage Ratios	Ratios that are used to measure the relative proportion of debt/fixed charge securities in the capital structure, and the firm's ability to pay financing charges.
Liability	Any obligation for payment or to render a service.
Liability On An Account	Legal responsibility to repay debt.
Lien	The right of the lender to take possession of an asset if the payment is not received in full.
Line of Credit	A line of credit is an agreement between a commercial bank and a business that states the amount of unsecured short-term borrowing the bank will make available to the firm over a given period of time.
Liquid Asset	Any asset that can be quickly converted to cash without substantial loss in the value of asset.
Liquidation	Dissolution a firm following predefined legal procedures.
Liquidity	The extent to which a company has current assets that are readily available to meet obligations.
Liquidity Crisis	Financial position in which a firm is unable to meet its short-term obligations.
Liquidity Ratios	Ratios that are used to estimate a company's liquidity position in the short-run such as the ratio of current assets to current liabilities.
Liquidity Risk	Liquidity risk arises from an institution's inability to meet its obligations when they come due without incurring unacceptable losses.
Lockbox	A lockbox is the most widely known and effective tool available for accelerating the collection of receivables. Lockboxes are post office boxes rented by the firm at one or more

locations near its customers. A nearby bank collects payments made to that address on behalf of the firm, deposits them, and sends a record of deposit, which may be a computer file, to the collecting firm. The lockbox service allows incoming payments (including credit card payments) to bypass corporate office and come directly to the bank. This process results in reducing mail, processing, and collection float.

M

Mail Float	Time period spent in the postal system.
Management/Leveraged Buyout	The situation when the management of a company purchases all the company's shares or assets.
Managerial Decisions	Decisions concerning the management and operations of the firm.
Managerial Finance	Managerial finance encompasses the functions of budgeting, financial forecasting, credit administration, investment analysis, and funds procurement for the firm. Managerial finance is the management of the firm's funds within the firm.
Market Capitalization	Total value of a company determined by the market price of its total issued stock.
Marketable Securities	Marketable securities consist of governmental bonds and bonds of high rated financial institutions. They are held for the purpose of investing in liquid funds and are not generally retained on a long-term basis. Marketable securities are stated at the market value. Adjustments in valuation are included in the income statement. Interest received on trading securities is reported as interest income.
Margin of Profit	It is calculated by dividing Gross Profit by Net Sales. It is measured to judge a firm's operating efficiency.
Margin of Safety	In working capital management it is referred as, the difference between the amount of long-term liabilities and the amount of fixed assets plus the permanent component of current assets.

Market Price	The price which prevails in the market.
Marketable Securities	Securities that can be easily converted into cash because of their high demand in the market.
Maturity Date	Date on which a debt is due for payment.
Money Supply (M3)	This refers to the total volume of money circulating in the economy, and conventionally comprises currency with the public and demand deposits (current account + savings account) with the public.
Monetary Policy	Government's policy which controls and influence the money supply or interest rates.
Monitoring Receivables	Keeping track of payments to try and spot potential defaults and possible problems to reduce losses.

N

Near Cash Assets	Assets that are easily convertible into cash such as government securities, bank deposits.
Negative Working Capital	Working capital is negative when current liabilities exceed current assets. It leads to technical insolvency.
Net Book Value	The current book value of an asset or liability after accounting adjustments such as depreciation.
Net Float	Sum of disbursement float and collection float.
Net Operating Margin	The ratio of net operating income to net sales.
Net Income	Earnings after providing for depreciation, interest, taxes and other expenses. It is also known as net profit.
Net Working Capital	Current assets minus current liabilities. Often referred to as net concept of working capital.
Net Income	The level of profit in a business after the deduction of income taxes, depreciation, operating expenses and other expenses.
Net Present Value (NPV)	A method of ranking capital budgeting projects. NPV is equal to the present value of future returns, discounted at the cost of capital, minus the present value of the cost of the investment.
Net Worth	Common stockholders' equity which consists of common stock, reserves and surplus, and retained earnings.

O

Open Account	Arrangement whereby sales are made with no formal debt contract.
Open-End Credit	Commonly referred to as a line of credit. It may be used repeatedly up to a certain limit, also known as Revolving Credit.
Open Market Operations	The Reserve Bank of India purchases and sells securities in open market to control the flow of credit in the country.
Operating Assets	Another term for working capital.
Operating Cash Flow	Earnings before depreciation but after taxes. It measures the cash generated from operations, not counting working capital requirements.
Operating Cycle	The average time between the acquisition of materials and the final cash realization from that acquisition. It is the length of time that the firm's cash is tied up in its operation.
Operating Expenses	The cost of doing business. It excludes depreciation.
Operating Lease	It is a short-term, cancealable lease in which the contract period is shorter than the life of the equipment.
Operating Leverage	The existence of fixed operating costs in a business's cost structure; the extent of fixed costs in comparison to variable costs in a firm's operations.
Operating Loan	A loan intended for short-term financing to cover routine operating expenses.
Operating Risk	Possibility that the firm's total revenues will be less than its total costs. Increases as the company increases its investment on fixed assets. It is caused by business cycles, competition, strikes, change in demand, change in technology etc.
Optimal Credit Policy	An optimal credit policy is one in which the incremental cash flows from sales are equal to incremental costs of carrying the increased investment in accounts receivable.
Outsourcing	Purchasing a component/service from outside suppliers.

Overcapitalization	It occurs when a firm is not able to service its debt holders.
Overdraft Facility	Usually provided by a bank, in which a depositor may write cheques in excess of the deposited balance in the account. Bank automatically extends a loan to cover the deficit.
Owners' Equity	The total funds invested in a business by the owners. This equity capital or net worth can be calculated by deducting the total liabilities from the total assets of a business.

P

Parent Company	A company that controls subsidiaries through its voting stock.
Participation Loan	A large loan made by a group of lenders.
Payback Period	Number of years required to recover the investment by net cash flows.
Payment Float	The time lag for the company-written cheques that have not yet cleared.
P/E (Price/Earnings) Ratio	Current MPS (Market Price of Share) divided by annual EPS (Earnings Per Share).
Permanent Current Assets	The minimum level of current assets needed to continue operations throughout the year.
Permanent Financing	Long-term financing using either debt or equity.
Pre-Authorized Cheques (PAC)	Cheques that are authorized by a payer in advance, and written either by the payee or by the payee's bank and then deposited in the payee's bank account.
Pre-Authorized Electronic Debits (PAED)	Debits to a bank account in advance by the payer. The payer's bank sends payment to the payee's bank through the Automated Clearing House (ACH) system.
Pre-emptive Right	Right of shareholders to maintain their proportional ownership control in a company when additional shares are issued.
Preference Shares	In the event of liquidation, preference shareholders rank ahead of equity shareholders for claims against the assets of the company. These shares are usually non-voting and have a fixed dividend rate.

Preauthorized Payment	Accelerating cash receipts by directly charging a customer's bank account.
Present Value	The amount of cash today that is equivalent in value to a stream of inflows to be received in the future. To calculate the present value, each future cash flow is multiplied by a present value factor.
Principal Amount	Refers to the face value of a loan or debt.
Private Placement	Sale of shares or bonds to a small group of investors that is not required to comply with the rules and regulations of disclosure.
Profit Margin	The proportion of each sales dollar that filters down to income, defined as income divided by net sales.
Profitability Index	The present value of the future cash flows divided by the initial investment. Also called the benefit-cost ratio.
Profitability Ratios	Ratios that measures the profitability of the firm such as profit margin ratios, rate of return ratios etc.
Progress Payments	Periodic payments to a supplier or contractor for the work completed, in order to reduce working capital requirements.
Project Financing	Debt financing provided by financial institutions for the development of a new project.

Q

Qualifying Stock Option	A benefit granted by a company that allows employees to purchase shares at a discount price.
Quarterly	Occurring every three months.
Quick Assets	Current assets minus inventories.
Quick Ratio	Indicator of a company's financial liquidity. Calculated by taking current assets less inventories, divided by current liabilities. This ratio places more emphasis on those liquid assets that can be quickly converted into cash. Also called the Acid test ratio.

R

Rate of Return	Return on invested capital (calculated as a percentage).

Ratio Analysis	Method of expressing relationships between a firm's accounting numbers and their trends over time that analysts use to make evaluations.
Raw Material	Material that is converted into a finished product for the purpose of sale.
Raw Material Supply Agreement	An agreement to furnish a specified amount per period of a specified raw material.
Real Cash Flow	Income adjusted for inflation and expressed in current purchasing power terms.
Real Income	The net income after adjustment for inflation.
Receivables Turnover Ratio	Total operating revenues divided by average receivables. The ratio is used to measure how effectively a firm is managing its accounts receivable.
Recession	A temporary downturn in economic activity, usually indicated by two consecutive quarters of a falling GDP.
Reorder Point	Reorder point is the amount of inventory which will indicate the next order.
Repo	A repurchase agreement or ready forward deal is a secured short-term loan by one party to another against some securities.
Restrictive Covenants	Provisions that place constraints on the operations of borrowers, such as restrictions on working capital, fixed assets, future borrowing, and payment of dividends.
Return On Capital Employed (ROCE)	Indicates the profitability of the firm's capital investments. It is determined by dividing Earnings Before Interest and Taxes by Capital Employed including short-term loans.
Return on Sales	A measurement of operational efficiency (Net profits before tax divided by net sales expressed as a percentage).
Retained Earnings	The amount of earnings retained in the business and not distributed to the shareholders as dividends.
Return on Equity (ROE)	A ratio used to find out the profitability of a business to the equity shareholders. Equity shareholders use ROE as a measure of how a company is using its money.

Return on Invested Capital	Measures the return on funds invested in the business by both long-term lenders and owners.
Return on Total Assets	The ratio of earnings available to common stockholders to total assets.
Revenue	Money received from the sale of products/ services.
Revolving Credit	A line of credit in which funds may be borrowed at any time.
Risk	Risk is the chance that actual outcomes may differ from expected outcomes. In financial terminology, the risk refers to the probability that actual future returns will be less than expected returns.
Risk-Return Trade-Off	Matching of potential risk with the potential return. As the risk varies directly with the return, so more the risk involved, greater is the potential return, and vice versa.

S

Safety Stocks	Safety stocks are maintained to take care of emergencies such as delayed delivery and higher demand than expected.
Sale	An agreement between a buyer and a seller on the price to be paid for providing a product or service.
Sale and Leaseback	Sale of an existing asset to a financial institution that then leases it back to the user.
Secondary Market	Also known as Share Market, in which securities are traded after they are initially offered in the primary market or new issue market.
Employed (ROCE)	Security Assets pledged as a security to back a loan/debt.
Security Interest	The right of the creditor to take property or a portion of property offered as security.
Seed Capital	The first contribution of capital toward the financing of a start-up business.
Share Capital	Total shares issued by a company.
Self-Liquidating Loan	Loan for funding of current assets. The sale of the current assets provides the cash to repay the loan.

Shares	Certificates or book entries representing ownership in a company.
Shareholders	Shareholders are the true owners of a company. They elect the board of directors, which has the ultimate authority to guide corporate affairs and set general policy.
Short-Term Investment	Investment with maturity of less than a year.
Short Term Financial Management	Concerned with the management of the firm's current assets and liabilities, and is one of the financial manager's most important functions. Managing these accounts wisely results in a balance between profitability and risk that has a positive impact on the firm's value.
Sinking Fund	Annual payment designed to amortize a bond or preference stock. The sinking fund is usually held in the form of cash or marketable securities.
Statement of Changes in Financial Position	A financial document that presents the increases or decreases in funds of a business.
Statutory Liquidity Ratio (SLR)	Banks in India are required to maintain 25 per cent of their demand and time liabilities in government securities and other approved securities.
Stock Dividend	A dividend paid in shares and not in cash.

T

Takeover	The transfer of control of a firm from one group of shareholders to another group of shareholders.
Tangible Asset	Any asset which can be touched and seen such as building, machinery, land etc.
Tangible Net Worth	Total assets less intangible assets, which include patents, copyrights, and total liabilities.
Target Cash Balance	Optimal amount of cash for a firm to hold, considering the trade-off between the opportunity costs of holding too much cash and the risks of holding too little cash.
Target-Profit Level	A pre-defined level of after-cost income a company targets to achieve from a given product.
Technical Analysis	Security analysis that observes and interpret patterns in past security prices.

Technical Insolvency	Technical insolvency occurs if a firm is unable to meet its payments when due.
Temporary Assets	That portion of a firm's current assets that fluctuates in response to seasonal short-term variations.
Temporary Financing	The sum of current liabilities.
Temporary investment	A short-term investment, such as a money market fund, Treasury bills, or short-term CD, which is usually held a year or less.
Term Loan	A loan with a maturity of more than one year.
Terms of Sale	Conditions under which a firm sells its products or services for cash or credit.
Time Value of Money	The value of money today is worth more than the value of money in the future, because the rupee received today can earn interest up until the time the future rupee is received.
Times Interest Earned Ratio	Measures the ability of the firm to meet its annual interest charges.
Total Assets Turnover	Measures the intensity by which the assets are used to generate sales.
Total Debt/Equity Ratio	Ratio of current liabilities plus long-term debt to shareholders' equity.
Total Market Capitalization	The total market value of all of a firm's outstanding securities.
Total Leverage	Total leverage refers to the overall sensitivity of earnings available to common shareholders to changes in sales revenue.
Trade Credit	Credit one firm grants to another firm for the purchase of products or services.
Trade Debt	Accounts payable.
Trend Ratio Analysis	The comparison of the successive values of each ratio for a single firm over a number of years.

U

Uncollectible Account	The payment from a debtor which cannot be collected by a company because the debtor is not able to pay or is not willing to pay.
Undercapitalization	When a business does not have sufficient equity in its capital structure.
Unit Sales	The number of products or service units sold by a company.

Unpaid Dividend	A dividend declared by the company that has not yet been paid.

V

Variable Rate	A variable rate loan or credit agreement, calls for an interest rate that may fluctuate over the life of the loan. The rate is often tied to an index that reflects changes in market rates of interest.
Venture Capital	The capital invested in a business that entails a greater degree of risk than is normally assumed in a business undertaking. Also known as Risk Capital.
Venture Capitalist	An individual or a firm investing in ventures that have an element of risk but offers high returns.
Vertical Analysis	The process of reducing all items in the balance sheet and income statement to a percentage of sales revenue.

W

Weak Rupee	A depreciated rupee with respect to other currencies, meaning that more rupees are needed to buy a unit of foreign currency.
What If Analysis	Analysis of the economic effect of possible future situations, such as economic downturns, demand changes, changes in interest rates, price levels, new technologies etc.
Windfall Profit	A sudden unexpected profit uncontrolled by the profiting firm.
Without Recourse Financing	Financing in which the right of recourse to the party receiving funds is forfeited to the party advancing funds.
Working Capital	Working capital is the excess of current assets (cash, accounts receivable, and inventory) over current liabilities (short term loans and accounts payable). Working capital represents the funds available to pay for the business's current requirements and a margin of protection for a company's short-term obligations. Working capital is essential for a company to meet the continuous operational needs of doing business.

Working Capital Turnover	Measures how actively the working capital in a business is being put to work to generate sales.
Working Capital Management	The deployment of current assets and current liabilities so as to maximize short-term liquidity.
Working Capital Ratio	Working capital expressed as a percentage of sales.
World Trade Organisation (WTO)	A multilateral agency that administers world trade agreements, fosters trade relations among nations, and solves trade disputes among member countries.
Written Down Value	The book value of an asset after allowing for depreciation and amortization.

Y

Yield	The percentage return paid on a stock in the form of dividends, or the effective rate of interest paid on a bond.

Z

Zero Balance Account (ZBA)	An account in a bank in which zero balance is maintained by transfers of funds from a master account in an amount only large enough to cover cheques presented.
Zero Base Budgeting (ZBB)	A budgeting method that disregards the previous year's budget in setting a new budget.